A Taos Mosaic

A Taos Mosaic

Portrait of a New Mexico Village

Claire Morrill

University of New Mexico Press

Albuquerque

ACKNOWLEDGMENTS

Chapter 3, "The Indispensable Bookman," part of Chapter 15, "Taos in D. H. Lawrence," and Chapter 19, "Piñon Smoke," are reprinted by permission from *Southwest Review*.

Chapter 14, "Three Women of Taos," is reprinted by permission from *The South Dakota Review*.

To
Genevitch and Johnny and Luis

At the Beginning: A Preface

> The White Rabbit put on his spectacles. "Where shall I begin, please your Majesty?" he asked.
> "Begin at the beginning," the King said gravely.
> —Lewis Carroll
> *Alice's Adventures in Wonderland*

Taos is a place to which all of its Anglo inhabitants came because they actively wanted to, not just because their great-grandfathers ran out of money when they got this far west, or their great-grandmothers finally got tired of those old covered wagons.

Actually I know only two Anglo Taoseños who were born here. Peggy Pond Church and Juanita Howell, when somebody asks what brought them to Taos, are able to answer "the stork." The rest of us have different replies and like to spend odd hours exchanging them. There seems to be endless interest in the subject. So perhaps I should explain what it was that brought Genevieve Janssen and me clattering over the mountain passes from Raton in that old Buick in 1947 to set up a book shop here.

It was quite a switch for both of us. I had long been managing editor of a daily newspaper in an industrial-chemical center in Michigan. She had been a psychiatric social worker.

A managing editor, I've always said, is someone who manages to edit a newspaper, and if you know anything about that sort of business, you know it's a rough-and-tumble affair, even in as well-behaved, industrious, and affluent a place as Midland, Michigan.

After seventeen years on this job and its predecessor, which amounted to about the same thing, I began to wish for a more serene life, closer to the belles-lettres and aesthetic. And I wanted a two-year breather from work, to do some traveling and figure out what to do next.

I had met Genevieve in Midland, where she was serving as director of a family service agency, though before I left she had moved on to become executive of a similar agency set up by five large suburban towns on Long Island. But we had occasionally kept in touch, and as World War II ended decided to take some time off to see a little country outside the United States. We would, we planned, spend the winter in South America, after which she would come back to the University of Oklahoma, where she was scheduled for a year of teaching in the graduate school. After that we would give the next year to an extensive jaunt into Europe and the Orient.

The South American trip went off as planned; so did Genevieve's year at the university. But our plans for travel in Europe and Asia were foiled by the fact of a still war-dislocated world. You could travel there, the State Department said, only if you had business to transact or were willing to be led around by the hand by some hearty minion of a Happiness Tour.

The result of this situation was that the spring of 1947 found us too frustrated to go on in our old grooves. We were ready for new pastures—I for a permanent thing, Genevieve for a brief fling before going back to her profession.

How about setting up a book shop, we asked ourselves, in some place with verve and color, a spot where we really wanted to live? But where?

About this time we began to hear of Taos, from faculty members who had vacationed or painted there and from an extensive spread in *Holiday* magazine. It sounded wonderful. While Genevieve enviously stuck to her university classes, I came out to see. For a week or so I looked around and then went back to report.

Taos was full of interesting people—Spanish Americans, Indians, and Anglos—in a magnificent setting. Its exciting four centuries of history had left it with a unique and beautiful architecture. It was a famous art center. An interest in aesthetics was woven into its contemporary life.

Taos was small, about eight thousand people living within a ten-mile radius. Taos was poor; whereas Midland had one of the country's high-bracket rates of per capita income, Taos had one of the lowest. It was a tourist center, but did tourists buy books? We didn't know. Taos, in short, was a wonderful place to lose your shirt. But we could not resist it. We came the following August.

Twenty-five years later we are still here, Genevieve too, for while she never lost her devotion to her former profession, she found she couldn't leave Taos either—a discovery she made when, in our third year here, somebody wanted to buy the shop.

viii

It has been a life of hard work, but much fun and a deep satisfaction. We have often wondered how we could have been so lucky that in the one major change we made in our lives, we both managed to guess right the first time.

Contents

List of Illustrations

1

The Time for Staying Still

As an old newspaper hand I found that a lot of the news from Taos is involved with the intangible, the aesthetic, and even the occult.

This reminds me of the time Mabel Luhan, Taos's late socialite and arts patron, wrote about a stay she had made in Ojo Caliente, a few miles away.

"A friend wrote me while I was there: 'I suppose you have no news, so I will send you some.'

"I replied, 'No, I have no news, nothing happens here but miracles.'" [1]

At the moment she was referring to the benefits of Ojo Caliente's mineral waters. But from her other writings one knows that Mrs. Luhan was always one of the most sensitive to the miracles that happen in Taos.

One of them is involved in the fundamental paradox of this village, in the fact that while Taos is one of the most intense communities one can find, so that a controversy here seems to be accompanied by a high degree of heat and action, still this remote town exudes a basic tranquillity that is hard to define or explain. Perhaps this is why community disagreements are so lively, since one can afford to operate more aggressively from a position of security.

Sometimes I think this inner assurance comes from living in a house whose floors are made of adobe, so that we are footed on the solid earth. Contemporary science, of course, tells us that the ground is not, as one used to say of the rock in the old doggerel, "just asettin' still," but that its atoms and molecules move busily about each other as if manipulated by some giant juggler. Still, we do not have any sensation of treading precariously on a quivering mass. We have a feeling that it's all pretty solid, and it does something for us.

Even in summer, when traveling visitors turn Taos into something resembling a metropolitan airport, one feels a fundamental serenity, a sense that is greatly heightened in winter, when visitors have returned to their homes or betaken themselves to the high ski slopes as the quiet snow comes down.

We may be conditioned for this winter feeling by that traditional hush at the pueblo beginning December 10 and known officially as "the Time for Staying Still." In Indian ceremonialism it is the interval between the death and rebirth of Mother Earth. She, Changing Woman, was young in spring, bore generously in summer, aged in the mellow autumn, and now in winter lies sleeping, building fresh strength for rebirth in the new spring. One must walk softly. She must not be disturbed.

The quiet is invoked by a kiva chief from the pueblo's highest house-top. Now all the Taos Indians must move back in from their summer homes in the fields at the base of the mountain. Now no Indian may dig in the earth, chop wood, or drive a car or wagon on pueblo land. These are the forty days, ending January 20, of the Time for Staying Still.

Perhaps when winter white blankets the braided mesa, the sloping foothills, the high ranges that cradle the valley, the ceremonial philosophy of our Indian neighbors pervades us all, throwing over us, too, the ritual blanket of quiet. It may be that winter is for us, too, a time for sleeping and renewal.

Perhaps it is a little easier for us in Taos to accept the tortured universe; though we know that in geological time the permanent-seeming mountains rise and sink, still they sit here now in rugged beauty and stability and will outlast us all.

And so in this secluded valley we have not attempted to reject the century nor ignore the ills that flesh inherits; there is something here that sustains and reassures. I report this Taos miracle because in anybody's language miracles are news.

2

The Eagle

If you are rugged, you can ride on horseback along the narrow, bald crest of Wheeler Peak, above the tree line at a height of more than thirteen thousand feet. From here, if you are brave enough to lift your eyes from the loose shale in which your mount is finding its uncertain footing, you can look to the full range of the eye's capacity. Here you are above it all, above the great uplifted mountains with glinting lakes in their pockets, above the limitless tableland, the Taos Valley.

From the upland ranches lying in the lee of the Picuris range, you can look across the Rio Grande at the woven texture of the eroded mesa, its carpet of gray-green sagebrush shimmering into lavender under the late sun's slanting rays. But though you look across it, you may not see the river's magnificent gorge, for except in two or three places the chasm snaking southward across the high plain three miles or so west of Taos is visible only from its brink.

But it is the great northern skyline of the Sangre de Cristo mountains that sets the drama of the Taos scene, a skyline the first startling sight of which, as one comes up out of the river's canyon onto the high plateau, has sent many a sophisticated traveler into an effulgence of admiration. Here, on this desert shelf a mile and a third high, lie the three neighboring adobe villages: the Indian pueblo of San Geronimo de Taos, the Spanish hamlet of Ranchos de Taos, and the Spanish-Anglo village of Fernando de Taos, the last known simply as Taos. The mountain range, an abstraction in pyramids, soars nearly seven thousand feet more above the mesa, circling to the east and south to partly enclose the cluster of hamlets.

It is a tale of geological excitement told here by this high plain, this deep canyon, this range and two more on the western horizon, the Jemez and Nacimiento mountains.

Disturbance is attested to by the surface exposure of both the newest and oldest rocks, the Tertiary and Precambrian, ranging in age from seventy million to more than six hundred million years and upthrust to their present height by subterranean convulsions continuing to geologically modern times.

In their day volcanic vents west of the Rio Grande in the Tres Piedras area have opened, covering the mesa with lava since overlaid with sediment.

Seas have several times covered the area.

The great river gorge, though its steep walls and jagged course suggest a crack suddenly opened by an earthquake, was formed by a gentler process, erosion—the river cutting deeper and deeper as the mesa rose during a mountain-building period placed in relatively modern times, an era not necessarily ended.

Alpine glaciers, identified as far as a hundred miles south, have crept down the region's mountains, and glacial ice still remains on the far side of Mount Blanca at the north.

It was up through a lake on Mount Blanca, some Taos Indians say (though another myth says it was up through Blue Lake on Taos Mountain), that they emerged to the upper world, after they had been created by our Father Sun.

Archaeologists believe that sometime between fifteen thousand and twenty-five thousand years ago, with one of the waves of Asian immigration across the Bering Strait, their ancestors came down the western mountain valleys.[1] One myth says that the Taos were looking for this place, Taos. They were led to it by an eagle. Where it dropped a feather, they made their home and some time later built the two great communal houses where they live today. They have been here a probable eight hundred years.

This was the land of journey's ending, and it moved Mary Austin, in a book by that title, to write:

> As you come up out of the river gorge into the valley of Taos, you see Pueblo Mountain standing toward the north, with thin storms of rain enfilading among the cañons of Star Water and Pueblo Creek, and the dance of the Rainbow Boys in and out of the storm's blueness. . . . Or suppose the rainbow comes forth, arching from foot to foot of Pueblo Mountain, moving as you move, while the Kachinas of the Middle Heaven water the pueblo fields, then you see how myths are made, out of the stroke on stroke of beauty.[2]

4

There the mountains, piled high in dramatic profusion, formed a protective back for the Taos people, throwing out arms to cradle the fields below and sending down a stream from Blue Lake to water the corn and squash.

And the people acknowledged the wonder. Mountains and lake were sacred. It was not that the Taos were grateful, for they were themselves part of this natural world. They spoke as later Saint Francis spoke: "My brother the wind . . . my sister water." They danced to the corn, celebrating the time of its germination, but the ulterior motive of gain was absent from this prayer, for they were themselves one with the corn.

Here for probably four centuries the Indians lived in peace. How long it was before the roving, the hunting tribes, Comanches from the eastern plains, Navajos, Apaches, and Utes from the north and west, began their raids on the peaceful and sedentary Pueblo Indians I do not know. Certainly the Taos lived in freedom from white encroachment for four hundred years before Barrio-Nuevo, scouting for Coronado's army, first saw the golden glint of the straw in their adobe houses late in 1541.

Taos has had many names since then, all dating back to the sixteenth and seventeenth centuries. Mary Austin's opinion is that its native name now is Tuatá, and that its place name is Yahlahaimu-bahutulba, Red Willow Place. She adds that though Taos is a Tigua town, the conquistadores came to it through Tewa country and with Tewa guides and interpreters, and so came to know it by its Tewa name of Tówih, of which Taos is a corruption.[3]

Purists insist that the name is pronounced with one syllable, rhyming with "house." But my ear has never been able to detect this harsh and purse-lipped pronunciation in everyday use, by Indian, Spanish American, or Anglo. Ta–os, we say, in two soft syllables, the first only slightly more stressed than the second, the *a* soft, the *o* long.

And what does it mean? "Does it," as Mabel Luhan wrote, "perhaps derive from the small band of devotees who followed Lao Tze westward out of China, imbued with his teaching of the Taos, the golden mean, the Middle Way? Are these Indians descended from those Taoes? Their religion closely resembles the non-aggressive, moderate politesse of the heart discernible in Lao Tze's few existent axioms." [4]

Nobody can say. But to anyone who knows the Taos Indian, and the orientalism inherent in his physical appearance, his language, and his symbolism, the suggestion will inevitably occur.

3

The Indispensable Bookman

I suppose that during those years ours was the only book shop in the country where you could buy a Gauguin monograph from a blanket Indian wearing his hair in two long braidlike rolls, the only shop where you could get a scarce item of Western Americana, a best seller, or a volume of Chinese poetry from a clerk who, though he spoke three languages, still could not read or write.

This erstwhile bookman was John Andrés Romero, Taos Indian and expert moccasin maker. He came into the book trade in 1950 when our book shop was merged with the famous old trading post known throughout the Southwest as the Mission Shop, and remained until 1960, when certain apparently unsolvable problems brought this connection to an abrupt and mutually regretted close.

As partners in the shop, Genevieve and I had inherited Johnny and his equally skilled moccasin-maker compadre, Luis Suazo, when we took over the Mission Shop from Rowena Meyers (Now Mrs. Paul Martínez), widow of trader Ralph Meyers, who had died two years before.

Ralph had been an extraordinary man—painter, silversmith, wood-carver, Spanish-Colonial-furniture maker, weaver and vegetable dye maker for his own fabrics. He knew as well as the Indians how to fashion moccasins from buckskin, which they scraped and bleached with sheep's brains to a snowy whiteness in the patio back of the shop. And under his training Johnny and Luis learned to vary their handiwork by the addition of calfskin in colors, and sometimes a cheerful Plains Indian ornament, tin jingles.

As for us, by the time of Ralph's death our new book business was outgrowing its first small alcove on the plaza, where we had nurtured it tenderly for three and a half years. At the same time we were learning, as booksellers learn everywhere, of the rugged necessity for a sideline, one that would do something to fatten the notoriously slim margin of profit to be made from books.

We had just returned one night from Los Alamos, some fifty or so miles away, where for the past three years we had staged an annual flourishing two-day book fair, when the offer to sell the Mission Shop came to us out of the blue.

All right, we decided, we sell the books on Indian silver; we'll sell the silver, too.

The historic adobe building to which we were going had not been a mission, in spite of the shop's name and the old bell swung from the niche surmounting its façade. It had instead been the home some century or so ago of a famous Taos socialite, La Doña Luz Lucero de Martínez. To brilliant events in her sala had come the major New Mexican figures of her day—Kit Carson and his wife from their home across the street; Taos's famed Spanish priest-politico, Padre Martínez, from his house west of the plaza; Archbishop Lamy, riding up from his episcopal palace in Santa Fe.

In 1950 its walls were hung with buckskin ceremonial robes and dresses, with old bullet molds and Ute and Navajo cradle boards, Navajo vegetable dye rugs, and silver concho belts. In the old carved cases which Ralph had made were silver-mounted ketohs (wrist guards from bow-and-arrow days), old silver bracelets, and Navajo squash-blossom necklaces pawned by the Indians and not redeemed.

To these we brought the books on Indian blankets, pottery, silver, and kachina dolls; the old histories of the state; and Willa Cather's great New Mexico novel, *Death Comes for the Archbishop* (for her fictional Archbishop Latour was in truth that same Archbishop Lamy who had dined many times in the old building, and part of the book had been written in Taos).

In this setting the regional books settled down comfortably, as also, we found, did the art books and general literature in which we were dealing.

We settled in comfortably, too, that cold winter, with Johnny and Luis working at their scarred old table before the wide windows of the moccasin room, visiting in the soft, almost accentless dialect of the Taos Pueblo, and the piñon smell from the fireplace blending with the fragrance of gray cedar smoldering on the top of the battered coal stove. And since, with Ralph's death, the old days for Johnny and Luis had been over for two years, they accepted the new regime with complete calm and an obvious eagerness to help.

Luis, after thirty years in the shop, still spoke no English; his tongues were Spanish and his native Tiwa, one of four dialects in use among the nineteen Rio Grande pueblos. His custom, if by any mischance he found himself alone in the front of the shop with an Anglo customer, was to beat a hasty backward retreat through the arch opening into the moccasin room, a horrified look on his weathered face.

Ralph once said that Luis was known to have spoken only two English words, a feat into which he had been startled by an incident during a visit to the shop by Queen Marie of Rumania. The queen had decided on a string of silver beads, and Ralph, while discussing the matter of restringing them on heavier cord, was nervously twirling the strand about in the air when suddenly the string broke and the beads flew in all directions over the old shop floor.

It was then Luis spoke his momentous words.

"Too bad," he said.

Our discussions with Luis, until his retirement at sixty-five, were confined to Spanish. Our contributions consisted of necessary words relating to his work, such as *zapatos* for moccasins, *colorado* for red or *amarillo* for yellow, the terms for widths and numbers, plus our understanding of a half-dozen other words and phrases such as *dos pesos* when he wanted a two-dollar advance on his wages.

But Johnny, to the extent of his needs, was a real linguist, and the fact that his three tongues included a wonderful telescoped version of English made him a source of considerable help in the book shop before we arrived in the mornings and during short periods when he was alone. He was known to sell not only impressive pieces of jewelry, but also on occasion forty or fifty dollars' worth of scholarly books, before we came in at nine on summer days.

Nor did the offices of moccasin making and selling mark the limits of his abilities. It was he who restrung, when necessary, the pawn necklaces of shell and turquoise, neatly winding the section that comes at the back of the neck with waxed cord, Indian fashion. It was he who looked after the building and cleverly built up small dikes of sand to channel the water from the winter's snow away from the shop's front door.

But his special gift was one for friendship. Old friends of the days when Ralph was here still came to see him. New ones added each year regarded an "in" with Johnny as a special mark of distinction. Boy Scouts hung fascinated over his shoulder to watch him at work, and small boys and girls came back year after year with apparently no other purpose than to see Johnny again.

As is true of all the Pueblo people, he loved children, and at forty-eight had two daughters and a quartet of roundheaded grandchildren who lived with him and his wife Lisa most of the time.

Of John's and Luis's personal lives at the pueblo we learned a great deal over the years. Of this Johnny spoke freely. Pastoral as their lives may seem—and in many cases are—in their farming community at the foot of Taos Mountain, they have their problems, most of them seeming to stem from contact with some of the least admirable aspects of the whiteman's way.

Of their secular community life we learned something as well. John once served for a year as War Chief Lieutenant, aide to the War Chief Captain. Wars are fortunately infrequent in this area these days, and their duties seemed to involve supervision of communal lands and other property (such as their herd of sixteen buffalo) and administration of justice in civil pueblo affairs. Since John received no compensation for these services, which took a considerable amount of effort and time away from his job at the book shop, he heaved a sigh of relief when his term of office expired.

Most of the Taos Indians are Catholics, but this comparatively new faith has been superimposed on their age-old ceremonialism, and while they perform their obligations to the church, it is their own animistic religion that is blended in with their everyday thought and action. Of this they are conditioned by centuries of reticence to say little, in the tribal belief that to reveal the details or significance of a ceremonial rite is to destroy its efficacy, its medicine. Johnny referred to such matters briefly as "Indian business."

But we know that he and Luis, during their years at the shop, each spent six weeks or so of one winter in the kiva, the underground ceremonial chamber (there are six in use at Taos Pueblo), instructing the boys who had reached puberty in the religious beliefs of their fathers and renewing their own ceremonial bonds with the group.

When John's turn had come and the weeks of his absence were nearly over we awaited his return with interest, for Lisa and Ben Couse, his friend, had both come into the shop and spoken of the matter.

"When he come back," Ben said, "he be different. You see."

"He be better," said Lisa, "he be more Indian."

And better he was and more Indian and more oriental, too.

His black hair, which had been worn in two rolls resembling braids and bound their full length with colored tape, had been pulled back into a chignon. In addition to his usual blanket, which when he left the shop he wore wrapped about shoulders and head, he had a second blanket rolled about his waist. From this hung a short apron of soft blue cloth such as a Chinese coolie might wear. And on his face was a new, calm look, as of a man who had just returned from another world—chastened, uplifted, and restored.

John told us many times that Luis is a big man at the pueblo, for he is

9

one of the grotesquely painted clowns called Black Eyes or Chiffoneta. We have seen him at the beautiful winter Deer Dance, his legs and upper body bare and painted with black stripes, his face painted, too, his head ornamented with corn husks, carrying his tiny bow and symbolic arrow of straw. He is one of the makers of fun—though not laugh-making fun, for its ritual meaning is deeply serious.

We are grateful for these glimpses of the Indian world. For the Taos are wise with an old wisdom, rooted in the earth, magnanimous through integration with the natural world about them; they draw from sources we cannot tap. On the few occasions when they come into any public meeting, first they confer among themselves in Tiwa, in a calm, almost somnolent flow of sound. Then the interpreter rises; his language is simple, his words well chosen. He reports what the governor and council have said on this matter. The statement is resolute and determined, for these are the Taos, "the proud, the rebellious," [1] but it is also dispassionate and reasonable.

Whatever the matter is of which we are talking, they have cut to the heart of it, putting to shame the Anglos who have spoken before them.

We are fascinated by the Indian's concept of the universe, his constant concern with keeping en rapport with it as the basis of his security.

We read the studies of the specialists who have written of the Pueblo Indians—Edgar L. Hewett and J. Walter Fewkes, Frank Waters and Elsie Clews Parsons, Mary Austin, Ruth Benedict, Matilda Coxe Stevenson, Bertha P. Dutton, Frank Cushing, and others since the time of the Smithsonian expeditions and the early army officers' reports. We watch the magnificent ritual dances at the Pueblos—the Taos Deer Dance, the Santo Domingo Corn Dance, the Zuni Shalako, and, perhaps the most beautiful of all, the Hopi Bean dances in February. They are ethnology, religious philosophy, and ballet, fused into a poetry of movement, sight, and sound.

But, study and watch and muse as we may, and work at close range as we did for years with Johnny and Luis, visiting with Johnny often on the peaceful winter afternoons, we have never been so rash as to think we have gained more than a faint glimmer of insight into the Indian tribal mind—still less, it seems, into the mind of one friendly and well-known tribesman.

One could never decide what were really the differences in approaches to things and ideas between Johnny and us. One could only ascribe them lamely to differences in cultures. And it was always easier to explain to ourselves why these variants in viewpoint existed than to state what they were.

But one thing was clear from the start: Johnny's approach to his relations with other people was more natural and wholesome than we were used to seeing in the Anglo or Spanish-American worlds. If we were on first-name terms with any customer, Johnny was, too. If he overheard any-one planning to drive to Santa Fe and if he needed to go there himself, he would not hesitate to ask if he might go along, no matter how slightly he knew the driver. Why not? He would be happy to do the same thing for him. And no employee need give any hint of special deference to his em-ployer, whatever his stature or position.

Mrs. Saul Harberg once felt it necessary to point out to her longtime Pueblo gardener that he was neglecting his duties. Not in the least discon-certed, he gave her a look of benevolent concern.

"Oh Effe," he said, "you getting old and cranky. You better go take a sleep."

Mrs. Harberg smiled back at him and went and took a sleep.

She was not an employer; she was just an old friend.

The Taos Indian, victim of two conquests, still retains his identity, his natural, unconscious pride. It is not an aggressive pride, but a calm assur-ance of his status as an individual—a status of equality and in fact (and this completely without arrogance) superiority.

Since Johnny's ancestors had originally come to Taos from Northeast Asia, we used to tell ourselves that it must be the Siberian in him that led him to call Genevieve "Genevitch." And it was commonplace to hear him call out from his chair at the moccasin table: "Genevitch, you come here!" It always startled her, but she always went.

We were hard put to it at times to maintain an equal status with Johnny. For one thing, we were the newcomers; his tenure in the old shop exceeded ours by fifteen years. So his loyalty and devotion to us (second only to that conferred upon Ralph and Rowena) carried with it a deep and at times highly inconvenient proprietary interest in the premises and a firm belief that in the event of his absence all wheels would come to a perma-nent stop. Nor did this viewpoint seem to him at all out of keeping with the fact that some of his personal problems were known to have kept him away from the shop for days and even weeks at a time.

On one occasion when a series of untoward events had goaded us into threatening him with the loss of his job—unless or until—he sighed, put his unfinished moccasin into his table drawer, reached for his blanket, and rose with mournful dignity.

"Aw right," he said. "You don' like me any more. I go. I go now, you don' wan' me. But," he added, "I te' you one fing. I gone, I sure fee' sorry for you gir's."

4

Part of the Earth

That I am part of the earth
my feet know perfectly
    —D. H. Lawrence
        Apocalypse

Restoring an old Taos adobe house is a lifetime affair. It will call for your own strenuous personal labor; for more patience than most people can readily summon; it will, you think sometimes, call for your heart's blood. And it will give you an inner experience that will last as long as you live.

We do not speak of our houses in these fulsome terms. We are only dimly aware of this feeling and could not explain it to anyone else. More-over, this is an honest, no-nonsense house that does not respond to florid comment. But we know ourselves that the feeling is here.

The Navajo prays in his Night Chant: "May it be beautiful all around me." It is such an envelopment in an aesthetic profundity that we some-times think we have.

This old Spanish house was literally molded and stroked into form by the hands of *los viejos*—the old ones. They fashioned it more than 150 years ago in the form that the first Spanish explorers found here as the homes of the Pueblo Indians. As the Indians had done, they built it with what was here: earth, water, and straw, surmounted by pine and aspen woods from the Taos mountains.

In this respect it is truly notable. Nowhere else in the United States can a style of architecture be found that traces its descent in an unbroken line from aboriginal American sources.

Its length sprawls along the earth, of which it is a part. Its floors, its two-foot-thick walls, are built of earth, and for warmth there is earth even above the pine beams and aspen rounds that form its ceilings.

Its primitive beauty evolves from its sculptured lines, molded and flowing, and the bulk and mass that are its strength and tie it in to the bare earth of the Talpa ridge.

Its lines do not give pleasure to every eye, of course. Many a Taos visitor, conditioned by the precision of contemporary architecture, sees in them only an untidiness, a disarray that calls for correction. But we should as soon call in a builder to straighten them as summon a cosmic landscape architect to cut to precision the irregular outline of Taos Mountain. The mere idea is, to us, all of a piece with G. K. Chesterton's fictional poor friend who went mad and ran about the country with an axe, hacking branches off the trees whenever there were not the same number on both sides.

In the matters of mass, line, and proportion the forebears of our Spanish neighbors seem to have been innate artists. So it is a gracious house that we found for ourselves in the country five miles from Taos. An upward, sculptured extension of the ground, it follows the natural inclination of the ridge, so that one long section slopes eastward and each room sits on a different level. Meanwhile the main room slopes toward the valley, requiring a division into two levels joined by a broad adobe step.

It is aesthetically impractical to hire the usual professional builder to stabilize and restore a classic Taos house. He is not *simpático* with it; he is not temperamentally equipped for the situation; he is not interested in maintaining its flowing lines.

"The first thing to do," he would say, "is to straighten that crooked window."

But we do not wish to straighten that shadowbox window or to replace a panel in an old door, to be rid of its open knothole and the crudely scratched cross that was put there to ward off sorcerers. We have no intention of raising the height of the three interior doors, all of them so low that even my own five-foot three-inch height cannot pass through unless I bend forward as if going into a cave.

Our restoration problem was solved by our next-door neighbor, Barbara Latham, artist and illustrator of children's books. Barbara had lived with her painter husband, Howard Cook, in an old adobe for many years.

"Get in some of the Spanish neighbors or Indians from the pueblo," she said. "They've lived in these houses all their lives and know how to handle them." We could, she said, just play it by ear—go along for a few days and see what happened. We could always find somebody else to help, if necessary.

So encouraged, we started out bravely with Johnny and Luis, our moccasin makers from the shop. Both had maintained their own houses at the pueblo for many years, had helped Ralph Meyers to keep the old shop in repair and rendered him similar service in restoring his house in Los Cordovas.

The two were delighted. Moccasin making, day after day, was a tedious business. Sure, sure, they knew how to do it, Johnny assured us. "Everything be aw right."

While we intended only to stabilize the house's exterior, there was much to be done inside, chiefly to provide for modern amenities and for a large window to open up the glorious view of the valley meadows with their backdrop, the old worn contour of the Picuris mountain range.

Genevieve being an executive type, it was agreed that I should stay with the shop that spring while she oversaw our two master builders and kept them supplied with tools and materials. Since neither of us had any notion of how much of anything would be needed—how many adobes, how much earth and straw for plastering, how many nails—she found that running the supply line, until she got the hang of it, was taking most of her time. For, to our helpers, if there were two nails on hand at 5:00 P.M., we had nails, even though two pounds might be needed at 8:00 the next morning.

Moreover, none of our problems was cut to standard size. We could not drive up to a lumberyard and buy adobe bricks, earth for plastering, and straw. We must find out by the grapevine who had been making adobes lately, track him down to his house, and bargain. But there was no earth for plastering there; that we must get from somebody else; and from still a third small rancher, out on the mesa, bags of straw, old and rotted so that, while it would add both strength and texture to walls and floors, it would not be stiff enough to protrude through their surfaces.

Finally, for any wood that would show, we would have to match the old wood of the house. Our first purchase was fourteen dollars' worth of old window frames and beams to cut up into sills and lintels, or if needed, to support the roof above a partition we planned to remove.

Johnny's first job was that of cutting a doorway through an interior wall. Genevieve, seeing him hacking busily away with a pickaxe, wondered what would happen to the section of wall above the aperture.

"Johnny," she told him, "you'll have to put in a support above that or the whole top of the wall will fall down."

"Oh, that be aw right," he said.

"But Johnny—"

"Don't you worry," he said, picking at another adobe. "Everything be aw right. I know what I doing."

But at this point Johnny suddenly had his first recognizable confronta-

14

tion with the law of gravity. The wall above the doorway began to sag omi-nously.

"Genevitch!" he yelled, "Go tell Luis bring me two-by-four!"

By the time Genevitch had found Luis in another part of the house, and he had located a two-by-four and returned with it, Johnny was sup-porting the upper wall by main strength, in a highly uncomfortable posi-tion he was forced to maintain until Luis could cut the board to the right length, hack out a slit at each side of the top of the hole, and slide the board into the slits.

This episode taught us that, while our friends evidently could build from the ground up, we should have the whole place down about our ears unless we could provide some knowledgeable supervision. All activity was suspended until we had recruited John Yaple, neighbor and friend and an artist at working with adobe, old wood, and rocks. He had a classic adobe house of his own; he had restored several others. He came and took over.

And he learned in a few days that our Pueblo builders had still not mastered the implications of Mr. Newton's idea. Arriving one morning, he found that, having finished another assignment, they had begun on their own the project of cutting a hole for a kitchen window.

"I don't know why the whole side of the house didn't fall down," he said later.

Our crew began to grow, with the addition of two more Indians to help Johnny and Luis, and two of our Spanish neighbors, Mrs. Tafoya and Mrs. Ortiz, who were experts in making fireplaces and plastering walls. Finally everybody was organized and working at full speed.

At this point in such a restoration project, an adobe house is a thor-oughly discouraging mess. Adobe stabilized is a firm thing, with a beautiful texture. But adobe dust seeps into everything, and wet adobe is just plain mud. In our house at this point, with walls coming down and walls going up, some people mixing mud and others plastering, and the cold May wind howling bleakly through open doorways, we despaired of ever capturing any of the order, the grace and charm we saw in our neighbors' houses.

It all got a great deal worse before it got even a little bit better. Next the plumber's men began digging a deep trench diagonally through the kitchen's adobe floor to run the water pipes from the sink to the bathroom. Electricians were doing the same on a smaller scale in a bedroom and chiseling shallow channels in adobe walls to conceal electrical cables. The telephone men followed suit. This last project fell afoul of Johnny Romero, busy with a plastering job on a wall where a telephone cable had just been installed. Finding the line in his way, he simply snipped it in two, cutting off telephone service from every house on the Talpa ridge.

Still Genevieve, frustrated and fascinated, slogged along at her unaccustomed job, with some help from me on weekends.

And then a new problem developed. Two transplanted New Yorkers, Joe Baum and Slim Bastian, had been retained to design and supervise sewage disposal arrangements. (Slim was an expert electronics technician and Joe a skilled photographer and fine violinist, so that the whole added up to a normal Taos situation.) The trench diggers for this project had proceeded only a few feet when they ran into a quarter-ton boulder. Use of dynamite to remove it was a touchy thing because of the proximity of the rock to our new living room windows. Joe and Slim circled the rock a few times, thought for a while, and came up with a homespun solution. They dug away earth, built hot fires under the boulder, doused it with streams of cold water, and struck it with heavy mallets. Large pieces cracked off. Several repetitions of this technique and our problem was solved.

As things settled down and the month moved along, we began, with Barbara's constant help and advice, to pull out of the slough. Mrs. Tafoya and Mrs. Ortiz had built a wonderful Indian corner fireplace in the living room, which we had designed in traditional style and for which Luis toted adobes and mixed mud and straw in a box. Except for rough plastering, such menial jobs were all the men were permitted to do about fireplace, walls, or floors. The fine craftsmanship involved in bringing these to a finished perfection was acknowledged as something which only women could do.

Over the rough adobe brick walls they applied a thick mud plaster. When it had dried, they filled in the cracks by hand.

They would finish with natural earth paint, to be brought from caves in the Picuris foothills. What color should we choose—the soft fawn of *tierra bayeta* or the equally beautiful, austere off-white of *tierra blanca* with its decorative glints of mica? For the main room, tierra bayeta, we thought, because of the warmth of its tone; for the rest, tierra blanca.

The earth pigments were mixed with water and spread on with pieces of natural sheepskin.

At last the rooms began to take on life, for the ceilings were undisturbed. They consisted of large, naturally round pine beams, called *vigas*, which supported the roof and protruded through walls to give interest to its exterior, and, between these, aspen rounds (*latias*) laid in herringbone pattern or, in some of the rooms, rough lengths of split pine of the old presawmill times.

Now our personal involvement with the house began to deepen. Genevieve had early begun to get her hands into adobe and had learned from the women to use the earth paints. And even at my greater distance from the intimate details of the craftsmanship being invoked, I began to feel more and more the creative pull of the house's coming into form.

But the greatest task still lay before us—two new adobe floors, one in a room which had not been used as living quarters, the other to replace one irreparably damaged. For this delicate project Mrs. Tafoya and Mrs. Ortiz declared themselves insufficiently skilled. This was a specialty; we would have to call in Mrs. Valerio from Llano Quemado, across the valley. She was *una vieja*—an old lady—and it was she who knew how to make floors.

Accompanied by her daughter, Mrs. Mondragón, she came—a small, fragile, black-clad figure with a dignified mien and a merry eye. She spoke only Spanish, but since Mrs. Mondragón and most of the rest of our crew were bilingual, this was no problem. While everyone else stood respectfully by to help, she took command of the job.

The Indians began tamping the ground in the room with a heavy cross-section of a cottonwood tree with upright handles attached. At intervals they sprinkled the area with water. When it was firm and level, Mrs. Valerio approved it and her own work began.

A dishpanful at a time, the mixture of mud and straw was brought in to her. On her knees she kneaded it with exquisite care, as if she were working bread dough, removing each straw that showed any stiffness and each particle of pebble large enough to be felt at all by her gnarled but sensitive hands. And then, a panful at a time, it went down on the tamped ground and was carefully leveled.

When the floor had dried, a few discernible cracks appeared, a development obviously expected by Mrs. Valerio, who nodded her head in approval. These she painstakingly filled with the same material, pushing it in with her fingers and smoothing it off to a perfect surface. Next a thin adobe wash was brushed on.

When this was dry, Mrs. Valerio came and surveyed it again. "Bueno," she said. Brushed with a red-brown paint made of pigment from a third Talpa cave, it was perfect. Mrs. Valerio's work was done, and we saw her off to Llano Quemado with cordial, respectful goodbyes.

Our two new floors had to be stabilized, and this, under Barbara's direction, we did ourselves, with three coats, one smoking hot and two cold, of a mixture of linseed oil and kerosene. With drying time, this operation took more than two weeks, but when they were over, the floors were like rich old leather.

We eyed them with satisfaction, for in Taos a good adobe floor is in much the same category as a fine Persian rug is elsewhere, and as jealously guarded. Spike heels are not welcome here, and party invitations are issued to female guests with a cheerfully accepted reminder to wear flat heels. After eighteen years, our floors are still virtually intact.

Our house was finished. Finished? Happily, no. It would never be really finished; an adobe house is a lifetime hobby.

For this is a complicated house; its imperfections are a part of its perfection, its faults built into its virtues. It is fragile, in that its four adobe hearths are easily marred, and permanent in that the mars are just as easily mended. Like an engaging but active child, it demands your continuous care and so enlarges your affection.

You are never finished and no one in Taos expects you to be.

Soon you will be hunting for an old Peñasco door to replace the cheap one brought for temporary purposes and used for ten years before you came upon an authentic old one. Perhaps you will find it in a mountain village, being used as part of a goat pen; perhaps it will turn up in an antique shop.

You will be scouring the area for old timbers, which you will use with adobe to add (the only exterior change you will make) a wide *portal*—a porch—which you will back up to the brisk southwestern wind, and into a corner of which Floraida and Annie Archuleta will build another small Indian fireplace to temper the cool air of the New Mexico summer evening.

For here during at least five months of the year you will have your morning and evening meals and stay on to smell the dew-moist new-mown hay in the valley or watch the moon move in its arc from the eastern foothills to go down near the flat top of Pedernal at Abiquiu.

Tony Vigil will split sections of pine logs, smoke them, and bring them to mend old ceilings in two of your rooms. He will make a delicate screen of aspen wands to help the lace vine mask the well house in the patio.

John Yaple will bring in lichen-embroidered volcanic rocks from the mesa to use with decorative gravel and native sage and chamisa to grace your section of the rocky Talpa ridge.

And Genevieve, that happy gardener, will get up with the magpies on summer mornings to set out trees and lilacs; to grub out the stones that lie scarcely under the surface of the ground and replace them with mountain soil fertilized with prized goat manure scrounged from her host at a cocktail party; and to produce, there or in a huge old copper kettle, or in canoas made from halves of hollowed-out logs, a riot of old-fashioned flowers.

You will find yourself helping her bring home, after a Sunday picnic, sections of turf from the river flats for a miniature lawn, to be of respectable size later and her pride and delight, but at first so small that for two summers she will clip it with kitchen shears.

As you ease the turf into place, you can look up across the valley and think how quiet it is here. It is a quiet that seems to be partly visual, for while there are a few houses on the opposite ridge, they are off at the right and too far away for their inhabitants to be seen. So there are just the mountains and the foothills and in the fields a few cattle and horses munching their slow way across the somnolent scene. They are needed—they and the sometimes moving clouds—to keep us knowing, should perspective fail, that this is a living landscape.

It is really to this peaceful house that I am writing. And thinking of Emily Dickinson and her ". . . letter to the world / That never wrote to me." [1] For my letter is answered as I write. This house and we who live in it are mutually involved, and we all know it.

5

The Land Grant, the Curse
of New Mexico

The first Spanish owner of our acre and a half of Talpa land left the place hastily one day 290 years ago, hotly pursued by a band of wrathful Pueblo Indians. Don Fernando Durán y Chávez and his son were two of the only three Spanish colonists in the whole Taos Valley to escape massacre in the Pueblo Revolt of 1680. They made it to El Paso and never came back.

I learned this from Rowena Martínez, who had been exploring the Santa Fe archives of the Bureau of Land Management for the Taos County Historical Society.

For the next thirty-five years, she said, the land just sat here, except that the Indians raised a few patches of beans in the creek valley just below us.

By 1715 the revolt was far behind—Diego de Vargas had recaptured the territory twenty-three years before—and new settlers had begun to come in. Cristóbal de la Serna put in a petition for the abandoned land (again to the Spanish crown) through Don Juan Ignacio Flore Mogollón, His Majesty's Governor and Captain General of the Kingdom. Don Juan thought he had better find out first if the move would be acceptable to the Indians. The proposal went to Juan de la Mora Pineda, lieutenant of the chief alcalde of the pueblo of Taos, who laid it before Indian dignitaries including the governor, cacique, and war chiefs. They had no objection, he found, to Serna's having the land. It was not theirs, anyway, they said; it already belonged to the Spaniards. They would just go down and harvest their beans and not plant there the following year.

So Serna took over the land grant, in a simple, symbolic ceremony that I sometimes envision as I look out over the valley. Pineda led him over the tract by the hand, pointing out its general boundaries. Then Cristóbal "pulled up grass, threw stones," and received two signed copies of the document, beautifully written in flowing script. All present then shouted (loudly and joyfully), "Long live the King!"

It was a small tract as land grants went here (the Maxwell grant, put together in the nineteenth century, was three times the size of Rhode Island), but still it was more than twenty-two thousand acres. Its boundaries were set in the document as "on one side the middle and on the other the hot spring and on the east an old landmark [*mojonera*] and on the other the mountain." The pastures and waters were to "be common."

I suppose the boundaries were definitely set when the grant was patented in 1903, or later, since it was surveyed three times, and I don't know when the "pastures and waters" were sold or otherwise assigned to individuals. I haven't tried to find out, since the Serna grant has apparently had a peaceful history. This situation bids fair to continue, although New Mexico's militant land grant organization has recently begun filing notices of "prior right of title" on this and twenty-eight other grants in the state. The action will cloud the titles, according to Santiago Anaya, president of the group, "if people believe in law and order." But nobody in Taos has even mentioned the move, as our area is not one of the state's trouble spots.

I don't really know what I'd try to do if it were—if someone were to come along and tell me that he owns our little piece of land himself by virtue of some century-old treaty; because of a faulty survey based on misreading of a document or misidentification of a landmark; or because of some fraud he claims was committed by a land speculator seventy-five years ago. I hope I never have to decide, and I probably won't, but there have been many less fortunate people in northern New Mexico, within a stone's throw of Taos. Complications like these, plus the eccentricities of inheritance traditions here and the general vicissitudes involved in some 450 years of history for individual pieces of land, have caused more than a century of litigation and rioting, arson, and murder during the last decade.

Matters of inheritance alone are enough to confuse the most astute and persistent attorney and abstractor in northern New Mexico. Here a man may have willed to his son a piece of land a few feet wide and a mile long, or part of a room or half a cow, not saying which half or what was to become of the rest of it, or half a mattress, again with no mention as to who could rightfully show up to sleep on the other half.

Old wills here make delightful reading. Louis H. Warner in the *New Mexico Historical Review* once mentioned a testator who divided a large residual estate into three parts for the benefit of "prisoners, bashful women and maidens, and the most unfortunate persons," the padre to choose the last two groups, the governor the first one.

But Warner devoted most of his article to some of the gems he found illustrating the Spanish patriarch's careful division of his land and other possessions among members of his family.

Division of rooms was the rule rather than the exception—so many vigas to each. Such bequests were made as these:

> To N thirty-seven vigas in the house, eight being in the kitchen, nine in the large room, nineteen in the parlor on the west side and three in the little room south of the parlor.
>
> Three parts of a tree.
>
> A wagon, to be divided equally among the children.
>
> Fifteen yards for pathways; eighty-two logs.
>
> Five dollars and eighty-five cents in cash, six feet three inches in a house, four feet three inches in a porch, two feet eight inches in a little house, and four feet two inches in a post corral.[1]

Even in a case where a man owned a whole room by himself, he could present a problem later if the rest of the family wanted to sell the house, a situation which arose here some years ago when California customers of ours wanted to buy an old adobe near Ranchos de Taos. All the heirs were willing to sell except Uncle Bonifacio, who owned and occupied the back room. But he was very old, the others pointed out, and couldn't possibly live very long. So our friends bought the rest of the house. Ten years later Uncle Bonifacio was still there.

The head of a Taos Spanish family would have no liking for the English system whereby the estate goes intact to the eldest son. What would the other sons do? They had no wish to leave the land, to which they had a deep emotional attachment, nor did anyone want them to leave. It was much better for everybody to stay here together. Because there was no money to buy more land for the children, the father arranged to divide the home place with meticulous exactness. To be fair, he cut it up into long strips, each strip fronting on the irrigation ditch and backing up to the foothills, where there were upland pastures and timber.

Over the generations the strips grew progressively narrower, until finally they reached the dead end of economic futility. One piece of property here is twenty-six inches wide and a mile and one-half deep and is owned by eight heirs. Another is twenty-seven feet wide at the highway and seven and one-half miles deep.

Complexities connected with land ownership in New Mexico have resulted in the fact that many a homeowner here has settled for a title so vulnerable it would horrify a land purchaser in any other area I know of. Not that it is impossible to secure what would normally be considered a firm title, if you work at it hard enough. William A. Keleher, Albuquerque attorney-historian who made New Mexico land problems a lifelong study, described the situation: "Confirmed by act of Congress or by the Court of Private Land Claims, with boundaries surveyed by competent surveyors and titles quieted and settled by able lawyers, there is every reason to say that many owners are vested with a title that is marketable and beyond any attack. But," he added, "every grant must be considered on its own merits, not only as to validity of title, but to all other factors prompting a purchase." [2]

But the situation may be even more complicated than that. Suppose a stranger decides to buy a piece of land in Rio Arriba County, next door to Taos. He buys it in good faith, pays for it, has it surveyed, puts through a suit to quiet title (which costs him a thousand dollars), and gets a warranty deed and an abstract as long as his arm. He has taken all the steps considered necessary for the legal acquisition of land. So he moves in, fences the land to keep in his herd of cattle, and builds a house and a barn. Before long, however, he is told by the owner of a small adjoining ranch that the land he thinks he has bought is not his, but belongs to his neighbor's family under the terms of the Treaty of Guadalupe Hidalgo, signed more than a hundred years ago. Whoever sold it to him, his neighbor claims, had no right to do so; the new owner is told that it had previously changed hands through forgery, known to have been practiced "as a fine art" in the Court of Private Land Claims set up in 1891, or through the machinations of the Santa Fe Ring. The term was applied to certain land speculators with a reputation, not always deserved, for knavery. [3]

The new owner of the Rio Arriba ranch has never heard of the Treaty of Guadalupe Hidalgo, the Court of Private Land Claims, or the Santa Fe Ring. He only knows that he has bought the land, paid good money for it, and taken all the normal procedures for transfer of real estate under U.S. law. He produces his documents and sits tight. Before long, however, his fences are cut and his cattle scattered; his house, barn, and haystacks are burned by night raiders.

This is the violent aspect of the movement of northern New Mexico's rural poor to recover from private ownership and from the U.S. Forest Service lands that they claim were unlawfully taken from their ancestors. This is the cause that brought Reies López Tijerina up from Texas to organize his militant Alianza Federal de Mercedes, known as the Alianza.

Tijerina startled the country one day in June of 1967 with headlines resulting from an armed raid by him and twenty of his followers on the courthouse at Tierra Amarilla, county seat of Rio Arriba. Two county officials were wounded by gunfire and two men held for several hours as hostages, though finally released unharmed. Tijerina was captured after the biggest manhunt in New Mexico history. He was tried and acquitted on charges growing out of the raid but went to a federal prison on an earlier charge of seizing federal property. Charges were still pending several years later against some of the Alianzans and two years after the incident the Tierra Amarilla jailer, Eulogio Salazar, who was to have been a witness, was found murdered.

No clue to this crime has been found, in spite of a tempting ten-thousand-dollar offer for information. There is still deep fear in Tierra Amarilla; no one is talking.

Such happenings give the Taoseño pause, for Rio Arriba is our immediate neighbor to the west. Moreover, Taos shares some of the same land problems and, among much of its population, the same deep poverty. From present indications it seems unlikely that the violence will spread to Taos. Still, in 1968 Tijerina leased a ranch in San Cristobal, twenty miles north of Taos, as headquarters for his Alliance. Two nights later the ranch house burned down. Arson was suspected, but state fire inspectors could find no proof. They did find a sizable cache of dynamite, though its owner said he had stored it for prospecting purposes.

What do the Alianzans want? They want the United States to buy back from individuals or take back from the Forest Service all lands that they claim were once included in northern New Mexico Spanish and Mexican grants and give them back to the living heirs of their original settlers. They would turn back the clock, in regard to many claims, to 1848, date of the Treaty of Guadalupe Hidalgo, which followed the end of the Mexican War and under whose terms New Mexico with all its lands was ceded to the United States.

Anything that has happened to land in the state since then was illegal, the Alianzans claim, if it served to divert it from possession by heirs of original grantees by any method—private or tax sale, inheritance, gift, trickery, or diversion to the Forest Service. For they maintain that the treaty guaranteed possession of the lands to the original grantees and their heirs. The fact that this would be an uncommonly complicated procedure is not their problem, they feel, for they charge that the United States permitted illegal actions and now bears the responsibility for correcting them.

What if the new land buyer in Rio Arriba has documents showing that he owns the land? They have documents, too, older ones. His documents are null and void, anyway, they claim, having been issued by some unit of the U.S. government, which they say has no jurisdiction. For while the Alianzans have never rejected the concept of their previous status as citizens of Spain or Mexico, they do not now regard themselves as citizens of the United States. "The United States is an intruder," Tijerina signs proclaim.

The Alianzans consider themselves citizens of the "Alliance of Free City States," each "free state" consisting of the lands and people involved in one of the old land grants. Each New Mexican Indian pueblo has this status, too, the Alianzans explain, but the Indians so far have not warmed to the idea, nor to the Alianza cause in general. "Go ahead and get the land back," they say, grinning, "and when you get it, we'll be right there waiting to take it back from you."

When you're thinking about land, you sometimes conclude that frontier New Mexico was run entirely by bungling amateurs and sly sharpsters. The honest, able pioneers and upright officials who overwhelmingly outnumbered them seem to fade right out of the picture.

There is, for instance, the matter of documents lost from state and federal archives. The Indians had done this sort of thing themselves, when in blind rage they destroyed every record they could find during their twelve-year occupancy of the Palace of the Governors in Santa Fe prior to 1692. Then in the 1870s and 1880s, when the Santa Fe Ring was at its peak, land documents mysteriously disappeared and false ones appeared. But much of the loss came about through sheer ignorance and carelessness. When Governor Lew Wallace (who wrote *Ben Hur*) moved into the palace around 1880, his wife, Susan, wandering about the building, was horrified to find state papers thrown about, torn, muddy, and waterstained, on the adobe floor of a dark inner room with a leaky roof. A previous governor, William A. Pile, is accused of throwing a mass of general state documents "down an outhouse," though some say it was sold as trash when he ordered a librarian to clean out a room.

But ignorance and chicanery were not confined to matters of state or federal archives. The fact that many of the ancestors of northern New Mexico subsistence ranchers were swindled out of their land has been too well researched and documented by too many scholars to allow room for doubt. One method that he claims accounted for 80 percent of the loss is described by Victor Westphall in his book *The Public Domain in New Mexico 1854–1891*.

Following the Treaty of Guadalupe Hidalgo the process set up by the U.S. government for guaranteeing titles in grants required the landowner to submit his evidence of title to the surveyor general, who held hearings and passed on his recommendations to the Congress for final decision. But many claimants, suspicious, were unwilling to present their documents and were encouraged by designing manipulators (some in high places) in the belief that such action would do nothing to secure their titles and would only result in more labor and expense. Furthermore, the complexity of the process involved was exaggerated by certain attorneys who, in the guise of benevolent advisers, offered to steer their claims through the mills at Santa Fe and Washington. Since cash was scarce, many of these attorneys offered to take their fees in lands. "Not all were relinquished in legal fees," Westphall concluded, "nevertheless, the same manipulators were involved throughout." [4]

There were other ways by which the illiterate villagers lost land. Some were induced to sell parcels of it at ridiculously low figures; [5] others saw it go to stores in payment for small debts. But some of it was lost through the villagers' own relaxed pattern of living—for instance, their failure in many cases to pay taxes.

This obligation sat lightly on these people. They were poor and cash was hard to come by. Hardly anybody paid taxes; nothing, it was felt, would happen if you simply ignored them. The county treasurer was most understanding about this. He was a friend of the family, perhaps a relative. He knew you couldn't afford to pay taxes; he wouldn't get tough about it.

Basically much of the loss of land happened through the imposition under U.S. domination of a new set of laws, which rural New Mexicans never understood and with which they were correspondingly slow to conform. Ironically, it was a repetition of the thing their forefathers had done to the Indians, imposing new laws that were foreign to their understanding and their whole way of living. The Indians, too, had ignored these new rules and not only had lost much of their land but had suffered worse penalties: imprisonment, beatings, and in some cases death.

As the long arm of the new law gradually reached into the remote Spanish villages, a new kind of community organization was decreed. The boards traditionally administering the common lands were dissolved, and the villages were ordered to incorporate under a new system. There was no provision for communal living, whereby each family had not only its own allotment of land but the right to pasture its cattle and sheep on lands owned in common. "No communal living?" the Alianzans ask wryly. "What about the Pueblo Indians, living communally in nineteen villages scattered along the Rio Grande?"

The matter of these common lands has been chiefly responsible for the longtime running feud between subsistence ranchers and the Forest Service. The problem began in 1891 when Congress authorized the president to reserve public lands for national forests. The nearly nine million acres included in national forests in this state were obtained by the government through purchase, trade, or transfers from the public domain. The potential for dissension lay in the fact that some of the purchases were made at tax sales or from banks that had foreclosed on mortgages, and much of the public-domain lands had achieved that status when claims were rejected by the Court of Private Land Claims, which turned down two-thirds of those presented.

Fundamentally the friction comes from two problems much talked about today: a conflict of cultures and a lack of communication. The situation has been well stated by Michael Jenkinson, former social worker in Rio Arriba County:

> The subsistence rancher, for whom bureaucracy was a thing to be avoided, now faced it at every turn. There were licenses to be bought for fishing and hunting. Permits were necessary to cut wood or graze cattle and sheep. And the Hispano soon discovered that these regulations, unlike many an earlier Spanish or Mexican edict, could not be ignored with impunity. A man could be fined for killing a deer to feed his family, or if his cattle strayed on national forest land.
>
> There was a formidable communication barrier. Many an Anglo forest ranger, suddenly thrust into a region where Spanish was the predominant language, could not understand the questioning people. Even had language not been a problem, the cultural isolation of the villagers would not have prepared them to accept many of the answers.

Overgrazing, a concern of the rangers, they understood not at all. "What did the number of sheep they grazed have to do with future water supplies for the city of Albuquerque?" And "why were Texans with polished boots and high-powered rifles hunting over the lands that were the birthright of the Hispano people?" [6]

The two biggest bones of contention in Rio Arriba County are the Tierra Amarilla grant and another called the San Joaquín del Cañon de Rio Chama. On the highway entering the village of Tierra Amarilla is an official state historical marker bearing this legend:

TIERRA AMARILLA
FOUNDED 1858

POP. 1,246   ELEV. 7,460

THE TIERRA AMARILLA LAND GRANT COMPRISING ALMOST 600,000 ACRES WAS GIVEN TO JOSÉ MANUEL MARTÍNEZ BY THE MEXICAN GOVERNMENT IN 1832. MANY DESCENDANTS OF JOSÉ MANUEL MARTÍNEZ STILL LIVE IN THE AREA.

And so they do, but they don't own much of the grant these days. Several historians say that before the turn of the century one Santa Fe attorney secured for his own possession 593,000 acres of it, some by purchase but much through sharp practices. Dr. Myra E. Jenkins, New Mexico State Historian, points out that the attorney was able to acquire much of the land through conveyance by one of the Spanish heirs, who sold out many of his compadres and got rich in the process.[7] But however it slipped out of their hands, much of it is now public domain land and much in the possession of individuals outside the original family, facts of which that highway sign must be a constant and abrasive reminder to the Alianzans. One of their most active members these days is a great-grandson of José Manuel Martínez.

The history of the San Joaquín grant is a different story and one of its major complications is directly due to government bungling. The grant was surveyed or its acreage officially estimated by the U.S. government several times and each time a different size area was reported.

The surveyor general in 1872 first estimated that it included about 184,320 acres, and upon that basis recommended that Congress approve it. Congress took no action. In 1878 a deputy surveyor actually surveyed the area claimed in the grant and came up with 472,736.95 acres. Still Congress failed to confirm it, though the figure had been approved by the surveyor general. Seven years later a new surveyor general, sent out to clean up land operations, took another look at the grant and pronounced the previous survey "manifestly and shockingly incorrect." This statement by the official, George W. Julian, appears in state archives in a document dated June 28, 1886. Julian ordered another survey, but made no conjecture as to the probable correct size of the grant. Finally on September 29, 1894, the Court of Private Land Claims approved a survey showing only 1,422.62 acres, and in 1905 a patent was issued for that amount.

So the size of the grant, as viewed by the government, was whittled down from a high of 472,736 acres to 1,422. Two maps were issued, an early one showing the large area and a later one designating the small final allotment.[8]

This is an oversimplified statement of the case, for the matter has been in and out of the courts and there are disputes over jurisdiction—Congress? The Supreme Court? The matter has been put up to Congress again recently, with no action expected. But the trouble obviously lies in the fact that government surveyors have disagreed inexcusably as to the size of the grant. If you were a descendant of one of the original grantees and believed yourself entitled to a huge slice of the original grant, which survey would you accept? Which map would you brood over in the long winter evenings?

28

Rowena Martínez, former chief resources clerk at Carson National Forest headquarters here and a student of land grants, believes the difference between the extremes came in an original allotment of the 1,400 acres to individuals, besides which they were given the right to graze their animals over a vast area. It was described vaguely as "On the north by El Rito del Cibolla [a stream], on the south by the Capulin [a mountain], and on the west by the *cojita blanca* [little white hill, interpreted as the Continental Divide], on the east by the boundaries of the Martínezes [the Martínez grant]."

The Alianzans today claim between 500,000 and 600,000 acres. In the presumably impossible event that such a claim should be allowed, some of it would have to be taken from the Jicarilla Apache Reservation, some from the Santa Fe National Forest, some from other public domain, and the rest from private owners.

"The land grant," said Keleher, "has been a curse to New Mexico." [9]

In October of 1966 things came to a climax with an attempt by Tijerina and 350 Alianzans to take over (as site for a new "San Joaquín free city state") Echo Amphitheatre, a scenic location in Carson National Forest that they claimed to lie within the old San Joaquín grant.

The move had been known about in advance and three forest rangers were there, with state police and newspaper reporters. One ranger of Spanish origin was not molested, but the others were hustled roughly over to a picnic table, where an Alianza "official" of the new "pueblo" pronounced them guilty of trespassing and sentenced them to jail terms and fines (to be suspended if they left the "pueblo" jurisdiction and remained out). Their trucks were impounded, though quickly released again.

The admitted purposes of the Alianza in deliberately staging the confrontation were publicity and the hope of making a test case of the land takeover. The government, however, lodged criminal charges instead: assault against the rangers and conversion of government property. Tijerina ultimately went to a federal penitentiary for two years on these charges and later his wife was convicted of burning a Forest Service sign. Meanwhile incendiary fires broke out in the forest and burning of ranchers' houses and barns continued.

Putting aside for the moment the fact that arson and murder are felonies and that the rebels have been ordered by the courts to cease harassment of private property owners and the Forest Service, have they a redressable grievance or must they write off any genuine losses as eastern Indians have wryly written off their sale of Manhattan Island for twenty-four dollars and a string of beads? Some Rio Arribans have done so, but many of those who have are educated and prospering; the Alianzans are not that fortunate and obviously not so minded.

What if their claims are based on a treaty signed 120 years ago? They know that a U.S.–Mexican border dispute growing out of that same treaty was settled within the past ten years. They know, too, that only recently the government made a multimillion-dollar payment to an Apache tribe in the Southwest for a huge tract of land bought by treaty late in the nineteenth century and not paid for until now.

From her minute examination of hundreds of New Mexico land grant documents, Dr. Jenkins does not believe the Alianzans have any real basis for their land claims, which she believes were settled in the Court of Private Land Claims, operating during thirteen years after 1891, and through procedures of the U.S. surveyor general for sixteen years before that. She believes many of their grant claims had previously been rejected by Spanish or Mexican governments and that many encroached on Indian lands protected by laws of both those countries. But she considers the Alianzans more sinned against than sinning and thinks they have been used by some landowners in Rio Arriba who have no connection with the original grantees.

One factor in the general confusion, Dr. Jenkins believes, was the fact that the American courts, while basically honest, did not understand the Spanish laws—and their big mistake was alienating and permitting the piecemeal distribution of the common lands. "They should have turned the commons back in to the public domain, and then made them subject to claim by individuals, giving prior rights to previous users," she said. "But the land grants are a dead issue now. Too many court decisions have been made, too many of them confirmed by the Supreme Court to be upset now." [10]

The trouble in Rio Arriba, though, involves more than the accuracy of Alianza beliefs. In all the tangle one hard fact appears, and Margaret Meaders, former editor of the university's *New Mexico Business* magazine, has stated it tersely: "Whether the Alianzans are right or wrong, if *they* think they've got a problem, *we've* got one." [11]

There have been two hopeful developments. The first is that Tijerina, released from the penitentiary on parole, while still dedicated to the cause, speaks in more moderate tones. Gone is much of the emotionalism that has seemed his main motivation—an emotionalism not surprising in a former fiery Pentecostal preacher whose early life as a Texas Chicano was marked by harassment and unbearable poverty. It seems that he is searching for logic in his approach. In the past he would turn to the government one day and the next day deny its jurisdiction; would rely on one clause of the treaty and reject another. He appeared to deny to even a legitimate grant heir the right to sell his land if he wished.

The most basic reason for hope that the land war may be due for a partial solution is the fact that the state, after years of neglect, has made a thoughtful and objective study of clouded land titles in northern New Mexico and southern Colorado, with specific recommendations for bettering the situation. In early 1972 the State Planning Commission published a massive report on the matter, reportedly at a cost of $80,000 furnished by the Four Corners Commission, a cooperative group set up by the four contiguous states of New Mexico, Arizona, Utah, and Colorado.

The study, made by a large legal firm in Santa Fe, covered a year and a half and involved approximately 150 interviews with landowners, large and small, prestigious land grant specialists and historians, and representative persons, both professional and at all levels of government, who deal with the use and ownership of land in the area.

The report covers the lengthy history of Spanish and Mexican land grants here, the provisions of the treaty and various related agreements, with a sharp look at the Santa Fe Ring and the Court of Private Land Claims, their uses and abuses, and carries on to analyze contemporary problems and complications.

It makes seven recommendations for correcting old complications (if possible) and preventing new ones. They include establishment of a network of primary monumentation in the unsurveyed areas of the land tied to the state plan coordinate system; preparation of individual tract surveys, preferably in large blocks; commencement of a voluntary program of title clearance through a legal system including an educational program; adoption of certain changes in the procedure for quieting titles; enactment of a marketable title act and various curative acts; provision for adequate state funds to assure that county clerks' offices are well staffed and maintain adequate records; and creation of a Land Title Clearance Commission, Land Survey Authority, and the office of State Surveyor.

Finally the report recommends a pilot program which would quiet approximately three hundred titles. The annual cost of the pilot program is estimated at around $330,000, of which nearly $60,000 would go for legal aid, in view of the current skyrocketing costs of clearing titles.[12]

If the recommendations are carried out and funds prove available, New Mexico's land troubles should see a gradual easing. But the framers of the report and the State Planning Commission which sponsored it are well aware of a problem that will dog the progress of the project. Of the persons interviewed, about 35 percent so thoroughly distrust any government arm that they resist title clearance on their land in the belief that it would only result in the disappearance of the poor ranchers' holdings into the hands of rich landowners. And how will they react when titles to lands they believe they own cannot be cleared to their advantage? They will listen only to someone they trust. The state's first job is to convince Tijerina.

At least authorities are trying thoughtfully to find a way in which some of New Mexico's subsistence ranchers can be freed from a lifelong, painful, and dangerous obsession with what, for many of them, must surely prove a lost cause.

What is needed now, as Dr. Jenkins points out, is a modern approach to land titles. And the state has taken the first step. But unless legislation is passed to implement the recommendations, the state funds and the enormous amount of labor that went into the study will have been simply wasted.[13]

6

Inside a Poverty Pocket

It was one of those moments of perception that startle, confuse, and enlighten, all at the same time. It came from a midwestern friend of ours, looking out from our house at one of New Mexico's most beautiful views.

"Do you know what I think," she asked, "when I look out there? I think: 'What a waste!'"

"Waste!" I thought. "Waste?" And then I caught myself. Oh. Of course. It won't grow corn.

I'm in favor of corn, for more than utilitarian reasons. It also is a beautiful sight—great, tall, green rows following the contours of the rolling Iowa countryside, bending with the wind and swinging back with ineffable grace.

But Taos land won't grow corn or much of any other field or garden crop. That is why, though this is one of the world's great beauty spots, it is also one of the country's worst poverty pockets.

It wasn't always that way. Seventy-five years ago this valley was called the breadbasket of the Southwest, a claim at least partly true. Helen Blumenschein, poking about in the old files of the Santa Fe *New Mexican*, ran across an August 1885 interview with Alex Gusdorf of Taos. His flour mills here, he said, were going strong; his stones had been idle only two months since March and he was expecting another bumper wheat crop. The Taos Valley, he said, would produce 275,000 bushels that season.

But times have changed. His stones have been idle for many years; there are a few around town used as doorsteps.

It wasn't the weather that changed. Over the centuries, the crops were not rotated; the land, unreplenished, was worked out. Watersheds, continuing their erosion, sent down less water for irrigation. Probably, the experts here say, you could build the land up again if you tried, but why try? In these times, when only large mechanized farms are profitable, the Taos farmer with his small splinter of land, faced with the added cost of irrigation, could not compete with Kansas.

Though the native Taoseño, whether Spanish American or Indian, is a farmer historically and by instinct, he can no longer make a living from his land. He must find some other way. Yet for one out of every twelve potential workers here, there is no other way. There are not enough jobs to go around.

Why, if he can't make a living here, doesn't he cut his losses and go somewhere else? He does, if he has to. But there is still that emotional pull of the Taos land. "Land to the Taos people is not just something they own, an asset to be bought and sold," says Father Benedict Cuesta, the Catholic priest at Arroyo Seco for a number of years. "Their families have lived here for centuries; their roots are in the land; their hearts and souls are there. The tie is really mystical." [1] This is a tangible factor, recognized in every study of northern New Mexico. "A man who sells his land sells his mother," they say.

So they will try everything before they will leave Taos—seasonal jobs harvesting potatoes or herding sheep in Colorado; fighting forest fires with organized crews. But finally, if they cannot find a permanent job, they will move away. During the decade before 1960 more than one-fourth of the population of the county, nearly all of them from the rural areas, left Taos, and the trend has continued. The emigrants were ultimately replaced and twelve hundred more added, mostly nonagricultural newcomers, living in or near the village itself.

The net result is that Taos is still poor. While, speaking in averages, New Mexico as a state is down at eye level in income with Appalachia, this county's per capita income is only 58 percent of the state figure. Forty percent of its families (which average four people) are living at below the poverty level.

Oddly enough, you usually can't single out the poor man here by appearances. A California tourist learned this the hard way a couple of years ago. Stopping at Santo Domingo Pueblo, a few miles south of Santa Fe, she felt she was seeing real poverty. Returning home, she generously gathered up a large bale of used clothing, which she shipped to the governor of the pueblo. The governor, startled and deeply affronted, immediately shipped it back, with a polite note saying in substance: "Dear Madam: We thank you very much for the gift of clothing you have sent to our people. But we are not poor and do not need it. There are poor Indians in California. We suggest that you send the clothing to them."

I don't know what the Taos governor would have done with the clothing, for the Taos Indian, like the Santo Domingo, is at the bottom of the heap economically, in spite of the fact that he gets free government medical service, has no rent or land tax to pay, and is subject to income tax only if he earns enough outside the pueblo to qualify. Yet some of the outward aspects that make him seem poor have nothing at all to do with his real situation. This is a matter of constant confusion to the casual tourist.

"Why don't you give these Indians overcoats to wear instead of those Penney store blankets?" he asks. And we know he doesn't really believe us when we tell him what every Taoseño knows: that they wear those blankets because they prefer to, because wearing them is a tradition and a ceremonial requirement, going back to the old days when the blanket was made of buckskin.

The visitor wants to know why the Indians have no electric lights and running water at the pueblo. Surely this is substandard housing, which antipoverty workers should move in quickly to correct. And this again is the way they want it. Only during 1969 was a minority group of young Indians able to get permission from the tribal council to run electric power to outlying houses, a permission granted after years of argument and with the stipulation that they bury the lines and bring them no nearer than 550 feet from the gate leading into the pueblo.

"So that explains that," the tourist concedes doubtfully, "but why do they still dip water out of the pueblo creek in pails and carry it up ladders to the upper levels of their buildings? Don't they get a lot of diseases from drinking raw river water?"

I checked this point again with Dr. William R. Kilgore, who worked at the pueblo for two or three years with the Indian Service.

"No," he said, "there's no more incidence of disease there than there is anywhere else in the state."

"Do they build up an immunity?"

"They don't seem to," he said. "They just keep the water sources free from contamination."

This is the Taos Indian's way of doing things, and no antipoverty worker is likely to change it—at least in the near future.

Certainly it is this preference for the traditional ways that has kept the Taos Indians from reaching out, as three New Mexican pueblos are currently doing, for commercialization and industrialization of their economies. Cochiti Pueblo has sold a huge tract of land to a California construction corporation for recreational purposes, utilizing a new lake made by damming up the Rio Grande (but filled with water brought through a diversion channel from the Colorado River). Tesuque Pueblo has leased a large tract for a multimillion-dollar housing project. Zuni Pueblo, with $55 million, mostly in government funds, has undertaken a five-year Comprehensive Development Plan involving one thousand new houses, an air strip, a shopping center, a battery of industries, and the restoration of four archaeological ruins for the purpose of attracting tourists. At the same time the tribe has restored a mission church and is improving its educational system.

In flanking its ancient houses with modern industrial plants and a supermarket, is Zuni surrendering its age-old culture to materialism? Is Taos preserving its cosmic values at the expense of an impoverished people? So far the question is not at issue here.

If it is hard to tell whether an Indian is really deprived by looking at him or his house, what about the majority of the Taos County population, whose ethnic roots are in Spain? They make up nearly three-fourths of the population, and they figure as prominently on welfare rolls as do the Indians. But you would never know it by looking at them, for they share with their European counterparts a strong pride in appearances. You hear this explanation in Spain itself when you ask how the reputedly poor peasant can look so neatly and comfortably dressed, and the explanation appeared again recently in a tongue-in-cheek book, *The Spaniard and the Seven Deadly Sins,* by Fernando Díaz-Plaja, which some of the Taos Spanish-American people have read with high amusement and a quick recognition of its truth. You will never see here, as you do in Guatemala, a little boy with his small derrière showing plainly through the shredded seat of his jeans. If the Spanish-American family must cut corners, it will cut them where they don't show.

Then there is the third so-called culture group here, the Anglos, who probably make up roughly a fourth of the population (just as in Utah any non-Mormon is called a Gentile, any New Mexican who is neither Indian nor Spanish is called an Anglo, whatever his hue or persuasion). In this group, too,.it is often hard to cut the poor man out of the herd, since many Taos Anglos share with the Indians a greater degree of indifference to certain material things than you find in most other parts of the country. If you're driving an old car, nobody wonders whether you can't afford a new one or just don't care enough to bother. If you have an old beat-up kitchen stove that you picked up twenty years ago for thirty-five dollars, you also have a wonderful huge wrought-iron key that you found in Taormina, and a four-hundred-year-old fetish dug up in Puyé. For this is Taos, to which many an Anglo has come, giving up an impressive income in New York or some other city for a simpler, more leisurely life with space, a magnificent milieu, and a much more selective approach to the things that he really wants.

36

But while it is possible to live here comfortably and graciously on a minimal income, you can't take a casual attitude toward the real poverty that afflicts forty percent of the population. It would be some small comfort if one could confirm Father Cuesta's belief that poverty here stops short of misery. But welfare department executives shake their heads when you ask them this question.

"There is misery, too," they say.

"On a wide scale?"

"On a wide scale." [2]

So we need industries, since we have only one, the Molybdenum Corporation of America, which employs 500 men (down from 600 two years ago). And there are four ski runs, one (the Taos Ski Valley) of major national importance, which make jobs for 150 more. But what industry could you bring in that wouldn't threaten the tourist volume, the area's lifeblood?

"Do you realize that New Mexico is one of the last places in the country where the air is still relatively pure?" asked Dr. Paul B. Sears, Yale ecologist and a new Taos settler, speaking at a recent meeting called to ward off air and water pollution, which now begin to pose a serious threat to the area.

Local action groups succeeded in blocking a paper mill that wanted to locate a few miles south of Santa Fe and would have made jobs for 250 men. Petitions have been handed around to prevent the Forest Service from permitting more cutting of timber, operations that would have set up a few more jobs. All this—and logically, one must admit—to protect ourselves and the tourist industry, although this is an industry from which much of our native population cannot profit directly and furthermore only resents.

The Forest Service, small ranchers here say, is more interested in where a tourist has his picnic (littering up the place with bottles and cans) than in where they pasture their cattle and sheep.

"How would you answer that?" I asked Paul Martínez, longtime forest ranger who for a number of years handled the matter of grazing permits in various parts of Carson and Santa Fe National Forests. I knew that he has considerable sympathy with the small ranchers who live on the forest fringes.

Paul thought a minute.

"You have to remember first," he said, "that these are national forests and so have to be administered for the general public and not just for local interests. And you have to remember that while the members of a family have probably increased in numbers, there's just the same amount of land, and it isn't as productive as it used to be. A man can still pasture ten head of cattle, but if he has ten sons, they can't each find pasture for ten head. It just isn't there."

But, you remind him, about a third of the land in Taos County is tied up in national forests.

"I know," he said, "and the Forest Service could do more to expand its policy of multiple land use. It's already done a lot. Great areas have been reseeded to make more pasture land. But it can reseed still more, and build more stock tanks and corrals.

"The point is that forest rangers have different interests. Some of them are interested in just the aesthetics, in keeping great tracts of open land and forest just to look at, camp in, ride through, and enjoy. Some are interested in mostly the wildlife, protection of game and fish, or in conservation angles involving water and timber. Some of them aren't stock-minded, just don't think in terms of cattle and sheep and don't even want to."

I knew what he meant, having just read Edward Abbey's article in *Life* magazine titled "Let Us Now Praise Mountain Lions," an emotional defense of these beautiful predators and a diatribe against sheep. Abbey is a western park ranger and author of several books, including the brilliant *Desert Solitaire*.

"Think of it," he wrote, "as a simple question of moral priorities: which is more important, mountain lions or mutton?"

The magazine itself had hedged with an editorial note: "This article is outrageously unfair to sheep, farmers, hunters, the U.S. Wildlife Services, and others. Nevertheless. . . ." [3]

The mountain lion is, of course, a magnificent animal. In a lifetime I've seen only two—one a forlorn creature you couldn't help wanting to let out of its cage at the Ghost Ranch Museum at Abiquiu and another that crossed the road ahead of our car one night as we drove home from the Taos Ski Valley. A great, lithe, beautiful animal, he gave us one casual over-the-shoulder glance and continued his leisurely walk across the highway to lope up the side of the canyon.

I don't know whether Abbey is right in saying that mountain lions don't attack people. But I do know that, out in this country, if I have to choose between a superb mountain lion and a flock of stupid sheep, I'll have to side with the sheep.

I'll say first that sheep make their own contribution to aesthetics, as everyone knows who has ever, driving along a country road, found himself having to wait for a huge flock running ahead. The rhythm and flow as they move from side to side and weave in and out make one of the West's great experiences. But aside from that, there is more to a sheep than mutton, for which I share Mr. Abbey's aversion. There is more than lamb, too (though a New Mexico leg of lamb is one of the world's great delicacies), and more than wool, one of man's basic commodities. There is what the income from these things means to New Mexico's rural poor.

Do we have to choose? Isn't there, in 451,000 acres of national forest land in just one county, room for grazing and selective timber cutting without endangering aesthetic and conservation interests? Paul Martínez thinks there is.

"Supervised grazing doesn't threaten any other interest," he says, "and selective timber cutting, properly managed, doesn't either. Some of those trees ought to go, for the good of the forests themselves. And if the cutting is properly done, everyone benefits, including a few more people who get jobs."

"You mean handle it as they do in the Black Forest in Germany?" I asked.

"That's a fair example," he said.

But if you put this problem to John Yaple, who's made these matters a special and knowledgeable interest for years, he takes the opposite view.

"The difference is," he says, "that most of the Black Forest sits on level land. Most of our forests out here are in mountain country. The trees ought to be allowed to live out their life span and lie where they fall, to decay, enrich the soil, hold moisture, and prevent erosion. The Forest Service likes a tidy forest, but this is wrong. The thing is just to leave the trees alone. Too many have already been cut here; the water tables are down. We'll have to learn not to meddle.

"The same thing is true about animals. A few years ago they put on a campaign in the Kaibab forest to kill off the predators and protect the deer. What happened was that before long there were so many deer that they killed a lot of the trees by chewing the bark."

"Then if you had to choose between sheep and mountain lions, you'd side with the lions?"

John would just leave the whole thing alone and let both of them take their chances.

Meanwhile, attacked by the small ranchers on one side and conservationists on the other, what is the Forest Service doing? Carson Forest, centered in Taos, employs 105 people most of the year (60 full time), a roster that rises to nearly 250 during peak summer seasons, and pays out roughly $952,000 a year in wages and salaries. It returns a fourth of its net income to the counties in which the forest stands. Yearly it issues permits making it possible for around 350 families to earn all or part of their income through the sale of such products as firewood and vigas.

39

It provides, it says, grazing lands at minimum fees on which 545 ranchers, mostly with small holdings, raise nearly 10,000 cattle and 32,000 sheep; has reseeded worked-out lands, increasing lamb weights in recent years by 30 percent; and has under way a ten-year plan to revegetate 88,000 acres in this one forest, with 500 miles of new fences and 285 water projects for stock. And, along with its program of thinning and reforestation, in 1969 the Carson Forest let contracts to private timber operators to cut 93 million board feet. The policy has continued on a similar scale.

Whether or not you object to this latter use of national forests, you see the point at which ecology and economics come into direct confrontation. It is clear to me that in a poverty pocket that is also a tourist area, in the midst of our belated, vital, and almost frantic crusade to protect the environment, somebody is going to have to hold a watching brief for the man who just needs a job. Whatever is happening here to provide income, it is still not enough, in spite of the fact that state and federal governments pour into this one county of 18,700 persons more than four million dollars a year in wages, salaries, and public assistance.

I think of this employment problem each time someone brings in a petition, such as the one recently circulated to prevent the paper mill from coming into northern New Mexico. Are they sure that, in spite of technological advances, you can't make paper without polluting the air and the Rio Grande? Are they sure there is no place to put the mill where it wouldn't deface the landscape? There probably is not, since a paper mill is a real problem child. Still, old conservationist and ecologically oriented though I am, I am not the first to see that, unless it is accompanied by a sincere and activist concern with finding an acceptable substitute, there are, in a too hasty brush-off of a possible source of employment, the seeds of a class war.

I know as well as the next one that many of our people are untrained for almost any job, a problem at which the government is currently nibbling. As of today any industry coming in would have to bring with it much of its labor force (or engage in a broad on-the-job training program), and in the meantime, what good does it do a man to train for a nonexistent job? If you add to these other problems the fact that we have the usual quota of apparently untrainable people and others who don't even want a job, you are stating the reason why fighting poverty is a highly frustrating occupation.

Our latest economic problem is our hippies. Ours seem mostly to be nonworking types who, learning that they can't live off the land, have found that so far, at least, they can live off the people, a viewpoint that Taos considers conspicuously unfair in a poverty area.

We do seem embarrassed about them and alternate between castigating magazine writers for mentioning them and calling public meetings asking state officials to help with the problem, thus bringing on more newspaper stories.

Our hippies are about like everyone else's, and have a few original theories I hadn't heard before. One of them came into the shop a while ago and told Genevieve that a few days before he had taken a pack of tarot cards without paying for them. He was sorry about it. He hadn't the money that day, but would be back the first of the next week to take care of the matter. That is the last we've seen of him.

Three others took some things from Georgette Ely's health food shop. Georgette indignantly followed them down the street and retrieved all of it that they hadn't already eaten. A few days later one of them came into the shop again.

"I'm the fellow," he said brightly, "who took some of your food the other day." He didn't offer to pay for it.

The hippies seem to have a sort of willy-nilly share-the-wealth theory. One of our friends, not a hippie though rather well oriented that way, has asked her neighbors not to lock their house when they go on vacation. "If people come in and steal anything," she explained, "it will be only because they need it."

That's probably why they've taken all the piñon wood from our back portal at the shop and one of them broke in one night and made off with our collection of handmade Indian jewelry. He finally admitted it officially, and early in the game sent Jim Mike Brandenburg, assistant district attorney, a lengthy memo titled "In Defense of My Crime." Without claiming that he needed the jewelry or money he might have gotten from its sale, he explained in esoteric terms how he happened to get the idea. The first thing was that the jewelry had gleamed and caught his eye. It reminded me of Kipling's fictional East Indian boy, Namgay Doola, explaining why he had cut off the cow's tail: It had swung in the moonlight.[4]

Not all of the hippies operate along these lines. One of our burglar's friends overheard him talking to two others just after he had climbed back out of our window and hastily notified the police, who retrieved most of the stolen items before morning. A few things were still missing, including two Indian pipe bags that had been used in Buffalo Bill's show. But a few days later a girl from one of the communes came in to bring them back. She hadn't had any connection with the theft, but had seen the bags and, hearing by the grapevine that some such things had been taken from us, just brought them in. This sort of thing has restored some of our faith in hippies.

I do have a genuine sympathy with them, in view of the boredom, frustration, and disillusionment that set them off. There was an early time lasting two or three years when, if there had been a hippie commune conveniently close, I should probably have joined it myself. It is true that they shook up American values, gave them a much-needed aeration. Yet Taos had already discovered some of those better values: a simpler, more loosely structured pattern of life, a need for space, and less dependence on things relating to convenience, comfort, and pseudo prestige. But most of Taos had kept a fundamental concept referred to by the Founding Fathers as a decent respect for the opinions of mankind, and had learned with Freya Stark the necessity for walking the narrow line between pattern and freedom.

And in an area more than a third of whose people are poor by circumstance, it is not easy to sympathize with a husky, poor-by-choice fellow coming out of the welfare office with a check, especially if he's going to cash it (as has happened) to pay ski tow fees. We would rather see the government use that money in further efforts to make it possible for the native Taoseño to live on his ancestral land with dignity and grace.

Our hippie situation seems to be fluid and their numbers have declined. At the same time our opinions about them vary from day to day. For one thing, some of the facts of life are beginning to register. One commune has not asked welfare help, wishing to break the chain of dependence. And, coming to see that northern New Mexico land will not sustain even its native people, they are passing the word on to others thinking of coming to Taos.

"Northern New Mexico is an arid terrain," wrote "Jasper Blowsnake" in one Taos publication, *The Fountain of Light*. "The wood is sparse," he continued. "The people are poor and are being invaded. . . . Don't come . . . and if you are already here with nothing to do—LEAVE!"

With most of our communes failing, many of our hippies leaving, and a 1972 ruling denying food stamps to "families" whose members are unrelated, this economic problem seems to be gradually solving itself.

This is probably the place to say that you will never understand the economic problem of the rural northern New Mexican of Spanish origin until you separate it from the Chicano problem of California, Texas, and metropolitan Albuquerque, Denver, and recently Santa Fe. New Mexican writers understand it fully enough; the distinction has been obscured by writers based on the East and West coasts, who have indiscriminately lumped our rebels in with the grape and lettuce strikers in California and Mexicans in Texas and Colorado.

For the northern New Mexican small rancher of Spanish descent is not a Chicano, a term seldom heard here except from newcomers. A Chicano is a Mexican, itself an appellation not often used here and then only as a term of opprobrium, though I have noticed that in recent months "Chicano" has gained a small measure of general acceptance.

But the Taos Spanish American will tell you that he is exactly that. As a matter of fact, on this side of the Rio Grande he doesn't even see the necessity for the longer term: "Why not just American?" he asks.

Johnny de Vargas, expert meatcutter at one of the supermarkets here, told a wryly amusing anecdote illustrating the point. Some years ago a high school friend of his, asked to fill out a questionnaire for entrance, wrote the word "American" in the space provided for nationality. But the superintendent demurred.

"Better make that 'Spanish-American,'" he said.

"I will," the boy said blandly, "if you'll fill yours in 'Jewish-American.'"

So, to confuse the sociologists, there is the fact that the Alianzan in Rio Arriba denies any U.S. citizenship, while the Taoseño insists on it, a situation which may deter Tijerina from making real headway in assembling a following here.

The true Chicano's problems are those of a displaced group of laborers, essentially migrants, coping with unionism, hours, wages, working conditions, and discrimination. The northern New Mexican of Spanish origin is a stay-at-home, with no union connections or aspirations and a minimum of discrimination to fight. He makes up no minority group. He is rather greatly in the majority here, holding at least 90 percent of the public jobs at all levels and in all branches of government as well as the teaching corps, and this with close to full understanding and consent of his minority neighbors, Indians and Anglos. In the professions, too, he makes his appearance. In Taos you can consult a Spanish-American physician, dentist, attorney, architect, minister, or banker, and find the roster of businessmen full of Spanish surnames.

The situations of the Southwest Chicano and the subsistence rancher of northern New Mexico overlap at only two points: their Spanish surnames and their deep poverty. Obviously a solution for one group will do little to help the other.

The northern New Mexican just wants to stay where he is, in a mesa and mountain setting whose beauty he treasures, on land to which his ties grow steadily stronger. He has no wish to move into an urban ghetto and add to his own and its complications. He wants what he has always wanted and what more and more other Americans want these days—elbow room, serenity, a life close to the land and to people he knows and understands.

His problem is that he has too little land, and that, while it is beautiful, it is unproductive.

This place, you can see, is no Shangri-la. A Taos—and there are many of varied kinds around the country—is a different thing, imperfect, beset with most of the problems that crop up anywhere else. But it is a place with which you are really engaged, so that if you are poor, you would rather be poor there than anywhere else; if you are ill or unhappy, better that it happen to you there than anywhere else you can think of.

And if you are happy, you are not surprised.

7

Dark Age Past

Modern times have brought doors and a few windows to Taos Pueblo, introducing a few bright patches of paint, green or that rich but muted tone known as Taos blue. Yet these small areas of color seem only to throw into prominence the overall adobe-ness of the two great multistory apartment houses, pointing up the historic necessity for protective coloration— tawny house against tawny earth, to escape the enemy eye.

But on San Gerónimo Day, the last of September, this study in monotones bursts into brilliant color.

Against the dusty plaza, upon the recessed rooftops of the truncated pyramid which is the north pueblo, the people gather in blankets and shawls of purple, lavender, red, white, or green with bright Roman stripes, the whole lively scene set against the verdant mountainous backdrop, surmounted by the blue dome of the autumn sky with its masses of cumulous cloud.

One is conscious of the upward thrust of the pattern in triangular planes. The tiny feet of each woman, encased in her folded white buckskin boots, carry the pyramidal form above them, its base the width of the skirt and shawl, a width narrowing smoothly upward to the small, shawl-covered head. Pyramidal figures against the pyramid of the north pueblo, and this in turn set against the study in triangular planes which is the Sacred Mountain.

There is a sun-drenched beauty about this San Gerónimo scene and a flavor of harvest plenty, as if the day were a planned collaboration of Mother Earth, deity and donor of the ripened corn, and our Father Sun, who created the people.

There is a flavor of amity among all things, the essence of the Taos ceremonial temperament, according with their courteous dismissal in the

seventeenth century of the militant Saint Michael named by Oñate as patron of the people and their invocation instead of that teacher of peace and
wisdom, Saint Jerome. And there are those who see in this choice a fine
blending of paganism with Christianity, in that from the hierarchy of Catholic saints they called one conforming with an ancient, persistent Southwestern Indian legend, of the Surpassing Being, the Fair-God, "apostle of
the larger kindliness," who should come to them out of the East, white
figure with long white beard and a dog at his feet. The doglike lion of Saint
Jerome? [1]

What seems peaceful coexistence in its generic meaning is pointed up
on San Gerónimo Day when in reverence the people bear the figure of the
Madonna from the adobe church and accord her a seat of honor in a high
bower of autumn leaves, before which they run their ceremonial races, to
spur the sun on its journey and direct the cloud people in their course to
bring the growing rain.

How true this fusion is, how well accepted today in diocesan councils
or Taos kivas I do not know. Is it regarded as practical concession to situation, regrettable but necessary compromise? Most infer, as indeed it seems
on the surface, a topsoil of Catholicism overlying the bedrock of Taos paganism. But whether uneasy peace or genuine acceptance, it was not
achieved without a century of struggle to root out the Indians' ancient beliefs and a half-century marked by fierce attempts by the Indians to defend
the faith of their fathers and destroy its attackers.

Northernmost of the Rio Grande pueblos, Taos was the last to be
reached by the probing fingers of Spanish exploration reaching up from the
south. But once begun in 1528, Spanish attempts to penetrate the country
by expeditions moved with such speed that in thirteen short years they had
reached this isolated outpost.

From the first the Indians learned to expect little good from these glittering strangers. It is true that Alvar Nuñez Cabeza de Vaca, first explorer
possibly to enter what is now known as New Mexico, seemed at first to be a
genuine humanitarian. But he found that roving bands of Spaniards wandering through the area adjacent to the present Mexican border had already earned for his countrymen a reputation for greed, chicanery, and oppression.

Although Cabeza de Vaca's protests, reported to the Spanish viceroy in
Mexico, caused the issuance of orders to later explorers to treat the natives
with kindness; although many of the early missionary friars were men of
benevolence; and although the first great colonizer of the Rio Grande
country, Don Juan de Oñate, maintained a consistent policy of neighborly
good will with its aboriginal dwellers, their intentions were not always sus-

tained by the moral and political climate of the times. For this was an era when on the one hand the question of the right of the conqueror to treat the conquered as he saw fit was solemnly debated in Spain, where Bartolomé de las Casas made considerable headway in his attempts to urge the human rights of captive peoples, even though scholars cited Aristotelian theories to combat him. But it was also an era when religious orthodoxy was in ironclad control, construing Indian rites as heathen ceremonies, to be ruthlessly suppressed. The rigid imposition of a religion which was foreign to their culture and of Spanish laws which they failed to understand set the twin bases of rising Indian discontent. Their kivas were closed and their ceremonial figures discarded, and for violations of the law, men and women were whipped and sold into slavery. Indeed this latter punishment was preferred by many of the Spanish colonists, since it provided them with a source of labor needed for their homes and ranches, as well as for backbreaking and dangerous work in the gold and silver mines that had been developed in various parts of the area.

By the middle of the seventeenth century the Indians had been reduced to slavery, and the inevitable reaction in a proud and once hospitable people had begun to set in. Revolts began in 1640, covering a period of four decades and culminating in the Pueblo Revolt of 1680. Its immediate cause was superstition.

In 1675 the superior of the great monastery of San Ildefonso, convinced as were many of his contemporaries that the Indians' medicine men were sorcerers employed in their subterranean kivas at rites of black magic, declared that he was bewitched and accused the Tegua people of causing his affliction. After an investigation by a special tribunal appointed by the governor of the territory, forty-seven Indians were convicted of the practice of witchcraft. Three were hanged, the rest imprisoned and enslaved.

The Pueblo people were whipped to a height of fury. A San Juan Indian named Popé, unable to induce his pueblo to spearhead a revolt to rid the country of its oppressors, established new headquarters in Taos, where in secrecy he fomented with his hosts a plot which burst into action in 1680.

All Spanish settlers and soldiers were killed or driven out of the country. None of the eighteen priests escaped martyrdom. The climax came at Jemez, where the old priest, Jesús Morador, seized in his bed at night, was stripped naked and mounted on a hog and so paraded about the village, taunted with shouts of derision. Then crawling on hands and knees like a beast, he was ridden about the plaza by his tormentors until, spurred and beaten, he fell dead.

The churches were burned; the sacred images desecrated. The kivas were reopened and the people returned to the ways of their fathers.

For twelve years Popé of Taos ruled the land from the governor's palace at Santa Fe.

Nor was the trouble ended when Don Diego de Vargas at the head of an army retook the capital for Cross and Crown. Twice he was forced to recapture the city and three times to march on Taos, the vortex of rebellion that for years kept the river country in turmoil.

The conflict was long and indecisive, and cessation of hostilities came only gradually, brought about by the increase in numbers of the Spanish colonists and the disappearance of one prime Indian grievance, when mining, proving unprofitable, was abandoned, and forced labor was no longer an issue.

But basically the ultimate peace between the Indians and the Spanish colonists was after all attributable to Bartolomé de las Casas. In 1542, just as the wave of conquest reached Taos, a reasonable and humanitarian code called the New Laws of the Indies, based on his earlier proposals, was enacted by the Spanish government. Its first salutary effects for the Indians of the New World died out after a decade, but the laws were reactivated after the Pueblo Indian revolt had shown the Spanish crown the failure of the old policy of repression.

The laws granted the Indians the right to organize their internal economy and practice their religious beliefs as they saw fit.

But the seventeenth century—the Dark Age for the Pueblo Indian—had waned before peace descended on the Rio Grande country.

What tribal memories do the Taos have of those years of more than two and one-half centuries ago? It cannot be assumed that they have none, for the Spanish are still unwelcome at Zuni, first pueblo to be captured by the mounted strangers from the south. But the Taos, proudest and most bellicose under oppression, are also in defeat the most magnanimous.

And so, on Christmas Eve, we hurry to the pueblo at dusk. Already the bonfires of pitchpine are burning all around the plaza and on the upper levels of the houses, billowing out clouds of black smoke and filling the winter air with their fragrance. Crowds of Anglos have already gathered outside the adobe church, where the priest from Taos is singing vespers.

The people are coming out now and we make a pathway for them, for they are carrying on their shoulders the figure of Mary Madonna, seated on a canopied litter. About them the night wind is swirling the clouds of smoke, so dense that they reflect back in ever-changing pattern the leaping flames of the *luminarias*. Rifle shots crack, their echoes flung back by the ring of foothills. Following the figure of the Madonna come the drummers and chanters. But these are Indian drums, and though the music has come from the church's magnificent repertoire, the words are in Tiwa.

The Madonna does not mind. Seen in the fitful firelight, her face is serene. I think myself she will not mind on her son's birthday tomorrow, when in the darkened church she hears the drums again and knows that the Taos have come from their kivas to perform before the gate of her house the great Deer Dance, celebrating in different and who knows how equally acceptable fashion the elemental life forces to which the Cristo himself paid the ultimate tribute.

8

Two Revolts

The eighteenth century appears as an era of peace in the Taos Valley, but it was far from an absolute peace. Though Indian and settler learned over the decades to live amicably together, the situation meant only a shift in the alignment of enmities. Now it was Indian and colonist joining forces against the hit-and-run raids of their common foe, the nomadic Indians of the plains, for whom the village-dwelling inhabitants appeared as easy sources of supplies, slaves, and wives.

The period was marked by repeated raids and countersallies, of which the most important in Taos annals was the massive attack in 1760 by Comanches. Erupting through the pass at the east, they carried off fifty Spanish women and children who were never recovered.

The Indio-Hispanic alliance carried over into the nineteenth century, and is seen in two bloody and abortive revolts, one in the third decade against the new republic of Mexico, another in the following decade against the newly imposed authority of the U.S. Army.

These were rebellions in which Taos both times played a leading role; in which twice Taos men, one an Indian and another an Anglo, ruled briefly as governor of the territory, and in which both died by quick violence, the first at the hands of a counterrevolutionary firing squad at Santa Cruz, the other shot and scalped at Taos by a group of infuriated Mexicans and Indians.

The century had begun, as indeed it ended, peacefully enough, though with a great surge of new activity, accompanied by the addition of other nationalities to the already mixed strains of the Taos blood.

The purchase by President Jefferson of the Louisiana Territory from Emperor Napoleon in 1803 opened up the Mississippi Valley to westward

Laura Gilpin

1. The great northern skyline of the Sangre de Cristos

Laura Gilpin

2. *The Rio Grande gorge, seen from the air*

Laura Gilpin

3. *North pueblo and Taos Mountain*

Mildred T. Crews

4. *The Rio Grande gorge*

Regina Cooke

5. *Johnny Romero (left) and Luis Suazo, with buckskin
hung up to dry*

Laura Gilpin

6. *Pueblo women plastering a wall*

Laura Gilpin

7. Genevieve Janssen (left) and author

8. *Talpa valley and Picuris range*

Laura Gilpin

9. *Old Peñasco door in the Talpa house*

10. *Ruins of the old Taos Pueblo church, destroyed in the rebellion of 1847*

11. *Blue Lake*

Laura Gilpin

12. *John Reyna, 1971 Taos Pueblo governor*

Laura Gilpin

13. Max Archuleta, aide to Pueblo Governor Reyna

14. *Old Zuni kachina doll (Shalako), author's collection*

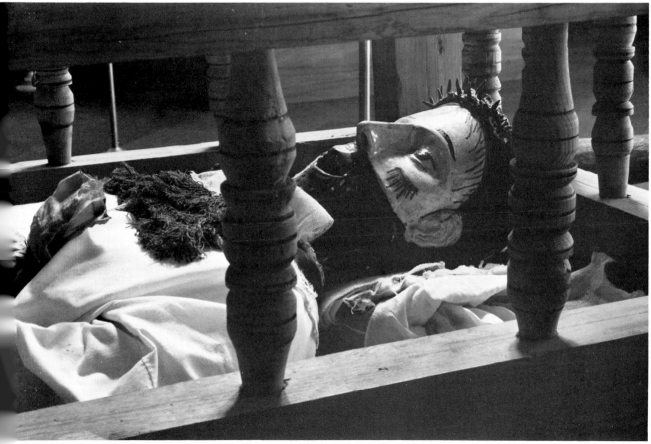

Laura Gilpin

15. The Cristo, collection Taylor Museum, Colorado Springs

*16. Penitente death cart, collection Taylor Museum,
Colorado Springs*

Laura Gilpin

17.   *The cross on the door protects against witches*

Laura Gilpin

18. *Andrew Dasburg*

movement across the plains, to meet in New Mexico the waves of Spanish colonization coming up from the south.

Enterprising Missouri merchants saw immense possibilities for profitable trading. First known to have come west to deal with the Indians on the northern plains was a Frenchman named La Lande, who penetrated as far west as a point north of Taos and turned south to Santa Fe. In 1812 a dozen St. Louis merchants launched the first sizable expedition, following La Lande's general route. This was followed by many others, growing in scope and volume of goods each year, selling their products in Taos, Santa Fe, and southern New Mexico and penetrating down into Mexico as far as Chihuahua.

As they scouted for shorter and more protected routes, they developed a shortcut that bypassed Taos at the east and went south through Las Vegas. Taos, however, having achieved eminence as a rendezvous for fur traders of the whole western area, was soon rejoined to this Santa Fe Trail by an alternate route, and for many decades was a prominent center for commercial activity. This was the era of the explorers, the guides, the mountain men, with names like Kit Carson, James Bridger, Louis and Antoine Robidoux; the merchants like Ceran St. Vrain, Charles Beaubien, the Bent brothers.

The newcomers again changed the character of Taos, for they came in numbers as trade on the trail grew by leaps and bounds. In spite of hardships and Indian attacks, the volume of traffic moving by horse, mule, and wagon mounted from a mere seventy men and $15,000 value in 1822 to an 1846 figure of 414 wagons carrying $1,752,250 worth of goods.

While this was happening, change of a different kind came from another direction. In 1821 Mexico declared its independence from Spain, and New Mexico became a part of the new republic. Revised laws made this area a department instead of a territory, concentrated power, and levied taxes which proved so generally unpopular that a smoldering spirit of revolt broke into open hostilities on August 1, 1837.

Led by a Taoseño known as General Chopón and the Montoya brothers, the insurgents established headquarters at Santa Cruz, and eight days later clashed head-on with the government's troops under Governor Pérez at San Ildefonso. From this engagement the governor was forced to retreat, and at the edge of Santa Fe his escape route was cut off and he was killed and decapitated by Santo Domingo Indians.

For the second time a Taos Indian sat as governor in the palace at Santa Fe. He was José González, elected and duly installed, and this accomplished, the revolutionary army disbanded. But though the acts of the rebels had been ratified by the General Assembly, composed of alcaldes and men of importance from the northern part of the river country, a counterrevolutionary force was assembled in the southern areas by Manuel Armijo and headed north from Albuquerque.

González thereupon retreated from Santa Fe to Santa Cruz, center of the revolutionary activity. Armijo occupied the capital, notified the Mexican government that he had quelled the rebellion, and was duly appointed governor. With an army quickly augmented by troops from Zacatecas, he marched on Santa Cruz, defeated the rebels, and captured their leader.

As the story is told, González was brought before Armijo on the outskirts of the village. On seeing the general, the Taoseño advanced with extended hand and, as was proper between two men of equal rank as governors, said, "How do you do, Compañero?"

Armijo replied, "How do you do, Compañero? Confess yourself, Compañero." Then turning to his soldiers, he ordered, "Now shoot my Compañero!" [1]

So ended the insurrection of 1837.

The bloody Taos rebellion of 1847 was an incident of the Mexican War. That struggle, brief and largely unpopular with the American people, had broken out in June of 1846, caused by a U.S. claim, disputed by Mexico, that when Texas had freed herself previously from Mexican rule and later had been annexed to the United States, all land claimed by Texas east of the Rio Grande had automatically become U.S. territory. This included the half of New Mexico in which Taos was located.

To back up the claim, the U.S. president sent three military expeditions into the West. One commanded by General Stephen W. Kearny proceeded from Fort Leavenworth along the general route of the Santa Fe Trail and headed for the capital. Governor Armijo, though at first determined to make a stand for the Mexican government at Apache Pass, suddenly through cowardice or resignation changed his mind, retreated to the capital without firing a shot, and continued his flight to the south toward Mexico.

In a bloodless conquest Kearny entered the city, declared the area U.S. territory, and as its first governor appointed the well-known Taos merchant, Charles Bent.

Convinced that the territory was safe from trouble, Kearny took a portion of his army on a military mission to California, sent another out to quiet the raiding Navajos, and left in Santa Fe only a small remnant of his troops commanded by General Sterling Price.

Trouble came swiftly on the heels of Kearny's departure. Scarcely a day had passed when word reached Price that plans were on foot for a general uprising against American authority.

At a meeting on December 12, 1846, those still loyal to Mexico had decided to strike a week later, but a postponement to Christmas Eve, when festivities would distract the authorities' attention, caused a leak in their plans. The further delay that ensued served only to result in a secret plot on a more extensive scale. It called for the killing or driving out of every American, as well as all Mexicans who had accepted offices under the U.S. regime. Although the plot had originated among the Spanish population, this time certain pueblos, including Taos, were enlisted.

In the meantime the authorities had relaxed their vigilance. On January 14, 1847, Governor Bent, thinking all danger past, left Santa Fe on the two-day journey to Taos to visit his family. On the night of January 19, his house was attacked by a large body of Mexicans and Indians, and the governor was captured and shot. A short few minutes later his scalp was carried around the plaza in triumph.

Other Taos notables killed in the massacre were Sheriff Stephen Lee, Circuit Attorney J. W. Leal, Prefect Cornelio Vigil, Narciso Beaubien, son of Judge Charles Beaubien of the Superior Court, and Pablo Jaramillo, brother-in-law of Governor Bent. Nine others in the area lost their lives, and a similar mass killing occurred at Mora.

Word of the governor's death reached General Price at Santa Fe the following day, along with advices that the Taos group, flushed with victory, was advancing down the canyon toward the capital, where it was to be joined by a similar group coming up from Albuquerque. Though he could assemble only 310 men, with five cannon (four howitzers and a six-pounder), on January 23 Price launched a desperate drive northward. He met the first opposition at Santa Cruz and routed it, with enemy losses of 36 men. Reinforced at Los Luceros by an additional force of 170 men under the command of Captain John Burgwin, rushed up from Albuquerque, he pushed on to Embudo, where he won a second engagement, and on February 3, in heavy winter cold and snow, he arrived in Taos.

Here he found that most of the Spanish elements among the insurgents had dispersed to their homes, leaving as defenders the Taos Indians, who had entrenched themselves in their adobe church at the pueblo.

Disposing his forces and artillery on west, east, and north sides of the structure, Price opened up with his batteries at nine in the morning. Two hours later, having been unable to breach the walls, he determined to storm the building. His report gives a vivid account of the tragic action of the day.

At a signal, Captain Burgwin, at the head of his own company and that of Captain McMillin, charged the western flank of the church, while Captain Angney, infantry battalion, and Captain Barber and Lieutenant Boon, Second Missouri Mounted Volunteers, charged the northern wall. As soon as the troops above-mentioned had established themselves under the western wall of the church, axes were used in an attempt to breach it, and a temporary ladder having been made, the roof was fired.

At this point, the report states, Burgwin with a small group left the protection of the church wall and attempted to force the front door of the building, but was cut down with severe wounds from which he died four days later.

> In the meantime, small holes had been cut in the western wall, and shells were thrown in by hand, doing good execution. The six-pounder was now brought around by Lieutenant Wilson, who at the distance of twenty yards, poured a heavy fire of grape into the town. The enemy, during all of this time, kept up a destructive fire·upon our troops.
> At about half-past three o'clock, the six-pounder was run up within sixty yards of the church, and after ten rounds, one of the holes which had been cut with the axes was widened into a practicable breach. The storming party . . . entered and took possession of the church without opposition. The interior was filled with dense smoke, but for which circumstance our storming party would have suffered great loss. A few of the enemy were seen in the gallery, where an open door admitted the air, but they retired without firing a gun.[2]

Price ordered the north battery to charge, but the Indians had abandoned the west section of the village, some seeking refuge in houses in the eastern section, some attempting to escape to the mountains. Of these, however, only two or three succeeded in eluding a mounted pursuing party, which killed fifty-one of their number.

After a quiet night during which the troops were quartered in abandoned pueblo houses, the Indians sued for peace and, as one of the conditional terms, surrendered one of their number, Tomás, who was believed to have instigated and been actively involved in the murder of Governor Bent and others.

After a few more skirmishes in scattered towns, the rebellion of 1847 was ended.

So far as is known, the Taos Indians have no written record of that grim battle at the pueblo in which 150 of their number were slain, along with 7 of the American soldiers. Mute testimony of the events of that winter day may be seen in the ruined tower of the old church, still standing after the passage of more than a century.

But death had not yet finished taking its toll of the Taos people. Still to come were the trial and execution of fifteen Indians and Mexicans—fourteen for the murder of the governor and others, and one for treason.

One eye-witness account of these proceedings has come down to us, written by a seventeen-year-old youth from Missouri who had just arrived with a trader's wagon train. He was a shrewd observer and his account of his journey into the Southwest, including the Taos episode, is one of the most valuable of the frontier chronicles. He was Lewis H. Garrard; his account is included in his book, *Wah-to-Yah and the Taos Trail.*

Garrard, too, took a dim view of the American role in what he termed "the discreditable Mexican war," and was clearly torn in his reaction to the trials and death penalties.

While he agreed that no fault should be found with the executions of those convicted of murder, he was forthright in his criticism of the haste with which convictions were secured and sentences carried out. The assistant prosecutor was "a great blow-hard"; the defense counsel "a volunteer private on furlough for the occasion." The jury in the first trial, which seemed to him both ignorant and prejudiced, returned, after an absence of only a few minutes, a verdict of "guilty in the first degree"—five men for murder, one for treason.

"Treason, indeed!" wrote Garrard. "What did that poor devil know of his new allegiance? . . . It certainly did appear to be a great assumption on the part of the Americans to conquer a country and then arraign the revolting inhabitants for treason."

As a matter of record, several others similarly accused of this crime were given presidential pardons on the ground that treason against the United States was not a crime of which a Mexican could be found guilty while his country was actually at war with the United States.

As the week progressed, the young Garrard's emotions swung back and forth. He visited the home of Governor Bent and was sickened as he learned of the savagery with which some of the assassinations had been carried out. He went to the jail and could not keep down an upsurge of pity for "the poor wretches" lying on the floor awaiting their executions. But he personally helped the sheriff to rub with soft Mexican soap the six nooses to be used for the first hangings.

As the jail was filled to overflowing, a date within the week was set for these first executions, which were to take place in an open field 150 yards away on the north side of the village, where a crude gallows had been hastily set up.

The day came, and Garrard, with his rifle at ready, joined the guard of eighteen soldiers and nine mountain men, as a government wagon with two mules attached was driven under the gallows. The Missouri youth's description of the scene is gruesome yet compassionate.

Standing in a row on a board placed from end to end of the wagon, the condemned were permitted to say a few words to their people.

Only one said he had committed murder and deserved the penalty. Four cringed before the imminent prospect of death. As for the man sentenced for treason, said Garrard, he "showed a spirit of martyrdom worthy of the cause for which he died—the liberty of his country."

The mules were started, the wagon was drawn from under the gallows. Garrard watched, fascinated and sick at heart.

But he was young and resilient; to his journal he made a curiously shocking addendum. Did it come from the sheer thoughtlessness of his late adolescence, or as simply an automatic human recoil from horror? "We made a collection among ourselves of five dollars," he wrote, "and dispatched a messenger to el casa Americano to prepare for us, when relieved from duty, an eggnog in honor of the occasion." [3]

The revolt of 1847 saw the last of bloodshed in the Taos Valley. Enough of terror had been compressed into a few short days to last to the present time.

9

The Indian Is the Deer

In 1971 the Taos Indians, after a court ruling and by congressional action, regained from the U.S. Forest Service full control of forty-eight thousand acres of wilderness surrounding the seat of their religion, Blue Lake. The shrine lies twelve miles from the pueblo itself, on the flank of Taos Mountain and at an altitude of 10,500 feet.

The U.S. Indian Claims Commission finally ruled that the Taos group held aboriginal Indian title to the land, which had been taken from it by the government in 1906, arbitrarily and without compensation. The victory by which they were awarded trust patent to this tract lying in the heart of Carson National Forest was many painful decades in the making. John Collier, Sr., and Oliver La Farge had done a great deal of work on the Indians' behalf. But at a day-long celebration here, attended by government dignitaries, John Yaple of Taos was given public credit as having done more than any other single man to secure the return of their land.

As the long struggle with bureaucratic Washington neared its close, newspapers all over the country gave considerable attention to this small group of about fifteen hundred Indians so bent on preserving their greatest religious shrine. But no reporter made any serious attempt to describe the real nature of this religion or the annual August rites that constitute the focal point of Taos Indian ceremonial observance. For this omission there is good reason. No white man or alien Indian has ever seen the rites. No Taos Indian will tell you anything about his religious beliefs.

The anthropologist Elsie Clews Parsons reported in a 1936 study of Taos Pueblo that once a white woman asked a Taos Indian: "What is Pueblo Indian religion?" His answer was "Life." Dr. Parsons interpreted his reply to mean "a means to life, that it covered life as a whole, and that, thorough animist as he was, everything significant was alive and a part of religion," and she added, "life, light, well-being, and, we must add, how to ask for it—that is indeed Pueblo religion." [1]

These, of course, are broad terms that could be applied to many religions, and they fail to satisfy the layman or ethnologist who wishes to learn how the Taos Indian pursues his quest for this kind of integration with life. The Taos certainly will not help the questioner, for his religion has not indoctrinated him with any feeling of obligation to tell; on the contrary, though many faiths insist on the duty of their adherents to "tell the glad tidings," the Taos has been conditioned by centuries of teachings handed down by tribal elders to say nothing specific to anyone outside his own pueblo about the great religious concepts on which his life is based.

Dr. Parsons dedicated this study of the pueblo to "my best friend in Taos, the most scrupulous Pueblo Indian of my acquaintance, who told me nothing about the pueblo and never will tell any white person anything his people would not have him tell, which is nothing." Since she was preparing to publish 120 pages of detail on the daily life and ceremonials of the Taos Indians, Mrs. Parsons was obviously getting information from some source. But she wanted to make sure this friend was not suspected of being that informant. For a breach of Taos traditional secrecy was such a serious matter that when her work was finally published, the identity of her informant was made the subject of lengthy investigation by the Pueblo council. When his name was finally learned, he proved to be a man who had died two years before the study was published. But his son, though not even suspected of having been involved, is said to have been deprived of his share of communal land. Moreover, whoever her informant had been, she was far from sure of the accuracy of the information, and he had limited it strictly to detail. No Indian had given her a connected description of any kiva ceremonial, much less any statement of the philosophy underlying Pueblo religious belief.

Of all the Pueblo Indians—those of the nineteen pueblos located along the Rio Grande, the Zunis living south of Gallup, and those of the three Hopi mesas in Arizona—the Taos are the most secretive. The tenets of their religion are passed on by word of mouth and from memory. There is a story, probably true, that upon the death of one Taos tribesman it was discovered that he had begun to set down on paper some Pueblo secrets, presumably related to the Emergence myth. The manuscript was burned.

It can, of course, be seen that, however great the degree of their secrecy, they cannot completely protect their ceremonial concepts from alien ears and eyes. For there is a central core of meaning common to the religion of all the Pueblos, and some have been more open to approaches of ethnologists. Two researchers, Matilda C. Stevenson and Frank Hamilton

58

Cushing, lived at Zuni for several years and learned its language. Cushing, in fact, who lived there for five years, so won the Zuni confidence that he was adopted into the Macaw clan, was initiated into tribal fraternities, was permitted to take part in religious rites, and was finally made Head Priest of the Bow, an office second in prestige in the pueblo.

From this position inside the tribe, Cushing set down his findings on Zuni thought and social, political, and ceremonial organization. His work was published in a report to the Bureau of American Ethnology and several important books. Stevenson, too, published a lengthy study on Zuni ceremonialism in a bureau report. The Taos believe that Zuni strength was seriously weakened by these revelations.

The studies indicated that the Zuni everyday life and work, as well as his ceremonialism, were woven into his understanding of cosmic mythology and symbolism. For instance, each of the house clusters represented one of the seven directions, north, south, east, west, the upper world, the underworld, and the midmost, the last a union of the other six. Each of the clans belonged to one of these groups, and its membership determined the part the individual clan would play in any council or ceremonial. The midmost was the cohesive factor in the organization, holding the Zuni together.

From these studies and those of other pueblos, it seems clear that Pueblo Indian religion is a body of thought based on the Indian's concept of his place in the natural universe and his relation to each of its manifestations.

Certainly Taos Indian life is firmly nature-oriented, as indicated for instance by a fragment of the Taos Emergence myth, obtained years ago by Dr. Aurelio M. Espinosa. His informant told him that the people came up from the lake at Mount Blanca, near Monte Vista, Colorado. Having been created by our Father Sun, they came up in groups corresponding to the societies to be found today in Taos kivas, and scattered to the places to which Sun directed them, with instructions to meet at the Canyon of the Red Willows, Taos.

First came the Feather People, who settled near Ranchos de Taos. Then came the Shell People, who went to a spot near the Colorado River. Then came the Water People, about whom an intriguing tale is told.

> They were first fish. They came over the mountain streams to the Santa Fe River. Then they swam up the Rio Grande and up the Taos River and to the Ranchos de Taos Creek until they arrived near the place where Fiadaina (Feather People) and Holdaina (Shell People) were living together. A Fiadaina girl went down to the river for water and saw the Water

People in the water and ran to tell her people. When they came down they saw all the fish there standing up in the water. "Those are some of our people," said Fiadaina and Holdaina. Then they got some bean plants and gave them to two girls. They told them to strike the fish with them. They struck them and they all became people.

Groups arriving after the Water People were Big-Earring People, Knife People, Sun People, People of Feathers in Cold Weather (otherwise known as Old Axe People), Big Parrot Feather People, Lightning People, and Day People. They all met finally at Taos.

It was thus that the world began for the Taos people. It will end, Dr. Espinosa was told, when they neglect their religious rites, and apparently by flood, when the hot springs north and south of Taos boil over.[2]

Whatever any white man learns of Taos Indian religion he must get from such bits of folklore, from what he can carry over from studies of other pueblos, and what he can infer from observation of the ceremonials performed here outside the kivas. And he must depend on his memory for details, since no photographs may be taken here (as at most pueblos) during a ceremonial, and artists are not permitted to sketch. If the observer wishes to go deeper, he must learn as the Indian learned (as Saint Francis learned, and Thoreau and Rachel Carson), by teachings coming out of the earth and the underlying waters, out of the cloud, the rain and lightning, from deer and coyote, sun, moon, circling planets, and rotating seasons.

These are the life forces that have surrounded and governed the Indian's life from prehistoric times, thousands of years before he heard from strangers of the saints and that great teacher from Nazareth, though these last he added to his pantheon willingly, after he had made sure they would not interfere with his relation to the fundamental forces he knew were vital to him.

Of all the Taos ceremonials we are allowed to see—the Corn Dance, Turtle Dance, Matachinas (based on the Montezuma legend and showing Spanish influence), the Feather Dance, and others, the Deer Dance is by far the greatest, a magnificent spectacle. But the August rites at Blue Lake are at the heart and core of Taos Indian religion. John Collier, Sr., longtime U.S. Commissioner of Indian Affairs, and a companion, James W. Young, came closer to seeing them than any other white men, witnessing a night ceremonial that presumably approached in nature and intensity the ultimate event at the lake itself.

It was in 1926. Collier had long been active in trying to secure the return of the tract surrounding the sacred lake to Indian control. In the course of the controversy loose rumors had been circulated that the rites to which the area was dedicated were not true religious observances, but erotic orgies, which should be sternly forbidden. To combat the rumors, the Indians reluctantly decided to permit Collier and Young to accompany them to the lake and observe the ceremonies. The two left Taos Pueblo with a caravan of about three hundred Indians—men and women with some babies in arms—and a large number of horses, though many of the old men went on foot.

But the two white men were not, after all, to see the Blue Lake rites. About halfway up the mountain the Indians found that they could not bring themselves to permit an alien eye to witness the ceremonials. Collier and Young were turned back after an overnight stay at the first ceremonial ground. But on that night they gained an emotional and religious experience of tremendous impact. Collier described it in a memo to the Senate and House Indian committees and afterward in his book, *On the Gleaming Way.*

His first impression was the sound of about two hundred horses, pastured in a five-acre glade, whinnying to each other and to new arrivals coming up the old, dark trail. The horses were descendants of those brought by the first Spanish explorations; otherwise, he felt, what transpired had remained unchanged from immemorial time.

He was aware of a supreme aesthetic quality. Log fires lighted up moving masses of human forms and thirty-foot aspen trunks, supporting huge canvases, which rose from levels of ground, tier behind tier and centering toward the fires.

On daises beneath the canvases were clusters of people who were not dancing at the moment, the firelight reflecting on the brilliant color of their shawls and blankets, their ornaments of wampum, turquoise, and silver:

> The fires lit the dance ground. Here were no colors, other than the fire's own color reflected from white or rusky robes. Here, with personal qualities shrouded, moved scores, hundreds of ghosts. They moved like masses of smoke, like wind made visible, like masses of cloud. . . . No casual motion, no gesture of one to another, ever appeared; all was a mass rhythm which changed a hundred times during the night. . . .
>
> The song went out from fifty, sometimes a hundred singers. From ten o'clock until dawn there was never a full minute's interlude. Only once were the dancers still. That was when the mass singing ceased and one powerful voice for seven minutes sang alone.[3]

Collier was transported by the experience. He had known something like this feeling before, every time, in fact, that he had witnessed any of the greatest of the Pueblo ceremonials. He had been especially aware of it during the Taos Deer Dance, during which any perceptive person felt the self retreating before an inrush of a strange power. But even that had been infinitely less powerful than this. He neither spoke nor understood the Tiwa dialect in which the chants were sung, but he felt he understood what was happening on this summer night in this vast mountain wilderness.

> That marvelous, ever-renewed, ever-increasing, ever-changing leap and rush of song was not only human song. . . . forces of the wild and of the universe had heard the call and taken the proffered dominion. . . . a strange release of energies took place. . . . the dynamic potentiality of ancient beliefs was realized, and . . . there was expressed a rejoicing, passionate and yet coldly exalted.[4]

In this he saw the spirit of Pueblo Indian religion. In this integration of human with mystical forces he could discern no asking, no adoration, no dread, but a simple sharing in joy.

Frank Waters in his work, *Masked Gods: Navaho and Pueblo Ceremonialism*, takes off from Collier's interpretation to point to a similar sharing evidenced in rituals among certain Mexican Indian tribes and a similar suprapersonal happiness seen in the Hindu darshan.

Waters, too, sees this exchange of energies between the individual and the universe as the secret core of all Pueblo and Navajo ceremonialism, and the great sings and dances as "but means to the end."

Whether or not one attempts to probe into their mystical symbolism, the major rituals of the Pueblos are great aesthetic experiences. And each observer brings to them his own background, the depth of his interest and perceptiveness, and the nature of his purpose in coming to witness them. So it is with the Taos Deer Dance, which we have seen many times, usually on Christmas Day, occasionally on January 6.

The deer come out of the kivas (the Old Axe and Water kivas, Parsons notes carefully). They come across the plaza and the bridge spanning Pueblo Creek in a long line of men and a few small boys wearing antlered heads and skins of deer, with a pointed stick in each hand to simulate forelegs. With them are buffalo and in some former years other animals, antelope, coyote, wildcat, and mountain lion. Seen with them are two Deer Chiefs, clad in white buckskin and carrying beaded buckskin quivers. The Chiefs bring the two Deer Mothers, moving in stately dignity in buckskin gowns and high white boots. The Mothers wear hair ornaments of parrot and eagle feathers; their cheeks are marked by a round black spot, with a black line following the line of the chin. Down the back of each hangs a mallard skin with feathers; each carries a gourd rattle, parrot feathers, and a sprig of spruce.

Completing the line come the Sacred Clowns, the Chiffoneta, legs and upper bodies bare and striped with black; they carry small symbolic bows and arrows.

In front of the church they form into two lines, the drums are heard, and the dancing begins.

The Deer Mothers preside, moving in classic dignity, sometimes shaking their rattles and holding high their eagle feathers and spruce sprigs, leading the other animals in simple patterns of circles, spirals, and diagonals. In their presence the lesser animals crouch or move back in obvious awe tinged with fear, giving out low animal cries.

At this point one of the other animals touches a deer, upon which a Chiffoneta shoots the deer with a straw arrow, slings it over his shoulder, and darts away. But he is pursued by one of the Deer Captains, who rescues the deer and brings it back. This byplay is marked by yelling and scuffling in the snow, but that the episode is more than a primitive sort of horseplay is clear from the fact that the watching Indians show no signs of amusement. There is obviously a ritual significance.

The dance is performed three times before the Deer Mothers lead the long column of animals back to the kivas.

Many veteran observers see in the Deer Dance a complicated symbolism, enormous psychological implications, occasionally interpreted with strong Jungian overtones. But viewed only in its simplest terms, it seems clear that not only on this winter day in this snowy plaza among these soaring mountains, but on any day and anywhere in the universe in which he seems to feel so much at home, the Indian *is* the deer; the deer *is* the Indian.

Each village of the Pueblo Indians has its yearly cycle of dramas, playing out its concept of creation and fertility, some of them small and intimate dances, others important, impressive spectacles, amazing survivals of age-old ceremonialism, done with dancing and chanting, drums and rattles, with altar rituals and poem choirs, with ceremonial racing, with complicated sequences done with exquisite precision and, in most cases, with rich and elaborate costuming.

One of the most spectacular is the Shalako, winter dance of the Zuni. The Shalako themselves are among the greatest of the kachinas, which are spirit embodiments of all mineral, plant, and animal forms of life, and like the saints serve as intermediaries between the Indian and his gods.

The Zuni were once a wandering tribe, seeking for the sacred middle of the earth. Once in crossing a stream they lost some of their children, who then became water people, kachinas, living under the Lake of Whispering Waters. But periodically they returned to the Zuni to bring rain. This continued until some of the mothers could not resist following their children back to their home. Thereafter the kachinas no longer visited the Zuni in person, but sent impersonators invested with their spirits. These we see today when in December they come to dance at the pueblo.

One early December day we drove to Zuni to see the six giant Shalako, who were to arrive that night.

Preparations for their coming had been spread over most of the year and six houses, new or renovated, had been made ready for their blessing, with prayer sticks placed inside and on the roofs. They had been preceded, we had read, by lesser gods; Long Horn, Rain God of the North, with his War Chief, Rain God of the South; two Warriors representing east and west; and two Whipping Kachinas to represent the other two directions, zenith and nadir.

At sunset the great Shalako crossed the stream and, after darkness had fallen, entered the village. They were magnificent figures, nine feet tall, dressed uniformly in white robes bordered with embroidered bands in red, green, and black. Eagle feathers surmounted their painted turquoise masks; their straight hair was long and black and they wore ruffs of raven feathers. Eyes bulging, long beaks clacking, they moved into the village with grotesque, rolling gait, and each entered his special house. We were not to see them again until nearly midnight. The interval was spent, Zuni ceremonial studies say, in questioning of the kachina by his host and family about his journey to Zuni and in hearing tribal history and the fertility invocation.

Finally, inside a house crowded with Zunis, Navajos, Hopis, and a few other Anglos, we watched the Shalako perform his queer, rolling dance. Except for brief intervals, which we had learned were arranged for food, rest, and a discreet and hidden exchange of impersonators behind the masks, the Shalako danced until dawn, sometimes accompanied by a small Fire God, the Long Horn, and his War Chief, sometimes by the Mudheads, small, squatty brown figures in black kilts and potatolike masks, who dance with a jerky, sidewise movement and are the idiot kachinas, warning against incest, which means marriage within the same clan.

We are told, although we did not see this, that Mudheads, Fire Gods, and Long Horns also have their own houses where they dance without the Shalako.

This is a very much simplified account of the great Zuni winter dance; the events of this one night are preceded, accompanied, and followed by lengthy and complicated ritualism, carried out with elaborate precision and with the use of such ceremonial factors as corn meal, Medicine Water, fire, food, and feathers.

One's sense of reality is blurred as he watches these majestic primitive dance rituals taking place in contemporary America.

On another night in February we found ourselves standing on the roof of a rough stone kiva on a high Hopi plateau in Arizona. There was no light but that of the winter stars and a faint glimmer coming up through the roof door of the kiva from the kerosene lamps inside.

Standing with us were a dozen or so people: a trader and his wife, a group of staff men from the Museum of New Mexico, and four of our friends.

The night silence was broken by faint sounds from a distance. The dancers came down the lane between the rows of houses; we heard the bells and rattles tied to their knees; we could see the fitful flashes of their lanterns and flashlights. Weirdly masked and costumed figures, they clambered up the ladder to our rooftop.

The night was a series of flashing impressions. In the kiva below they were initiating the young girls who had just reached puberty. On the roof where we stood the new arrivals had erected an altar, before which they were manipulating the kachina puppets.

So far as I know, the Hopi are the only Indians in the Southwest who will permit a non-Indian to enter a kiva. We had arrived too late to go down into this one, which was already overcrowded. But, this ceremonial ended, we drove to another kiva several miles away, where after another lengthy wait, we were able to find a minute unoccupied spot among Hopi women and children. The kiva was a small, plain room, warmed by a little stove and again lighted with kerosene lamps, where we sat bolt upright on the floor with our feet straight out before us in a position painful to maintain. But we would have maintained it indefinitely to see the incredible figures—clowns, ogres, and other kachinas—in this bizarre ceremonial.

At five in the morning we gave ourselves a brief rest, but were stirring again by midmorning, since the famous Whipping Kachinas were roving about this Hopi village. We kept a sharp eye out, having been warned that upon sight of one of them, all spectators must immediately get into a building where they could not be seen, in order to avoid the kachinas' whips.

Fortunately we were near a small Hopi store when they came into view, and for an hour were impounded there with a roomful of Indians, who pulled down the window shades and maintained almost a complete silence until they considered it safe to leave. A half-hour later we repeated the performance, this time ducking into a house, where we were courteously received and spent another hour sitting on the floor with a group of Hopi women and children.

Finally on this mild, sunny afternoon we stood on the flat roof of a stone house and saw in the placita below us the most beautiful Indian ceremonial of our experience, a Bean Dance.

I was not then nor am I now concerned chiefly with the detail of costuming or the choreography of this dance, at once primitive and sophisticated, in which I suppose two hundred Indians participated. I remember that their basic costumes were immaculately white, that the foxtails that swung at the rear of their kilts would have done credit to the finest furrier, that they carried slung across their shoulders rectangular baskets filled with beautiful bean sprouts in a delicate shade of chartreuse. But I remember most clearly the rhythm and grace and flow of their movements.

I wondered how the choreography had evolved in the Indian long ago. But I was not surprised at the quality of the production. A preoccupation with beauty is an indigenous factor in the southwestern Indian world.

10

The Peyote Cult

The peyote cult, at least from the standpoint of numbers, seems to be less important in the Taos Indian's religious life than many people suppose. While some ethnologists believe there were more than 130 peyote cultists here thirty-five years ago and that the number has grown to more than 300, informed sources here now say there has never been so large a group involved, and that fewer than 50 Taos Pueblo Indians are peyote users at the present time.[1]

Taos is the only Pueblo group that seems to be interested in peyote, though individuals from both Acoma and Santo Domingo often attend Taos meetings. But the cult is flourishing among the Navajo, as it is among nearly all Plains Indian groups of the United States and parts of Canada. Organized into a sort of federation known as the Native American Church, it has a membership of around 225,000 Indians.

Peyote is a small, spineless, carrot-shaped cactus native to the Rio Grande Valley and areas on southward. Numerous studies have been made over the years of the history and use, ritual and secular, of this hallucinatory plant and the controversies it has sparked with tribal leaders and the courts. One of the soundest of the studies is that written by Weston La Barre, based on work begun in this area in 1936, published as an anthropological treatise by Yale University Press and updated in 1968.

Peyote, otherwise known as *nahautl* or *peyotl,* is identified technically as *Lophophora williamsii Lemaire.* Laymen know of it, La Barre says, as mescaline, its major activating factor. It is said to contain nine narcotic alkaloids of the isoquiniline series, some of them strychninelike in their physiological action, the rest morphinelike.

Mexican Indians were using it in prehistoric times, but it appeared among U.S. tribes only about 1907, though one isolated instance is recorded in 1720, when a Taos Indian was prosecuted because he had eaten peyote and "disturbed the town." It reached the Plains Indians first and was brought to Taos in 1910 when several Taos Indians visited an Oklahoma tribe.

La Barre did no original research on Taos peyote use and had to depend for this information on Dr. Parsons and C. B. Dustin.

The standard ritual involves an all-night ceremony, complicated and precise, around a crescent-shaped earthen mound and a small fire. In use are a drum, gourd rattle, and carved staff, which are passed around in prescribed fashion, after smoking and purifying ceremonies, each person singing four "peyote songs." At midnight and dawn there are water-bringing ceremonies. As day breaks, there is a curing rite and then a ceremonial breakfast of parched corn, fruit, and boneless meat. During the meeting there are prayers, curative rites, and sometimes public confession of sins.

During the night each person eats several (usually four to seven) of the plants, chewing the peyote first, then rolling the pulp into a ball in his hand and swallowing it. The first effect is exhilaration (produced by the strychninelike alkaloids), then depression, nausea, and wakefulness, at which point the morphinelike alkaloids come into play, bringing brilliant color visions which last for several hours.[2]

Some groups introduce Christian elements, Pentecostal in nature, into their meetings, but this does not seem to be true in Taos.

Since peyote is not habit-forming and has no deleterious physiological effects, it is not a narcotic, the Association of American Indian Affairs, headed by the anthropologist Oliver La Farge, declared in a published statement dated 1961.[3] The view is supported by most anthropologists. As a result, it has come into use by various tribes for secular purposes ranging from finding lost objects to the cure of a wide range of diseases. At Taos it has been considered historically as a specific for counteracting the effects of snake venom.

Though laws in some states still brand it as illegal, New Mexico law was amended in 1959 to permit the ritual use of peyote, and in 1960 an Arizona court ruled in favor of a Navajo woman, a member of the First American Church, who had been arrested under a tribal law forbidding its use.

In line with the changing general view, Taos tribal authorities have also tempered their former violent objections to peyote. No longer are "peyote boys" subject to such severe penalties as were sometimes inflicted thirty years ago: heavy fines, floggings, and ejection from their kivas. A member of the cult may now hold high religious or secular office.

Peyote has inevitably proved attractive to some commune dwellers in Taos, but the Indians have not welcomed them into pueblo groups. One

Taos Indian who attempted to bring a hippie into a meeting complained loudly when his friend was turned away. But at least two Taos Indians are known to have attended a peyote ceremony at a nearby commune.

The peyote cult, among the relatively small number of Taos Indians who have aligned themselves with it, seems to coexist easily with their age-old animistic religion and the Catholic faith that they later adopted.

11

The Penitentes

On a bitterly cold Holy Thursday in 1894 a Denver newspaper reporter, D. J. Flynn, arrived in Taos by train and stagecoach, hired a team of horses with wagon, and set out to drive four miles south to the Spanish village of Ranchos de Taos. He was trailing a story for *Harper's Weekly* on the contemporary status of one of the weirdest phenomena in all New Mexico's history: the flagellant rites of the Penitentes or Brothers of Light.

Though for two months he had been in correspondence with Americans in New Mexico on the subject, his efforts to secure information had met with scant success. Some had told him that, though they had lived in the state for many years and heard persistent rumors of these ceremonies, they had never witnessed them, since they were held at night and in secret and the presence of outsiders was not permitted. Others said that the advance of civilization had watered down the "barbaric rites."

These are much like the answers he would have been given in the 1970s, almost eighty years later. But what he actually saw on that Holy Thursday and Good Friday on a spot within two or three miles from my present home was quite different from what I have been able to see during twenty-five Holy Weeks spent here of the activities of this offshoot of the Catholic Church, of the Third Order of Saint Francis of Assisi.

Flynn had brought with him from Denver another man and two women. In Taos he picked up three of the six Anglos then living here—all men—and in his lumbering vehicle proceeded along the dirt road that ran below the foothills of the Sangre de Cristo range until he saw what he was looking for: about four hundred Mexicans (as they were then called), men, women, and children, drawn up in a straight line extending from a small adobe hut at one end of a field to a large cross standing about a quarter of a mile away. Doing his homework later, he learned that the adobe hut was a *morada,* a Penitente church.

Flynn's arrival with his party of seven appeared to be highly unpopular as he neared the line, a fact indicated by scowls and vocal advice to turn back. But with the essential persistence of his calling he drove to within 125 feet of the line, halted his horses, and settled down to await developments. As a result of his temerity, he got for his magazine that afternoon the only eyewitness account I have been able to find of a Penitente service in the heyday of the order in the Taos area.[1]

Flynn's account of what he saw here has, I feel it only fair to state, been downgraded to second class by George Mills and Richard Grove in a thoughtful study of Penitente material sources, published by the Taylor Museum of the Colorado Springs Fine Arts Center. Here it has been relegated to a class of witness credibility described as "between the reliable accounts and hearsay . . . much useful information contained in pseudonymous, anonymous, and second-hand eyewitness accounts." This, the two authors point out, is inadmissible as evidence in a court of law, but useful to one aware of its limitations and dangers.[2]

I find it hard to understand their classification of Flynn's account as dubious. It does not conflict in essentials with many another description which they do accept of Penitente ceremonies in the state; furthermore, Flynn completely omitted any attempt to attribute to the order activities such as death by crucifixion which over the years have proved most controversial. Here, in essence, is what the newsman said he saw.

A band of men emerged from the morada, the leader carrying a crucifix and the next in line playing a weird and solemn tune on what Flynn called a piccolo, but what we know as a *pito* or reed flute. Next came six chanters followed by two men wearing only white cotton "drawers," with black bags over their heads and foreheads bound about by red bandannas. Streams of blood were running down the backs of these two, from deep cuts, he later learned, which had been made ritually with pieces of flint or glass. Barefoot, the two stumbled along across a mesa covered with thorn cactus, sagebrush, and stones.

Now this pair began to flagellate their own bare backs with cactus whips, bringing them down at every step, over first one shoulder, then the other. So sharp were these *disciplinas*, Flynn reported, that they could with difficulty be wrenched from the bleeding flesh. Still the flagellants maintained a stoical silence. The blows increased in rapidity and intensity until, he estimated, about five hundred had been inflicted on each before they reached the cross. There the members of the entire party fell upon their knees, still chanting, while the two scourgers began to move in a wide circle about the cross, still applying their knouts. This done, they resumed their line of march, still flagellating.

Flynn was surrounded by Mexicans at this point and so unable to train his camera on the lacerated backs. But he described them. "So sharp and knife-like were the whips that the entire covering of flesh had been torn off, leaving the bones of the ribs exposed to full view."

This party now entered the morada and was replaced by a large one, in which, following the chanters, were two masked men bearing on their shoulders crosses about fifteen feet in length, made of rough timbers about twelve inches in diameter and weighing, he estimated, between three and four hundred pounds.

"As this procession started, two men armed with whips took their places behind the cross-bearers, and at every step applied vicious blows upon the naked backs of the men in front. Behind these followed a party of eight more flagellants, followed by a dozen or so men carrying elevated in front of them primitive figures of saints."

To the sound of whipping and occasional chants, while the crowd stood in reverence, this processional made its way to the cross and returned. "The blood flowed in torrents down the backs of the flagellants, staining the drawers to the ground and leaving the subjects of this terrible sacrifice so weak they were hardly able to complete the journey."

That evening, visiting the office of a Taos doctor who had originally directed him to the Ranchos de Taos scene, he sat discussing the day's lurid scene when the physician was called to attend one of the Penitentes who by reason of the flogging and exposure to the chill March weather had contracted pneumonia. Flynn seized the chance to accompany him as he followed the sick man's father to "a wretched hut beyond the town." As they neared the house they saw a lantern moving in the distance and heard again the strain of the pito, indicating that another rite of the Brothers of Light was in progress.

Finally reaching the one-room house, they saw the patient lying on a mattress on the adobe floor. "I cannot describe the condition of his back, but it looked as though sharp knives had been drawn across it in all directions and the flesh torn out with pincers."

The following day Flynn repaired to the Ranchos de Taos mesa again to witness the dramatic reenactment of the crucifixion. Having grown bolder, he drove to a point directly behind the crowd and within twenty-five feet of the principal actors.

In the center of the area stood the cross, the figure already suspended from it. That day it was a wooden figure, though in other instances both before that date and in early days afterward, a man had been tied to it, by ropes or thongs of wet buckskin, and in a few instances (though many sources dispute this) fastened to it by nails driven through hands and feet.

Beside the cross that day stood a man holding a spear, representing the soldier who had pierced the side of Christ. Around his head was a band of white cloth into which an American flag had been stuck, and his face was streaked with red and white paint. The service of the day was read at this point by a man using an old and dilapidated notebook.

At this point Flynn reached for his camera, which he had hidden among the blankets in the bottom of the wagon. In his party on this occasion were two men whom he identifies only as a civil engineer and one of Kit Carson's captains of scouts. The captain immediately protested Flynn's use of the camera, fearing trouble from the crowd and threatening to leave if the newsman persisted. But Flynn, too sorely tempted, did persist, and the scout left in haste.

"Placing the camera under my arm," Flynn wrote, "and shielding the lens with my traveling cap, I watched for a favorable moment, and then dropping the cap for an instant, the civil engineer pressed the button, and the cap once more arose to its office. The click of the spring, however had been heard by those in the crowd nearest us, and curious glances were turned upon us that were far from reassuring.

"Our faces, however, betrayed nothing, and a few minutes later, when the procession carrying the effigy had started, several more snaps were secured in like manner."

The cross bearer led the procession, followed by ten little girls representing the Wise Virgins, these "carrying all sorts and conditions of lanterns, ranging from an orthodox burglar's to a discarded and abandoned track-walker's." Next came three slightly older girls robed in somber black, the three Marys; then men carrying figures of the Blessed Virgin dressed "as a Mexican lady of fashion." Last came a group of chanters and four women bearing on their shoulders a bier on which reposed the figure of Christ.

The procession marched down to the village of Ranchos de Taos, and back, returning the Cristo to the morada.

This ended the reporter's observations of the rites. He had seen, of course, only part of the Holy Week Penitente reenactment of the Passion of Christ, details of which have excited immense curiosity and proved over the years to be enormously difficult to authenticate, because of the secrecy of the participants and their resentment of efforts of nonmembers to witness the bizarre ceremonies.

The gentle Saint Francis of Assisi—though himself a Penitent—would have been confounded had he known the lengths to which in this remote northern portion of the New World some of his followers would carry his belief in salvation through penance.

He had set up two previous orders, the Order of Saint Francis of Assisi in the year 1210, and the Second Franciscan Order of Poor Ladies (Poor Clares) established in 1212 after an appeal by one of his Assisi disciples, Saint Clare. In 1218 he organized the Order of the Brothers and Sisters of Penance, now known as the Third Order of Saint Francis, for the laity who, without leaving the world, might take modified vows.

Later an offshoot of the parent order was established in Spain, known as Los Hermanos de Penitentes. Franciscan in origin and sponsorship, its route to northern New Mexico can easily be traced. In 1500 the Franciscan friars came to the New World, and in the sixteenth century penetrated these northern fastnesses with the vanguard of the Spanish conquistadores.

Definite attestation to this fact is contained in the *Historia de la Nuevo México*, written by Captain Gaspar Pérez de Villagra, published in Spain twelve years after he saw penitential rites observed in New Mexico on March 20, 1598, by the first great colonizer of the northern country, Don Juan de Oñate.

Of Holy Thursday, Villagra, who had accompanied the expedition, wrote:

> The night was one of prayer and penance for all. The women and children came barefoot to pray at the holy shrine. The soldiers, with cruel scourges, beat their backs unmercifully until the camp ran crimson with their blood. The humble Franciscan friars, barefoot and clothed in cruel thorny girdles, devoutly chanted their doleful hymns, praying forgiveness for their sins.
>
> Don Juan, unknown to anyone except me, went to a secluded spot where he cruelly scourged himself, mingling bitter tears with the blood which flowed from his many wounds. This continued throughout the camp till early morn. . . . Gerónimo and I took example from these worthy ones and underwent like punishment.

As the Franciscans spread throughout the area, pursuing with devout zeal their work of maintaining the faith among the Spanish colonists and Christianizing the Pueblo Indians, the Penitential order spread with them. And since it stemmed from the Spanish offshoot of the original Third Order, its rules and laws departed from those of the original order in some respects, notably those regarding flagellation.

That by the late eighteenth century the mother church in New Mexico was having at least faint misgivings regarding the trend being taken by the Penitentes is shown in the first church document in existence regarding the matter in this territory. The manuscript, seen at the cathedral in Santa Fe and dated September 17, 1794, is headed "Information given to Governor Chacón by the Reverend P. Custodio F. Cayetano José Bernal." The document contains the following statement: "It [the venerable Third Order of Penitentes] is established with the previous permission of the Prelates of our Holy Religion, as of right its immediate Superiors; Furthermore, to them pertains the right to know and regulate its affairs as necessarily follows from many declamatory and confirmatory Bulls of many Popes of Rome." [3]

Their misgivings were justified. On these isolated northern fringes of the Spanish-dominated territories, Old World trends were maintained and intensified. They were furthered, as it happened, by the fact that at the end of the Mexican revolution, which brought freedom from Spain, all Spanish-born Franciscans were ordered out of the country in 1828. This left the religious guidance of the small mountain villages in the hands of laymen, without the moderating influence of the mother church. At this time, records show, virtually every non-Indian New Mexican was not only a Catholic but also a Penitente.

And in their isolation, the hold of the Brothers of Light upon the religious affairs of the area was maintained, even after the return of the padres. Roads and trails were difficult, often impassable in bad weather. And there were not enough priests, so that one was assigned to a group of villages, visiting them in rotation. This meant that masses were infrequently said; ministrations to the sick and dying and the conducting of funeral services were still in the hands of laymen. So the Penitentes flourished and their penitential excesses continued.

In 1886 the church took a definite stand to curb the order, when Archbishop J. B. Salpointe of Santa Fe issued a circular letter which he ordered sent to the Hermano Mayor of each Penitente group, demanding that the members leave off their flagellation and return to the original laws of the Third Order of Saint Francis. When this move brought small results, another letter was sent out two years later:

> With regard to the Society called Los Penitentes we firmly believe that it fully deserves all blame. Consequently, it must not be fostered. This society, though perhaps legitimate and religious in its beginning, has so greatly degenerated many years ago that it has no longer fixed rules but is governed in everything according to the pleasure of the director of every locality, and in many cases it is nothing else but a political society. We therefore desire. . . .
>
> That mass must not be celebrated in the chapels, where the

75

Penitentes observe their rights and abuses. Moreover, we command that the following rule be observed by our Priests toward the Penitentes who celebrate the wake over the dead bodies, with scourgings, not excluding eating and drinking and despised our ordinances and penalties, published to that effect in the year 1886. They are to be deprived of the Sacrament until they amend.[4]

But moderation of the Penitente rites came slowly. It is obvious to a resident of the area that it resulted in great measure from a gradual improvement in communications brought about by automobiles and trucks, better roads, newspapers (some of which were printed in Spanish), telephones, and radios. These brought the people out of their extreme isolation and also diverted their interests somewhat from the community organization which had constituted the hard center of their religious life and, to a great extent, their social life as well. An improvement in education was also a vital factor—education, which must have been practically nonexistent in the nineteenth century in isolated sections of the state, in view of the fact that, even as late as 1940, 63 percent of the population of the Taos area had not progressed as far as the sixth grade in school.

It was not until 1947, the year of my arrival in Taos, that the Penitentes here were accepted into the good graces of the church. And even then the order of admission carried a stern warning. Archbishop Edwin V. Byrne of Santa Fe granted the order the blessing of the Catholic Church, "if the Brethren proceed with moderation and privately under our supervision."

He pointed to the "excesses and abuses" which had occurred in the order in the past, and admitted that some individuals and groups were still guilty of them, referring especially to "this or that group" which "still makes itself a political football, thus giving a bad name to the Brethren."

He approved acts of physical and spiritual penance, provided they were to stop short of injury to health, adding that these are "not acts of sadism or masochism, as modern wise men wish to say in these days, softened by luxury and comfort."

The archbishop pointed to the Penitentes as "a pious association of men joined in charity to commemorate the passion and death of the Redeemer," and credited them with the preservation of the faith during the trying period when the Franciscan friars were in exile.

But he cautiously inserted in his order a statement of strict jurisdiction: " . . . we have the authority and power to suppress this association just as we can and must suppress any other pious association in the church which goes counter to, or exceeds the laws of God and His church, or the dictates of reason." [5]

Some of the excesses to which he referred may be seen in an explanation of the duties of the ten officers of each morada, who were collectively designated as Hermanos de Luz or Brothers of Light, and were elected annually. They were:

1. The Hermano Mayor, head of the organization
2. The Celador or Warden, who looked after the building and also carried out sentences imposed upon a brother for some misdeed
3. The Coadjutor or Helper, who cleansed the scourges used by the flagellants and washed the bodies of the Brothers after completion of their penance
4. The Infermero or Nurse, whose duty it was to do works of mercy and see that a sick brother received proper attention from the group
5. The Mandatorio or Collector, who served as secretary
6. The Maestro de Novios (Teacher of Novices), who was required to examine a prospective new member and to direct the Mandatorio in instructing him regarding the obligations, chief of which was strict observance of secrecy in regard to the proceedings of the organization
7. The Secretario or Secretary, whose duty was to read to a member any rule about whose meaning he was in doubt
8. The Sangrador or Pricker, who inflicted the seal of the Penitentes upon the backs of the members—three gashes in full length and three the width of the back, at right angles to each other, cut with any sharp, rough instrument, usually a piece of flint or glass; the Sangrador also whipped certain members with a heavy rawhide lash
9. The Resador, translated as One Who Prays, who marched with the flagellants, praying for them while they were whipping themselves
10. The Pitero or Fluter, who played during the greater part of the ceremonies; his was the only instrument used, except for a wooden rattle called a *matraca*, consisting of a stiff stick and a notched wheel, which, when whirled, gave out a dull clicking sound [6]

A man could not become a full-fledged member, and hence not an officer of the Penitentes, until he had whipped for five years. After that he was not required to flagellate except on the occasion of some special penance.

There have always been two points of special controversy among specialists in Penitente material and in the minds of residents of northern New Mexico and southern Colorado, areas to which the order seemed to be confined. These questions are the sincerity of the flagellants and the extent of their excesses.

That the order's basic tenets involved a genuine piety and a desire to help each other in time of need is shown in a Taos document dated February 23, 1861:

> The members of the Pious Fraternity of the County of Taos should know that our intention since old times has been devotion to the Blood of Christ, which was shed to save us sinners, for so did God give His only Son to be offered in sacrifice for sinners.
>
> The principal object of our organization is to serve God our Creator in the belief that Jesus Christ is the Saviour of the World, according to the teachings of the Holy Gospel; to keep the Ten Commandments of the Law of God; to live humbly; to adjure discord and unjust dealings with our fellow men; to shun saloons and all of the temptations the world offers, for "what does it profit a man, if he gain the whole world, but suffer the loss of his own soul?"; to act toward one another with charity and mutual love like brothers in Jesus Christ; to provide a good example for each other, helping in illnesses, afflictions and time of need, pardoning one another's offenses, and mutually tolerating our weaknesses; to follow the humble life given to us as an example by Our Lord Jesus Christ, and to recognize and respect each other as members of a body that is Christ Jesus, our Redeemer, and to say as says the Gospel of Saint Matthew, Chapter 11, verses 25–26: "I praise Thee, Father, Lord of heaven and earth, that Thou didst hide these things from the wise and prudent, and didst reveal them to little ones. Yes, Father, for such was Thy good pleasure." [7]

This was certainly orthodox enough as a statement of Christian faith and an intention to love and help their neighbors. Opinions as to the sincerity of the members in carrying out the tenets range from one extreme to the other. Charles F. Lummis in a chapter in his famous Southwestern travel book, *Land of Poco Tiempo,* written just before the turn of the century, gave an extremely unsympathetic view, believing that the order included too many rascals enduring extreme penitential suffering in order to proceed spiritually unscathed with further nefarious deeds. But Lummis based his comment on remarks from certain non-Penitente bystanders who had seen two malefactors among the flagellants that day.

Others, including researchers, credit the participants with genuine sincerity in their stated beliefs, and point to their aid supplied to any member in need of help of any kind, and to the pressure to mend his ways placed upon any member inclined to wander from the path of moral rectitude. A sifting of any information available inclines one to the opinion that the Penitentes must be judged as individuals, and as individual local groups.

But, whatever this situation was, one must certainly accept the archbishop's statement that there were numerous instances in which the considerable power of the Penitentes, both as individuals and groups, was used for political purposes.

This was inevitable. As an agrarian people in an arid country, they were desperately poor. Any employment that might be available was usually obtainable only through political string-pulling. So most New Mexicans were politicos. And since at the same time they were Penitentes, a political jefe was also likely to be a leading Penitente and so had a double-edged weapon of influence.

As further commentary on their sincerity, it is noted that the Penitente dramatization of a popular interpretation of the passion and death of Jesus was a response to the same urge that has produced the Passion Play at Oberammergau, as well as medieval miracle plays, and in New Mexico such folk dramas as the Christmas play, *Los Pastores*, and *Los Comanches*, commemorating the raids of that roving Indian tribe on the sedentary Spanish and Indians of the Taos Valley.

But though some works on the Penitentes have stressed the folk play angle and discount accounts of torture, self-torture, and death as a major part of the activities of the brothers, there is no real doubt that during the three and a half centuries during which the rites have been held in remote areas such as Taos the Penitentes did exceed the bounds of reason, inflicting cruel and unusual punishments upon themselves and each other and reenacting the Crucifixion with sometimes lethal exactness.

Accepting only well-authenticated accounts, one learns of a Penitente whose naked back and chest were bound with cactus, over which his arms were folded. Both legs were tightly bound with horsehair ropes and he crawled on his knees over a path of cactus. Another Penitente was similarly punished, with the addition of chains fastened to his ankles.[8]

There is an authentic account of a crossbearer who fell to the ground, and lying there with the cross arm resting upon his neck was given fifty blows with a whip until he was helped to his feet and resumed his burden. About to sink again, he was revived with kicks.[9] Well-supported reports of Penitentes who collapsed during the rites are many. One, carrying the cross from the Calvary to the morada, whipped during the processional and jerked this way and that by means of four short ropes in the hands of attendants, fell just before reaching the building.[10]

Though the cactus whip was itself a torturous weapon, it is known that some groups tied to it bits of glass or pieces of iron or wire, or used chain whips equipped with sharp metal claws.

One credible witness saw a Penitente buried upright in the earth with nothing above the ground but his head, remaining in that position two days and nights.[11] Another reported seeing a Penitente who traveled two miles with a pole placed across his shoulders and the back of his neck, and his arms extended and strapped to the pole. In each hand he held a sword, the points resting upon his thighs and piercing his flesh at any misstep or unevenness of the ground.[12]

That deaths did actually result in at least a small number of cases to men chosen for the honor role of the Cristo in the Crucifixion seems well established. But researchers seem to have discredited an often-heard tale that in such a case, the man's family learned of his death by discovering his shoes on the doorstep the next morning. There are also authenticated reports of nails used to fasten the man's hands and feet to the cross. To one statement that, where he was bound to the cross by cords or thongs, a supporting platform was used to help support his body, researchers who claim to have surveyed the whole field of testimony on the matter claim there is no record of the use in this area of any such ameliorating provision.[13]

Lurid tabloid accounts might have well resulted, as in fact they did, from one emotional phase of the Holy Week rites, known as the Tinieblas. This was held in the morada chapel, and as reported in authenticated accounts reached a calculated frenzy, intended as it was to symbolize the chaos into which the world was thrown after Christ's death, lasting until His resurrection.

Ruth Laughlin in her book *Caballeros* reports that some of the men worked themselves into a fury, forcing some in the room to stand by seizing them by the hair. She reported women fainting, others crouched against the walls in fear; sounds of whipping from the adjoining room; the sound in the darkness of prayers for souls in purgatory; cries of frightened children; clanking of chains; banging together of pieces of tin; chanting; the eerie strains of the pito and the clacking of matracas.

Another feature of the primitive drama was calculated to strike fear into the heart of a nonmember, or at least to add a macabre note. This was the use in some processionals of the Death Cart, or Carreta del Muerto, a heavy, low, wooden cart, with solid wooden wheels, upon which sat a carefully carved skeleton clothed in black and holding a drawn bow with arrow in place. This a Penitente dragged by a horsehair rope passed over his shoulders and under his arms.

In view of the nature of the rites, the extremes to which they were

80

sometimes carried, and the secrecy in which the membership sought to keep them shrouded, it is small wonder that they continuously attracted the attention of tabloid writers and incited exaggerated versions of their activities in the minds of their neighbors in northern New Mexico. Even now it is difficult to know whether the fervor of the Penitentes has abated entirely to normal Catholic rituals or whether in the remote mountain villages some vestiges may still remain of the earlier, savage self-punishments.

It seems, though, that the old days are past. About 1965, for the first time, there was no Penitente service in the little morada near Mabel Luhan's house. In the old days—the twenties—she had been awakened in the Good Friday nights by the singing voices as the faithful marched up to the Calvary; by the thud that punctuated the wild anguish of the *alabados*, the chants; the nervous whinnying of the horses; the barking of the dogs, who could hear, though the people in the valley could not.

We, too, have seen the diminishing of the Penitente zeal, though it was already much diminished when we came here in 1947. The Good Friday rites in the little morada that I pass each day on my way to the book shop are less impressive each year, the decline marked by the arrival of a Denver news photographer doing a documentary on the Penitente survival. Since then I have observed the Good Friday ritual at Rio Chiquito, two miles away and now thought to represent the strongest remnant of survival in the immediate Taos area. It depicted the road to Calvary and the Crucifixion in symbolic terms. It was simple and somehow moving. But there was no hint of flagellation or real emotional involvement and the service on the mesa was attended by only about thirty persons, many of them teenagers and children.

Though in New Mexico one is never sure of what may lie behind the next mountain, all indications I can see in an informal continuing inquiry are that the Penitentes are content with the symbolism of the mother church, or in cases where they continue to exist as separate lay entities, carry out their dramatic reenactments without the fanatical zeal that marked their rites up to and beyond the turn of the century.

From the Brothers of Light have come some of New Mexico's finest primitive art treasures. Left by the withdrawal of the priests to handle their own religious affairs, they developed an iconography of beauty and power. To have pictures and figures of the saints, it was necessary for them to make them. Great *santeros* among them carved three-dimensional figures, called *bultos*, and painted *retablos* on wood or tin. While regrettably the people themselves no longer seem to treasure these magnificent *santos*, their indifference has served to enrich museums and private collections of great value and interest.

Several monographs have been put together on the subject by E. Boyd and others, just as Dorothy Benrimo has recently published a camera study of the beautiful crosses of wood, stone, and metal in infinite variety which were made by Catholics of that era to mark the graves of their dead.

To these treasures they have added a reservoir of religious folk music in their alabados or hymns. The words, copied into small notebooks, hark back to medieval Spain. The music, apparently entirely transmitted by memory, is somewhat reminiscent of Gregorian chants, but, plaintive, shrill, and punctuated by though not accompanied by the pito, seems eerily dissonant.

So the Penitent Brothers, in isolation, out of an excess of piety and some facets of their temperamental heritage, wrote one of the most fascinating chapters in the rich history of New Mexico.

12

The Prevalence of Witches

It's probably just as well that my inquiry into the matter of witchcraft in New Mexico, though it has covered a span of nearly a decade, has been both relaxed and sporadic. Poking one's nose into this kind of thing, even when motivated by only a sort of benevolent curiosity, is rated as a hazardous activity in an area where, I was told a few years ago by a New Mexico university folklore specialist, it is not too much to say that "witchcraft is the second religion." [1]

For this state has relegated to the status of a mere trifling incident Salem's brief foray into the exorcising of witches by hanging nineteen women. Populations of whole villages here have been decimated by executions for sorcery. At Zuni Pueblo witches were still being hanged as late as 1911, and, it is suspected, even to 1920. Confessions were being forced up to 1939.

Nor do the Indians have a monopoly on this brand of superstition. In his memoirs, only recently published, a reputable Albuquerque physician, Meldrum K. Wylder, wrote that a belief in witchcraft is widespread among our Spanish-speaking people and "seems to be here to stay." Wylder, after a lifetime of ministering to the ills of thousands of patients in the state's largest metropolitan area, bolstered his statement by numerous incidents told to him of sickness brought on by evil supernatural power.

"Many times," he wrote, "in serious cases when the patient continued to grow worse, I have been told, 'No doctor can do anything for this patient. This is an *infermedad puesta* [i.e., a disease that has been put on by someone else]. The only way that this patient can get well is to find the witch that put this sickness upon her and get her to take off the spell.' " [2]

While fear of sorcerers and constant use of methods to combat their power have been present historically in Taos, this pueblo is blameless of the charge of putting any to death, according to Elsie Clews Parsons. The reason, she said, was not humanitarian forbearance, but rather an unreasoning fear of the witches, since even a doctor would be afraid to identify the witch who was injuring his patient.

Parsons was sure that even in the late thirties Taos was subject to the depredations of not only traditional witches but also a local variety called *yiapana* or "sleepmaker." These, however, came only in January and were considered merely a nuisance, not actually harmful. Wearing their hair down over their white-painted faces, they seemed to confine their activities to stealing fresh meat and "putting you to sleep." For protection, you carried a stone or "medicine to spit." [3]

Superstitious credence in the powers of both good and evil spirits came into New Mexico with the conquistadores, who found that indeed it had been here before them, the resultant admixture causing some of the most savage violence in the known four hundred years of New Mexico history. It was an accusation of sorcery against Pueblo medicine men by the superior of the *convento* at San Ildefonso that set off the Pueblo Revolt of 1680, in which all the Spanish colonists were driven out of the country and a hundred, including all the priests, were put to death. And in turn it was three "infernal spirits" in an underground *estufa* at Taos who advised and directed that bloody revenge.

There is also the 1630 *Memorial* of Fray Alonso de Benavides, first custodian of the New Mexico missions and first agent here for the Holy Office of the Inquisition. In this report, written expressly for the eyes of Pope Urban VII, the father set down an account of a curious Taos Pueblo incident:

> And in the bygone year of one thousand six hundred and twenty-seven, the Lord confirmed the Holy Word by a miracle among them. And it was thus:
>
> It went hard with them to give up having many wives as they used to have before they were baptized; and each day the religious preached to them the truth of the Holy Sacrament of Matrimony; and the one that most contradicted this was an old Indian woman, a sorceress, who, under pretext of going to the country for firewood, took out four other women with her.
>
> These were good Christians and married according to the rule of our Holy Mother Church; and going and coming, she kept persuading them that they should not consent to the method of marriage which the Father taught, for that which they used to use in their gentilism was better, the which argument the

good Christian women steadily resisted. And as they were arriving again already near the pueblo, the sorceress not ceasing from her sermon, and the heavens being clear and serene, a thunderbolt fell and slew that infernal Mistress of the Demon, right between the good Christians who were resisting her evil doctrine.

Now, more than three hundred years later, accusations of witchcraft appear in testimony in New Mexico court trials, fear of the evil eye persists in some areas, and Taos itself has a practicing witch doctor who claims to be skilled in removal of spells from unfortunate persons who are *embrujado* —bewitched.

This middle-aged, well-dressed gentleman with a Spanish name is the original of the witch doctor in Frank O'Rourke's Taos novel, *The Man Who Found His Way.* Here he was credited with having removed a spell cast over one of our villagers by a witch living in Questa, twenty-five miles to the north. Jimmy Valentine of Taos told me that the witch, a well-known Questa character, had since died, but that the witch doctor was still living in Cañon, a settlement two miles east of us. He was sure I might confer with him if I wished. A few days later the witch doctor came into the shop and for an hour or so we talked in a back room, a conversation conducted in guarded tones and suspended entirely whenever anyone came near.

His services, he feels, are much needed in the community, where people do not know how much witchcraft is going on among them. Afflicted with sickness or bad luck, they are unaware that they have been bewitched.

He gave an example of a man in Lower Ranchitos a few years ago who had hired an Indian boy to tend a small herd of cattle in a neighboring pasture. Contrary to his instructions, the boy, bored with his job by late afternoon, began bringing the cattle in an hour or so early. The owner of the cows, after he had several times roundly scolded the boy for his disobedience, began having severe headaches every afternoon. Finally he realized what was happening, questioned the boy, and got a confession that the child had learned from his grandmother how to bewitch him. He had made a small effigy of his employer and each afternoon had been sticking pins into its head. After confessing, the boy did not dare to continue his nefarious practice and the headaches were never repeated.

While this man had been able to diagnose and cure his own case, most are unable to solve their problems alone, the witch doctor said, and require the help of one who is skilled in these matters.

However, at this point he expressed himself as unwilling to contribute to research on witchcraft, having previously furnished background material for two novels without any sizable financial benefits to himself. For this reason I was unable to learn the extent of his practice, the nature of his treatments, or the source of his training. He is reputed, however, to be particularly skilled in the use of native herbs and relieving of ailments responding to manipulation.

The late Dr. R. D. Jameson of Highlands University, told me that two loci of witchcraft in this area are the villages of El Abuelo ("The Grandfather"), near Mora, and a spot vaguely designated as "up north of Taos." Jameson said that in these two localities witches are known to hold periodic Sabats, roundups in the nature of orgies. But my efforts to learn anything definite about the satanic conventions have so far proved futile.

I have broached the subject to various persons most likely to know of these affairs, once even finding someone who claimed he knew the spot where the Sabats are held and even knew when one was to be staged in the near future. His promise to go with me to the scene of the orgy, however, dissolved as the day grew near. He had, he explained, out-of-town guests coming; it would never do for so many to invade the scene of the Sabat. I suspect he felt that a witch would have small trouble spotting even one or two of us skulking in the sagebrush.

But I have pursued the subject of witchcraft in other quarters, once sitting in as the sole spectator at a court hearing in which a Taos woman was accused by a Santa Fe couple, Mr. and Mrs. José R. Rivera, of failing to fulfill her promise after they had paid her to cure them, by occult means, of certain ailments, and by the same method to help them to find a treasure she had told them was buried in their patio.

Since in these legally enlightened times there is no such crime as witchcraft in New Mexico and hence no law against it, the accused, Mrs. Teresita Ferguson, was charged with having obtained money under false pretense. She was acquitted in district court in Santa Fe, after retaining as defense counsel one of the state's most able attorneys, David Chávez, later a justice of the New Mexico Supreme Court. The jury was convinced that the money paid to her had been only a loan.

But the witnesses claimed that Mrs. Ferguson (mother of a New Mexico State Corporation commissioner) had promised to cure them—the man of "miner's consumption," the woman of high blood pressure—by removing an evil spell, which she said had been laid upon them. Her treatments, they said, involved the use of candles, prayers, a glass ball, measurement of parts of their bodies, a leather belt for the husband to wear, and for the wife a copper necklace consisting of a chain hung with U.S. and Canadian pennies (this was produced in court) and ribbons of stipulated colors. The latter, the woman testified, after having been worn beneath her clothing, were burned and the ashes were buried to complete the cure.

In the course of the treatments, which were given in Taos, the couple said Mrs. Ferguson volunteered the information that a treasure of $30,000 lay buried in their patio. To obtain it, they said, on the Taoseña's instructions they spent several hours each night for six weeks pulling on a rope tied to an iron stake driven into the ground. They said Teresita helped with the project, during which "sometimes she mumbled and sometimes we could hear her say, 'There are three spirits. Can you see them?' " She told them, they added, "that her glass ball showed her that half of the treasure was in silver, half in gold."

When neither the cures nor the treasure materialized, in spite of the payments of $134 they had made, the two lodged a court complaint.

"Did you think you were suffering from witchery?" Chávez asked the woman.

"One cannot know these things," she replied.

"Do you believe in witchery?"

"There are witches, but the trouble is to find out who they are."

"You believed she could cure you?"

"I didn't believe it, but I didn't doubt it, either."

This state of suspension between belief and disbelief in witches was brought into strong light in the strange case involving "the Frog Man of Mora." [4] Actually it was not a frog, but a toad. It was by a slip of the tongue during the early hours of the court hearing that District Attorney E. R. Cooper transformed the supernatural amphibian into a frog, his error perpetuated by newspaper reporters, whose adoption of the term can possibly be credited to the popularity at that time of a comic strip involving a frog man. "The Frog Man of Mora" attained headline billing in newspapers from Las Vegas, New Mexico to San Francisco during the week of December 23, 1939.

But it was really a toad, fourteen inches long, that leaped into the bedroom of Mrs. Avelino Espinosa that night, knocked out three or four of her teeth, attempted to strangle her, inflicted several deep facial scratches, and finally leaped out through the closed window without breaking the glass. Outside it drew a large circle in the snow, marked a cross inside it, and disappeared into the New Mexico winter night.

Mrs. Epinosa was not the only resident of El Abuelo, three miles from Mora, who participated in the event. Her sister, Mrs. Adelido Cisneros, with whom she was sleeping, also saw the toad, as did the sister's husband, who came running in response to the women's screams and chased the toad about the room with a broom before it made its escape through the closed window.

Mrs. Espinosa was not deceived by the shape of the thing which had subjected her to this terrifying nighttime attack. Shapeshifting, she knew, is a traditional talent of witches, who can appear as goats, owls, or any one of several other animals or birds. She knew her assailant to be her husband, Avelino. She had known for some time that he was a *brujo*, and besides, in the thick of the fracas both she and her sister had heard his voice in the attic.

To all of this the three testified in a four-hour court hearing at Mora a week or so later before Justice of the Peace Vincent Romero, when Espinosa was brought in on a technical charge of mayhem. The latter appeared without a lawyer and took the whole thing as a joke. Justice Romero dismissed the case.

One fine April morning, Genevieve and I made the fifty-mile drive over the mountain to learn the details of the matter from the justice and his niece, Mrs. Adelina Rudolph, Mora county health nurse.

"I didn't believe the whole damn thing," said the keen-eyed official, who is a graduate of Notre Dame.

In the witch-ridden village of El Abuelo the Espinosas had lived with their epileptic son, then nineteen. His mother believed the son's condition was due to a spell cast by his father.

"She had got the boy so afraid of his father," said Mrs. Rudolph, "that every time Avelino came into the room, he would have a fit."

When finally the boy died, the mother would not permit her husband to attend the funeral or the two-night wake that followed. After the second night she left the house, first burning all the food, which she felt was bewitched, and as an extra precaution placing a cross made of needles above the door, and went home with her sister and brother-in-law. It was during that night that the toad appeared in her bedroom.

"The doctor who was called in to examine her injuries," said Justice Romero, "was an osteopath, Dr. R. H. Husted. His theory of what happened that night was that after having lost two nights' sleep because of the wake, the sister had had a nightmare and attacked Mrs. Espinosa in her sleep. There was no denying the fact that she had lost three or four teeth and that her face looked as if claws had dug into it. The scratches were all infected by the next day, too, which was another funny thing."

But in spite of the fact that they could and did explain the frog man case in natural terms, the justice and his niece, two educated, well-oriented

88

residents in the world of contemporary thought, were not prepared to write off completely the possibility of witchcraft as a force for evil.

"Do I believe in witches?" Mrs. Rudolph repeated my question. "No, I don't. But just the same, there are some people in Mora who everybody thinks are witches, and I will say I wouldn't eat any food they gave me, unless I could cook it." Here she explained a technique employed by sorcerers throughout their worldwide history—obtaining power over a victim by supplying him with food to be eaten without further cooking.

"I would eat meat given me by a witch, because I could cook it," Mrs. Rudolph went on, "but I certainly wouldn't eat a pie, for instance, which was already baked."

And her uncle, Justice Romero, said, "I don't believe in witches, either, but I sure wouldn't take any chances."

They told us of several instances of black magic in Mora. One concerned a man who, although married, had become infatuated with a schoolteacher in the village, with whom for some time he had carried on an open affair. When she died after a short illness, it was found that she had kept a small rag doll made of a piece of one of his shirts, by which means she had retained her hold over him. Her lover did not mourn her death, our informants said. He was like a man waking from a sleep. She had bewitched him; now the spell was broken.

After this conference my partner and I drove on to Las Vegas, where we sought out Dr. Jameson in his office on the university campus and heard his startling statement, "It is not too much to say that witchcraft is the second religion in New Mexico." In his classes in the study of folklore, he said, he had interested himself in drawing out students from the area on the subject of belief in witchcraft in this northern mountain section.

"When they first come to college, they are ashamed of the beliefs of many of the old people, call them old wives' tales. But after a while they say they just don't know."

As for us, stalled for six hours that night in a snowstorm in an isolated mountain section, we wondered whether we had ourselves incurred the malice of the local brujos by our curiosity about their affairs. A mile from the top of Holman Hill—a good-size mountain, in spite of its name—the car slewed sideways and came to a stop with its rear wheels only two or three inches from the edge of a soft shoulder over which we could look straight down for what seemed a thousand feet or so. All efforts to move it only increasing the danger, we finally set the brakes and waited for someone to come.

It had been an open, sunny late April day. Now at 5:00 P.M., black clouds swung low and in dead silence threw down a thick blanket of unseasonal snow. The road disappeared. It seemed to us that no one had ever traveled this way, that no one would ever come.

To reinforce the brakes we put the car into gear, so depriving ourselves of the use of the heater, and, huddled on the front seat to keep the weight away from the dropoff, shivered every time our dog even flapped her tail as she crouched trustingly on the seat behind us.

Black night came on; hours passed and, sitting on our chilled feet, we fell into fitful sleep. It was not until eleven o'clock that we were rescued by a Catholic priest driving home to Mora from Taos. Since he was going down the mountain rather than up, he took us back to Mora, where he aroused the owner of a small hotel and found us lodging for the rest of the night.

Like witches all over the world, the New Mexico agents of Satan enjoyed considerable mobility. At night they could be seen rolling along the road in lighted gourds or flying through the sky like balls of fire, for these noctural sallies wearing their own bodies but taking the eyes and legs of coyotes, cats, or other animals. A hazard involved in such substitutions was pointed up in a case reported in 1888 in the *Journal of American Folk-Lore:* "Juan Perea, a male witch, who died here in San Mateo some months ago, met with a strange misfortune in this wise: he had gone off with the eyes of a cat, and during his absence a dog knocked over the table and ate up Juan's own eyes." Juan "had to wear cat's eyes all the rest of his life."

If you were on good terms with a witch, she could carry you with her on her back to New York in a second. You were blindfolded and enjoined to strict silence. If you uttered a word, you found yourself alone in a vast wilderness; if in an excess of fright you cried out "God save me!" you fell to the ground from a great height, though luckily you were not killed by the fall. "There are," the *Journal* reported, "several courageous people in the territory who have made journeys thus upon the backs of witches. At least they are ready to swear so, and they find ten thousand believers to one skeptic." [5]

There were some unique features about New Mexico witches. At Taos Pueblo they injured their victims by blowing into their bodies such things as a feather, thorn, arrow point, porcupine quill, or poisonous snake. These had to be sucked out by the medicine man.

Another singularity of witches throughout the area was that anyone named Juan or Juana could catch them. Some thought that no one else had this talent, except a priest with holy water. The procedure Juan followed was to draw a nine-foot circle on the ground, turn his shirt inside out, put it on again, and cry, "Venga, bruja!"—"Come, witch!"—whereupon the witch perforce fell inside the circle and into his power. There was a be-lief in some circles that Juan seldom made use of his specialized skill, since, if he captured a witch, all the other witches in the country joined hands and whipped him to death.

However, the theory that only Juans, Juanas, and priests with holy water could trap a sorcerer was fairly well disproved by the fact that the pueblos of Nambe, Zia, and Santa Clara owe their extensive decline to the large number of executions for purported practices in witchcraft, a statement attested to by Adolph Bandelier, one of the most famous of the specialists in the study of the Pueblo Indians.[6]

As for Zuni Pueblo, "It is impossible to make even a speculative esti-mate of the probable number of witches killed at Zuñi over a given period of years," according to Watson Smith and John M. Roberts, in a 1954 mono-graph published by Peabody Museum at Harvard University. "But," they added, "the relative frequency of the cases reported during those times when white observers were present suggests that they may have been fairly numerous." [7]

Mere trials and executions were carried out by the Bow Priests, who constituted the tribunal handling cases of sorcery, which was the only of-fense, except for cowardice in battle, punishable by death.

Frank Cushing, one of the ablest of the Zuni specialists, who made that pueblo his home for a number of years, reported that "Should the crops fail, wind storms prevail, or a man threatened by another die (even from natural causes) the reputed wizard would be dragged from his bed at night by the secret council of the A-pi-than-shi-wa-ni, taken to their secret chamber, and tried, 'long and fairly.' " [8]

Here the method of punishment was to hang the suspected witch from a horizontal bar set up in the plaza, by his feet or thumbs or by his arms tied together behind his back. He would be continuously urged to confess, with periodic clubbings by the Bow Priests. If he refused, he might be clubbed to death, though occasionally, and most unaccountably, he was re-leased.

According to Smith and Roberts, seven members of one family were clubbed to death, suspicion having originally fallen upon them because one member was given to unexplained wanderings and at one time had been followed by a sheepherder, who had reported that his tracks at one point were eighteen feet apart, as if he had flown.[9]

Another old man was said to have planted prayer sticks decorated with owl feathers, which are used only by witches and had caused sand-storms, killing the corn.[10] Others were found guilty of having caused mea-sles or smallpox or droughts or of robbing graveyards for turquoise. One who did not subscribe to the ancient beliefs irreverently threw a stone into a deep pit in a sacred cave where a ceremony was being held, thus offending the spirits, who "made a great noise."

But by 1897 white intervention was at least effecting a decline in the number of beatings and executions. Anglo anthropologists, teachers, and Indian Service employees were taking an active part in offering asylum to Indians accused of witchcraft, and soldiers from nearby Fort Wingate appeared on the scene.

Irving Telling, quoting from official records of the time, told of the 1897 arrest of four Zunis for dealing roughly with an elderly person accused of witchcraft. "The school matron, Miss Mary E. Dissette, had cared for the abused victim in defiance of the Indians, and one troop [of soldiers] remained at the pueblo to protect the white staff against possible retaliation. But when more Zuñis were taken into custody in September, the natives became so restless that the troopers began a six-months vigil to protect the Anglos in the town." [11] Soldiers remained there until March 14, 1898.

By 1920 Parsons thought the Zuni suspect was no longer persecuted, but only "talked to" by the Bow Priests, though as late as 1939 confessions were still being forced.[12] However, another ethnologist, Ruth Bunzel, felt that even in 1920 there may have been secret executions. Witches were still being tried there, she found, and she suspected that some were done away with, unless they escaped to other pueblos.[13]

How much is left of these superstitions among the New Mexicans—the Pueblo Indians, the Navajos (persistent believers in witches), the Spanish Americans?

In 1947 L.S.M. Curtin, in a fascinating treatise on the healing herbs of the upper Rio Grande country, described a method of warding off trouble from sorcerers among the Spanish villagers in isolated areas. You wired two large nails together to form a cross, which you placed in the fire. When it was red hot, you placed on it a small string of hearts of chili, then sprinkled over the whole some Mexican rock salt, with a motion describing the cross, and added a little kerosene. The resultant flame was intended to burn up all the witchery that might have threatened you.[14]

In the Jemez area some still believe in the evil eye. But who now believes what Blanche Grant, late Taos historian, reported with tongue in cheek in 1934—that "little people" live in a group of old deserted houses called Buena Vista, five or six miles west of our village? [15] Who still believes that there the witches swing out of chimneys in flame? Who lately has seen that big white brujo come up out of the Rio Grande canyon and make his way along the road? And who has seen, north of Taos, that assembly of sorcerers, shapeshifted into bats and goats, sullying the clean mountain night with their blasphemous Sabat rites?

There isn't so much said about these things in New Mexico any more. But it is plain there are many who still believe in witches, and many more who, if they don't believe, don't *not* believe, either.

13

The Non-Artist's Life

The Painters Discover Taos

Taos has been rediscovered several times by successive groups that
have radically altered its pattern of living and its public image. Its original
discovers, the Pueblo Indians, were followed by the Spanish explorers, the
padres, and the colonists. Next came the Anglo trappers and traders.
Finally, just before the turn of the last century, Taos was discovered again,
this time by a specialized group from the Anglo culture, the painters. This
influence also took root and flourished, resulting in Taos's international
fame as an art center. Today this small village of about twenty-five
hundred people has more than eighty art galleries and probably more than
one hundred resident painters working on various levels of competence.

The four pioneer Taos painters were still here in 1947, all hale and
hearty and actively painting, though they must all have been in their middle or late seventies. They were Ernest L. Blumenschein, Joseph Henry
Sharp, Bert G. Phillips, and Oscar E. Berninghaus. Victor Higgins, who
had come later with Walter Ufer, was here, too.

The first four were all small men who dressed in neat business suits.
With the exception of Blumenschein, all managed to combine gentleness
with strength. But Blumy, as everyone called him, relished his reputation
as an eccentric and even a difficult man. Since he and Berninghaus both
had long-handled German names, newcomers often confused their identi-
ties. Once at a public affair Blumy, addressed as Mr. Berninghaus, pointed
across the room and said, grinning, "That's Bernie over there. He's the nice
one. I'm Blumy, the stinker."

As Taoseñas we soon ran into the problem of trying to explain why so
many painters since 1898 have come to this one small, dusty village. The

question still comes up so often that whenever a stranger comes over to one of us wearing a look of uncommon bewilderment, we can usually guess he is working up to asking this question. It is probably unfair that it does not particularly endear him to us. But we know that, if only to be polite, we shall have to make some kind of answer, and we know, too, that he will leave as puzzled as when he came. For the fact that he asks at all means he is not particularly impressed with Taos. He finds our adobe houses untidy and wonders why we don't rid ourselves of that old corral with its weathered, leaning sides. He is sure it is not the town that has brought the painters to Taos, nor is it the countryside, for there are mountains, mesas, and canyons all over the West. And we know that if he sees nothing here that he thinks should interest an artist, there is nothing we can tell him that will change his mind.

Even the painters themselves have not done too well with words, though several tried not long ago in response to a newspaper reporter's question. A mystical quality of light, they said, and limitless spaces; the warmth, vigor, color, and relaxed pattern of life here among extraordinary people in a magnificent setting; involvement in a creative search for an approach to the area's triracial heritage; and, more particularly, freedom from interruption at work and the comparatively low cost of living.

Andrew Dasburg, dean of Taos painters, said he came from New York more than fifty years ago in answer to a telegram from Mabel Luhan: "Wonderful place. You must come. Am sending tickets. Bring me a cook."

When he got here at sunset on a snowy day, Taos Valley seemed like the first days of creation. But though it seemed lonely and far from the world, he felt an immediate sense of belonging.

We do have quite a lengthy account from Blumy of why and how he came, with Phillips. They both told it many times, so that it grew into a local legend of "the broken wheel," which is usually represented in the parade at the July fiesta. Blumy finally set down his account for Laura Bickerstaff as an introduction to her book, *Pioneer Artists of Taos*.

He said he first heard about Taos when he was studying in Paris, from Sharp, who had once sketched here for a couple of weeks. A short time afterward Blumy, following a preliminary trip into the Southwest on an illustrating assignment for *McClure's Magazine*, started out from Denver with Phillips for a leisurely sketching trip intended to end in Mexico. Traveling south with their gear in a horse-drawn wagon, they had reached a point about twenty miles north of Taos when one wheel of the wagon slipped into a deep rut and collapsed. Blumy, having lost in the flip of a three-dollar gold piece, mounted one of the horses and, holding the broken wheel before him, set out for Taos to get it repaired. Holding a wagon wheel on horse-

back proved a grinding ordeal, but soon he had almost forgotten his problem in the excitement of the country through which he was riding. Sharp
had tried to tell him but had not been able really to bring it to life. This
landscape, these people, were quite different from those of Colorado, from
which he had just come—were different from any others he had ever seen.
Here was painting material as fresh, as exotic, as anything Gauguin had
found in Tahiti.

By the time he returned to rescue Phillips, he had decided to live and
to paint in Taos. Phillips was equally enchanted. Later they were joined by
Sharp, and except for short intervals, all three spent the rest of their lives
here.

Four of the survivors among the six earliest painters we knew only
casually—Sharp with his little goatee; gentle Mr. Phillips; Higgins, the
Beau Brummel of the Taos artists; and Berninghaus, with the benevolent
twinkle in his eye. And we knew Mrs. Berninghaus, who remained here
until her death, a notable landmark, holding the chronically strained fabric
of the Taos Art Association together by sheer determination and the fact
that she had never been intimidated by man or beast. Before her marriage
she had been one of the famous Harvey Girls who had guided tourists
around New Mexico, and after that was manager of Gerson Gusdorf's magnificent Don Fernando Hotel here, which burned in the twenties and
which Taoseños of that era remember with sharp nostalgia.

But Blumy we knew a great deal better than the other veteran painters because of our early and continuous friendship with his daughter
Helen. And through Helen we came to know Mrs. Blumy on occasional visits to their huge old adobe house. I can see her now, in her chair before the
piñon fire and in later years resting in her big bed in the west wing of the
house, a delicate, patrician lady, beautifully groomed to her last day. They
were a family of painters and the Blumenscheins had met and married as
students in Paris.

Blumy and Sharp were both Ohioans, Phillips from New York State.
All three had had extensive training at top academies both in this country
and abroad and were professional painters of recognized stature by the
time they settled in Taos. Blumy had had to decide between two careers;
he was a violinist of sufficiently high caliber to be chosen as first violin by
Anton Dvorak when, as director of the New York National Conservatory,
Dvorak organized a metropolitan symphony orchestra.

Berninghaus, from St. Louis, was largely self-taught, except for night
classes at Washington University, but had already achieved national prominence when he first saw Taos. He came by narrow-gauge railroad and
stage. The railroad, known affectionately as "the Chili Line" from the huge

96

loads of New Mexican chili it transported, wandered down from Colorado to Santa Fe. Berninghaus was sketching scenery from the flat top of a freight car when a friendly brakeman pointed out Taos Mountain and told him about the little Mexican village and Indian pueblo that sat at its base. So vivid was his description that Berninghaus left the train and set off over a primitive trail on a twenty-five-mile wagon trip that brought him to Taos. It marked the first of many visits until in 1925 he settled here for good.

Sharp was responsible for the arrival here of the fifth of the early painters, E. Irving Couse of Michigan. Couse had studied in New York and Paris, where he, too, heard Sharp's description of the Taos scene as fresh material for painters. And finally came W. Herbert Dunton, known as "Buck." Dunton, a Maine farm boy, studied in Boston and New York. Running into Blumy, who was teaching at the Art Students League in New York, he, too, heard about Taos, where he settled finally in 1912, after several years of painting and working as a cowhand on ranches from Oregon to Mexico.

The two artists who came next, Ufer and Higgins, are included in the first six who established Taos as an internationally known art center. Ufer had left Louisville, Kentucky, to study in Munich and somehow had landed in Chicago. Higgins was there, too, over from Shelbyville, Indiana, to study at the Chicago Art Institute. By this time the original Taos painters were overcoming the economic disadvantage of their isolated base by organizing the Taos Society of Artists and as such taking their work on national tours. Contact with their annual exhibitions in Chicago galleries brought Ufer and Higgins to Taos.

Dunton, an old ranch hand, became the "cowboy artist," but the others found themselves drawn to the Spanish people and the quiet and introspective Pueblo Indians. Some probed beneath the surface of life here; some romanticized it. One—Sharp—saw it with an anthropologist's eye, with the result that many of his Indian paintings were acquired by the Smithsonian Institution.

They painted with distinction, with vigor and affection. Spurred by their traveling shows and the active interest of the Santa Fe Railroad, which for years used Taos paintings in its national advertising, their sales were tremendous, their reputations made, and Taos established as a major art center. Though they never caught the public fancy in quite the booming fashion of Remington and Charles M. Russell, their work is still avidly sought and little can be found for sale, though eastern and regional dealers continue to search.

It had obviously been the visual aspects of the country and people that had brought and kept them here. It was Mabel Luhan who changed the direction of Taos painting, a change which began with her telegram to Dasburg. He had been painting in Paris for several years and brought to Taos his interest in cubism and the new rhythms of Cézanne and Picasso. He came first in 1916, returned repeatedly to Taos or Sante Fe, and finally settled here in 1930. And, again Mabel's doing, he was followed by others whose interest was focused on aesthetic rather than illustrative reality. At one time or another for short periods Robert Henri, John Marin, Maurice Sterne, Marsden Hartley, and Georgia O'Keeffe were painting in Taos.

They set the young painters here off on a search for new meanings through a more subjective approach, and they in turn attracted others.

Where is Taos going as an art center—forward, backward? Just standing still? If you put the question out among some of the new and old hands, the answers are typical of the place:

Taos isn't what it used to be, even a few years ago.

Taos (Epaminondas-like) never was what it used to be.

Taos painting grows more and more vital, while that in New York and San Francisco grows steadily more sterile.

Taos is both better and worse than it used to be. It's worse because in the past few years it's had a great influx of potboiler stuff and of commercial watered-down modern painting, flip mannerisms taking off from established contemporary work. But Taos is moving forward because while this has been happening, there has been an addition of a small group of fine, serious modern painters.

In any case, Taos isn't innovating—no op, pop, camp, funk, minimal painting. Painters say all the avante garde movements of the twentieth century have started in the big centers, such as Paris and New York. It is a matter of sheer numbers; it takes a lot of painters to start a new movement. And only the poor painters just jump on the bandwagon. Anyway, they point out, in every new movement only a handful of the great ones survive.

Taos, then, is not in the mainstream of American painting?

No.

Is that good or bad?

It is good. There are other streams.

But what schools of painting are foremost here?

None. Taos is full of lone wolves, and this includes even the bad painters. Except for the representational and so-called Westerns, you can't pigeonhole anyone and the only factor the artists see that they have in common is the influence on them all of the light and the space, which each one puts to his own use.

"Of course," one of them hastens to add, "we all derive from some outside source. There aren't many original visions, like Paul Klee's, for instance."

While some of them miss the excitement of what is going on in the big centers, the things they really miss are seeing more of the big shows and the magical communication that comes from contact with top-flight critics, who seldom find their way out into the mountains. But they feel they can do their best painting here, and they've made the choice. It doesn't seem, though, to be a real hardship. A lot of them show in important galleries on both east and west coasts, get sizable commissions and prizes, and teach in major universities. And their volume of sales in Taos alone is big enough to impress even the *Wall Street Journal.*

Dasburg himself is pleased with the way painting is going in Taos. "When was it ever more vital?" he asks.

Virtually all of the Taos artists are Anglos, though art in various forms is indigenous with the southwestern Indians and, to a lesser extent, with the Spanish people. But the Taos Indian is a farmer and in that respect a great disappointment to tourists because, unlike the Indians of most other parts of the state, he makes no jewelry, weaves no blankets or rugs, fires no pottery, and paints few pictures. His deep concern with beauty comes out only in his architecture and his ritual chants and dances. He has so far taken little part in a magnificent development focused in Santa Fe at the Institute of American Indian Arts, where three hundred students from eighty tribes in twenty-eight states have startled even their hopeful federal sponsors with a remarkable response to a chance to give free personal interpretations of their individual tribal cultures and contemporary lives.

But in Taos itself almost the only Indian painting to be seen is shown in the "Navajo Gallery," directed by a Navajo painter, R. C. Gorman.

Moreover, the Spanish Americans today seem almost completely uninterested in carrying on the creative handicraft of their fathers. And there is again a good reason, the fact that their arts and crafts, beautiful in their primitiveness, grew out of utilitarian need which is now a thing of the past. There are no great santeros now, painting retablos and carving wooden figures of the saints and the Cristo, for you can buy bright plaster figures in the stores. Why take the time and the trouble to make a fine blanket chest for yourself, when you can buy one ready-made at the furniture store? Except for two or three wood-carvers, there are few Spanish names on the art roster in Taos, and the current important resurgence of crafts has been until lately almost entirely an Anglo development, led by Rachel Brown's weavings of museum level.

Recently, however, under government sponsorship, attempts have been made to revive the Spanish-Colonial crafts and to encourage the Taos Indians to develop handicraft skills. The real potential in these two groups seems to lie in the children. Constantine Aiello is so pleased with the work of his small students at the pueblo day school that he has published a collection of their paintings in a book, *Oo-oónah Art*. The Indian word means "child," and proceeds from the sale of the book go into a fund to provide an art center at the pueblo, where the children may paint and exhibit their work.

Slings and Bear Traps

There are special aspects of life in an art center, and a few of them we could do without. One is that problem the whole country tries to cope with, especially in places where much store is set by aesthetics and historical background. Shall we or shall we not allow neon signs? Shall we let a new four-lane highway run through that pastoral section between us and the Sacred Mountain? Shall we leave undisturbed our narrow, crooked streets, the soft lines and flat roofs of our houses?

So we argue about the nature of progress; about the economic hazards or advantages in a poverty area of trying to preserve Taos as a "museum village"; about the possibly stultifying effect on the creative instincts of new architects of too much emphasis on the pure forms of our indigenous architecture. Even among painters there is likely to be disagreement as to what is beautiful, what in good taste. And we run into stout resistance to restrictions as to the uses a man can make of his own land. Eyesores develop—such as junkyards—which nobody seems to know how to avoid or eradicate.

A case pointing to the complications that can result from an honest disagreement came up when the parish of the great mission church of Saint Francis of Assisi at Ranchos de Taos set out to restore the magnificent structure.

Its date is controversial, but it seems to have been built in 1730, though not registered with diocesan headquarters in Mexico until 1772, when it was stabilized after a period of neglect.

The church is 120 feet long, its adobe walls 13 feet thick at the base, growing progressively thinner as they reach its great height. In its original construction burros hauled the huge adobe bricks up earth ramps. The form of the building is anchored to the ground by massive buttresses, and there are two towers, one slightly taller than the other, in true Taos lack of precision. During all of its nearly two and a half centuries it had kept its adobe plaster, both inside and out, so preserving its soft texture and sculptured lines. In its restoration both were lost when, by order of the parish priest, the archbishop concurring, it was given a hard cement coat.

In the accompanying protest from a big sector of Taos, Genevieve was

100

directly involved, since she had organized and at that time was chairman of a group called "The Friends of Taos Valley," dedicated to the preservation of the area's beauty.

But the parish, though it had many dissidents, stood firm. Its council had, in fact, begun the project in secrecy, in order (it frankly admitted) to get it as far along as possible before the plan for hard plaster became generally known.

"The artists always complain when we make any changes," the padre said.

And try as they did, at their diplomatic best, "The Friends," backed by other influential citizens of the area, were unsuccessful in their efforts to get a reconsideration. The council was tired of the perpetual attention the soft plaster required. The priest had recently come from Ecuador, with its beautiful stone jewel-box churches. To him an adobe structure was an indication of poverty, improvidence, and probably even a lack of respect to the faith. Hard plaster to him was a status symbol, as it is to many of his parishioners.

There was more involved than this. One could sense in this predominantly Spanish-American parish a definite, instinctive pullback from what seemed like Anglo interference in its affairs. To a firm offer of funds raised by one group of "The Friends" to defray the annual expense of refinishing the church with soft plaster, the parish returned a courteous refusal.

"My people feel," a spokesman said, "that if we let you give us money to maintain the plaster, you will try to tell us when and how we must do it." He went on to point out the basic difference in viewpoints. "To you this is a beautiful building and an historic monument, but to us it's our parish church. You probably think we should keep on using candles, but if we do, our old people cannot see to read."

The church was hard-plastered, but there have since been two hopeful developments. At a dedication mass for the renovated structure a diocesan official hinted that as the old church had seen many changes, so it doubtless would see many more, including perhaps at some time a return to soft plaster. And later Archbishop James Peter Davis of Santa Fe appointed Reverend Benedict Cuesta as chairman of a new organization to protect and preserve Iberian colonial art belonging to the Catholic Church in New Mexico. The choice of Father Cuesta as chairman is hailed here as especially fortunate, since he recently restored, with volunteer labor of his parishioners, the little Catholic church at Arroyo Seco.

The prestige and known views of the new organization's members give sound reason for belief that not only will the great church at Ranchos de Taos some day be restored to its former beauty, but that the furor accompanying its temporary disfigurement will result in future security for all of New Mexico's ecclesiastical art and architectural treasures.

With such problems as this, and they are many and diverse in nature, we pay for the pleasure of living in a village devoting so much of its thought to aesthetics. But we think it's worth it, especially on a night when a husky young painter comes in as a dinner guest, grinning broadly, clutching a tall brown paper sack, and announcing, "Champagne! Celebration! The gallery sold four paintings for me today."

An Act of Enchantment

You don't have to be an artist to live an imaginative life in Taos. And the reason for this isn't just the fact that over the years you pick up an increasing familiarity with the styles of great painters, from Fra Angelico to Modigliani, and find yourself spending more and more vacation time prowling through libraries, galleries, and museums, primitive ruins and Spanish-Colonial and Gothic cathedrals. Nor is it entirely related to the aesthetic interests and talents of many of the people who come here to live or to visit. Basically it's the fact that day-by-day happenings here seem to have special qualities. An ordinary picnic can be an extraordinary event, if you drive down the steep winding road into the Rio Grande canyon, cross John Dunn's bridge, climb up the intimidating switchbacks of the canyon's west side to reach the high mesa, build your fire among the volcanic rocks, and picnic among the stars, while the round moon picks up the thin thread of the river six hundred feet below and the thinner thread of Hondo Creek coming down through its own slitted canyon to join it.

A wedding reception can be something special, and there are two of these I shall never forget.

One was the wedding of Johnny Romero's daughter, Mary, to the son of the governor of San Juan Pueblo. After the service in the pueblo church, for whose restoration Johnny had made some of the adobes, there was a feast at his house. On a long table, covered with oilcloth, was everything Johnny and Lisa like best: lamb stew and coarse Indian bread, chili, canned peaches, a huge pink cake, bowls of red jello, and bottles of orange and red drink. The men, standing around the long table, were served first, and then it was our turn. Finally, the food cleared away, came the real purpose of the gathering. For an hour, on straight-backed chairs ranged around the walls, we sat in full silence as a half-dozen of the pueblo's blanketed elder statesmen, sitting in dignity with their eyes closed, delivered one by one in the murmurous Tiwa dialect their sage advice to the bride and groom.

Our other most memorable wedding party was given by one of Taos's distinguished hostesses, Mary Hamlin Goodwin, for one of her beautiful daughters, Lisa. It was a throwback to true New Mexican colonial elegance. The reception was held in the patio of her great adobe house, for which she herself had served as both architect and contractor. Two hundred or so guests were dressed in fashionable New York clothes or swirling Navajo skirts with velvet blouses, in Indian blankets or little black Spanish shawls. Under the wide portals were champagne and turkeys and hams, huge shrimp and smoked oysters, guacamole salad and *cabrito* (young kid) that all day had been simmering in a tall clay *olla* or pot, spiced with red chili dried against some adobe wall at Chimayo. Indian drums throbbed in the background and guitars filled the summer night with seventeenth-century Mexican serenades. Around the little dance floor the low piñon trees were filled with white paper birds, and outside the wall sheep were grazing.

Sometimes on summer evenings you drive up to the Hotel St. Bernard at Taos Ski Valley, nine thousand feet high. Here Chilton Anderson has based his summer Taos School of Music, which has an advisory link with New York's Mannes School of Music. You can sit around a blazing fire to hear a student concert of chamber music. The next night the faculty will come down to Taos to play Bach and Mozart and Bartok.

We are especially glad about this development, for it is a professional one and Taos historically has been short of music, having had to get by with occasional concerts arranged by a community organization, by the Wurlitzer Foundation, or (some years back) the few times when Mabel Degen brought in a Juilliard string quartet and presented it for her friends.

Some of these special Taos events come as complete surprises. You go over to Ben Hazard's, a half-mile or so down the road, to find that Ben and three of his friends have spent the past four days whipping up thirty or more paintings, takeoffs on the work of prominent Taos artists. One of the guest-painters, in flowing robes and with a red mop for hair, is impersonating a well-known gallery director. The lampoons are hilariously identifiable, and auctioned off by Louis Ribak bring in two or three hundred dollars, which finally goes to the animal shelter.

One day during a July fiesta we saw an intriguing sight in a shop window. It was an enormous mural of the plaza, complete with two hundred Taos characters. Four painters had worked on it for six weeks— Becky James, Dorothy Brett, Barbara Latham, and Tom Benrimo. They had been aided by Frank Waters, Taos writer, and his wife, Janey; Dorothy Benrimo, designer and silversmith; and Bob Gribbroeck, Hollywood animation cartoonist.

The mural has finally gone to the Millicent A. Rogers museum. Mrs. Rogers, Standard Oil heiress and for years listed as one of the country's ten best-dressed women, maintained one of her three houses in Taos and spent her last years here. After her death more than a decade ago the museum was set up by one of her sons, Paul Peralta-Ramos of New York, to exhibit her extraordinary collection of southwestern Indian and Spanish-American art objects.

There many people spend an hour or so identifying the characters in the Taos mural. And if they take the trouble, they can find the Book Shop Girls standing in front of La Fonda Hotel. We were vastly pleased at finding ourselves there. Perhaps that made us real Taoseñas.

But I guess the thing that will best show the special flavor of Taos happenings is my own little Christmas tree, which I have only because I happened to be standing in the right place to be struck by this benevolent streak of lightning. It came about at all only through an instinctive and typical Taos response to what Lawrence Clark Powell would call an act of enchantment.

I am the eighth Taoseño who over the years has been the recipient of one of these jewellike miniature trees inspired and engineered by Dorothy Benrimo. Dorothy, whose late husband was the artist Tom Benrimo, is a Taos designer and silversmith of such distinction that her work has toured the country in month-long showings at galleries and museums under the sponsorship of the Smithsonian Institution. She has served on the faculty of Pratt Institute and Carnegie Tech, and has done research in design for Tiffany's. She makes beautiful liquid silver jewelry on special commissions, and recently published a distinguished camera study of northern New Mexico's primitive Spanish cemetery crosses.

At a friend's house I was engrossed in admiration of the latest miniature tree she had done when Dorothy came by.

"It's enchanting," I said.

She gave me a quick look. "Well," she said, "I think it's your turn next year."

"How do you decide it?" I asked.

"I don't," she said. "It just happens. It's a happening."

I was enchanted all over again and equally appalled. For where did all these exquisite miniatures and marvelous little decorations come from? How many would there have to be?

She was quite casual about it. "Oh, there have to be six or seven hundred. You pick them up yourself all year and I will, too, and then before Christmas I'll send out postcards to your friends, people you know well, to anyone we think would like to bring in some little thing. And then some day in December a few of us will get together and have dinner and trim the tree."

"Six or seven hundred things," I said, faintly.

"Oh, sure," she said, "don't worry about it."

But I did worry about it. All year I hunted for miniatures, a half-inch to three-quarter inch in size, and they seemed to elude me. I began to alert close friends and my sister Anne, who came up with wonderful little treasures, tiny mushrooms and ladybugs, ducks, chickens, and geese.

In December Dorothy came in with sixty miniature gift packages she had made, rich in foil, ribbons, seed pearls, and tiny sequins. With these to go by, and aided by a whole boxful of glittering miniature decorations from helpful Chicago friends, Genevieve and I managed to make forty more.

Dorothy by this time had sent out the cards to people who might consent to having their arms twisted, and in a day or so Genevieve had a telephone call from a friend in the Midwest.

"Look," she began in guarded tones, "I've just had this card about the tree. Is Claire ill?"

"Mercy, no," said Genevieve. "Dorothy's done seven of these before. It's just one of those wonderful things that happen in Taos."

And soon there arrived a cunning little globe, a half-inch high, that swung on its axis, with all the continents showing.

The eleven of us who gathered to trim the tree included a friend of Lib White's from Norway who, though a complete stranger to me, had spent most of the past week mounting tiny sequins onto the tips of small weed sprigs and with paints transforming dime-store angels into little celestial musicians.

Dorothy had brought the fifteen-inch artificial tree, which she had mounted on a round tray revolving above a music box. With tinsel and glue the trimming began. There seemed no end to the wonderful miniatures coming out of their boxes: tiny original Taos paintings, sculptures, ink drawings, weavings, and santos; animals, birds, flowers, and insects; miniature train and painted Sicilian cart; bells and musical instruments; typewriters, midget dictionary, and replica of the front page of the *New York Times;* stereo records and books (one of them entitled *Inside Taos* by Claire Morrill); and dozens of other things. Kenny Anderson, who was seven, had parted with one of his real treasures, a tiny hot dog, and my great-niece, Barbara, had written a distinguished little poem on a tree-shaped paper.

We eight Taoseños who have these exquisite trees don't wait until Christmas to bring them out, admire them, and show them off. And if by any mischance we should ever have to leave Taos, we will have to console us these small glowing symbols of what it really is like.

14

Three Women of Taos

Towering over the human landscape in Taos for around four decades
—and as Brett still does—was that amazing triumvirate of internationally
famous women brought into confrontation here by D. H. Lawrence. They
were Lawrence's wife, Frieda, Mabel Dodge Luhan, and Dorothy Brett.

Mabel had come in 1916 and had soon abandoned her painter husband, Maurice Sterne (her third in sixteen years) in favor of a Taos Indian,
Antonio Luján, whom she later married. Fascinated by this mysterious and
complicated land, she had summoned as its interpreter the controversial
English novelist, Lawrence. He had come with Frieda in the early twenties
for the first of three periods of residence, the last ending in 1925. With
them on the second of their visits had come Brett, an English painter,
daughter of Reginald Lord Esher, and a devoted Lawrence disciple. Then
by 1925 they had gone—the Lawrences—to resume their wandering life
abroad, leaving Mabel and Brett here; and then came Lawrence's death in
France in 1930 and Frieda's return to Taos.

The story of this turbulent involvement with Lawrence as storm center
is too well known to repeat here, told in his letters, in books by all three of
the women, and in many other works by Lawrence biographers and critics.

That the three continued to live here in close proximity to each other
after the publication of their books has proved over the years to be the subject of endless curiosity on the part of visitors to the book shop. For in
print they had openly revealed the details of their varied attachments to
Lawrence and the naked savagery of their mutual antagonisms.

Side by side on the shelf were the books: Mabel's *Lorenzo in Taos;*
Frieda's *Not I, But the Wind;* and Brett's *Lawrence and Brett: A Friendship.* And here were the three women, immured in the small Anglo social
world of an isolated mountain village.

Did they continue to see each other? Did they, in fact, even speak? Or had Lawrence's death and the passage of time dulled the sharp memories of their quarrels? Interest in these questions never flags, though it all happened more than forty-five years ago and most of the books have been long out of print. I am realizing now that, though questioned continually on these points, neither Genevieve nor I had seemed to summon sufficient interest to attempt to verify the impressions we had inevitably and unconsciously drawn. Yet the impressions themselves are perhaps worth telling.

Until Frieda's death in 1956 and Mabel's six years later they saw each other often, both casually and by design. The memories of their shared experiences, with the Lawrence phase as a major factor, had, I am sure, woven a bond among the three stronger than any of them consciously felt. Yet their opinions of each other had never basically changed. Each was, to the others, a "troublemaker."

To Frieda, married a few years before her death to Angelino Ravagli, Brett was still "too much with us"—an inveterate early riser who painted in the first few hours and was free to visit the rest of the day. And Brett made no secret of her resentment of Frieda, a point made amply clear after Alfred Alvarez, then married to Frieda's granddaughter, Ursula Barr, visited Taos in 1961 to tape material from those who had known her best for a television program planned by the British Broadcasting Corporation.

"I suppose," Brett said to Spud Johnson, "you all said she was a wonderful woman. Well, I didn't. I said she was a bitch, and she was."

Such unflattering opinion was a three-way affair among them, yet we noticed that each was quick to defend the others against any adverse comment from outside their ranks. There was, I think, among them a sort of group loyalty which, while it permitted internecine derogation, rallied each of them to the defense of the others against attack from anyone else. And I am interested now in the fact of never having seen any evidence of rivalry among the three for position in the Taos or outside social or cultural world. Each simply was what she was.

Profiles here of the three as I knew them will not show them as of that earlier day. Those portraits they sat for many times, and each has added her own version. They came off as strong, jealous, possessive women, certainly not intellectuals; Brett and Mabel frustrated; Mabel unabashedly uninhibited, living her life in conformity with only the bohemian mores of which she was a leading exponent; Frieda living hers only according to her own belief in what, at the time, was relevant.

Such early portraits of Mabel, Frieda, and Brett may be seen in many places and concern me here only as background. This triptych will show three women of Taos, mellowed by the passage of time and their varying degrees of fulfillment—no longer really wayward, not gentled either, but undeniably vital.

Mabel

Had there been in Mabel Dodge Luhan any of the teacher, any of the prophet, certainly any of the charlatan, she could have gathered about her in Taos a veritable cult. For as public interest has never waned in her involvement with Lawrence, still less has it flagged in her image as that of a young, wealthy, sophisticated woman who abruptly abandoned a monumentally successful career in Florence and New York as socialite and arts patron, retreated to this primitive village high in the Sangre de Cristo Mountains, married a blanket Indian, and apparently found what she was searching for in sufficient degree to hold her here for the rest of her life.

Mabel had been a few days in Santa Fe, much of which she disliked, and had heard very little about Taos, most of it negative, when she arrived here one snowy evening in 1916 with Maurice Sterne, whom she had married that year. But in the first hour or two of winter darkness, after a negligible dinner in a squalid hotel, she surrendered impulsively to what Lawrence was later to call "the curious otherness of Taos," and decided to stay. Before the evening was over, she had made inquiries, had found her way with Sterne through the dark, muddy streets to the home of "Doc" Martin, and (over her husband's aggrieved objections) had rented a house.

Predictably her marriage with Sterne was soon ended. She turned instead to Tony Luján, a man of great dignity and presence who was nevertheless an untutored Indian, his hair worn in two long rolls like braids and wearing the traditional blanket. Seven years later their liaison was legalized. It was a marriage that lasted until her death nearly forty years later.

What had she found in Taos that others might find? In over twenty-five years in the book shop we have heard this question continually and directly implied in the intense interest shown in Mrs. Luhan on the part of a large segment of the public that visits Taos. From their approach it was obvious during her lifetime that these were people hoping somehow to establish contact with this woman who seemed to have found what they themselves were looking for—a means of absorbing something of what they vaguely sensed as the healing influence of the Taos (probably the Indian) way. They came, men and women, not only the curious but the dissatisfied, the disillusioned, the groping, in the hope of taking the first step.

Such contacts Mabel firmly rejected. Fan letters, if the writer had

108

made the approach by asking how to obtain her books, she promptly turned over to us, with a memo: "Dear Book Shop: Please cope."

They were fan letters in the classic sense, ranging from the dignified to the maudlin. And that the writers were interested in the author and not in the books became evident when we learned early to expect no replies to the notes we sent out quoting prices of the titles for which they had asked.

Mabel had no wish to be identified in the shop when strangers were present. No one, please, was to be directed to her home.

That her gate bore the sign "No Tourists Admitted" was, I think, more than a natural and indeed necessary protection against the hordes who would have disrupted her life. She had, I am sure, little interest in people at large. And she was not by temperament a cultist, in spite of a touch of the flowing-robe complex shown at one time by copying from Isadora Duncan and later in clothes designed for her here by Adrian of Hollywood.

What, as a matter of fact, had she found in Taos? Was it anything closer to a religious philosophy than a belief in "the good spirit of Taos," to which she sometimes referred, which released the creative powers? She never explored the question in any of her published work. Perhaps she has done so in the three-quarters of a ton of unpublished manuscripts (four of them) and correspondence which in 1951 she turned over to Yale University. But at her stipulation these books are not to be published until after the deaths of the principals involved.

To her would-be devotees Mabel was a woman who had summarily dismissed the half-gods and turned her face to the gods. Had she really seen them? She has not said, unless a failure can be construed in her summons to Lawrence to come and give the land a voice.

In writing later that he had never fulfilled this commission, it seems to me now that this usually perceptive woman had somehow missed the great precept which Lawrence clearly saw stated in the Indian life-way: "Thou shalt acknowledge the wonder." This she had either missed or rejected. Or perhaps she had accepted his conclusion that no white man can identify himself with the Indian consciousness.

In any case, if the gods had not arrived for Mabel, who can dismiss all the half-gods? And actually, what was required? Though the Pueblo Indian's life is simple, he has obviously not imposed on himself the real austerity, such as the order set forth in the *Upanishads* to "give up all desire, then give up that by which you gave it up."

So Mabel's considerable wealth she brought with her. The adobe house on the edge of the village to which she originally came was developed into a sprawling, impressive, and beautiful hacienda. Here with Tony, her son John Evans part of the time, and a retinue of servants she lived in a kind of simple but feudal comfort. She did not try to merge herself with the Taos Pueblo Indian world. Rather, it was Tony who came to live with her in her world of electric lights and plumbing.

There is an interesting sidelight on this in an incident that happened not long after World War II. The young men of the pueblo had come back from military service after having lived in barracks with modern conveniences. It was hard to go back to the old primitive ways. Why should they not have inside plumbing and electric current for lights, refrigeration, and washing machines?

But the old men objected. The controversy grew hot and finally broke into print. Other people got into the act, including Mabel. In a letter to a Taos newspaper she expressed her opinion that the old ways were best.

This brought a scathing rebuttal from one of the young Indians. If the old ways are best, he wrote, perhaps Mrs. Luhan would like to try them. He would himself be glad to give her the opportunity. He would trade houses with her. He would live in her home with its electric lights, refrigerator, and warm inside bathroom. She might live at the pueblo, dipping water in pails from Rio Pueblo and carrying it up the steep ladder; she might in the cold winter night visit the outhouse near the corral.

This terminated her share in the controversy, though it raged on for some time. The old men finally won out. Their argument: it is not just a matter of having electricity; it is the fact that in its train come the refrigerators, the electric washing machines, the radios. These, they said, mean debts, which the Indian cannot deal with.

Mabel's life, in certain basic practical aspects, was not much different than it had been before she had come to Taos. Moreover, although she had left behind her the brilliant salons over which she had presided in New York and Europe, she gathered about her in Taos at various times such great ones as Stokowski, Brill, Lawrence, Mary Austin, and Thornton Wilder. And in addition, as all the rest of us had done, she had brought herself.

But still she had found something here which had held her restless feet for forty-six years. Perhaps it was simply the fact that at last she had found work to do. For it is well known in Taos that few are happy here unless they are busy. And Mabel during these years was far from idle—witness the eleven books she wrote and her huge volume of correspondence. Perhaps her analyst had been right in recommending writing her memoirs as a useful therapy.

Perhaps her anchor in Taos was Tony, to whom she remained bound for over four decades. For although the marriage was far from serene, she was uneasy out of his sight for even an hour or two.

110

There is, though, a curious footnote in the fact that on her death in the summer of 1962, Mabel, by her own wish, was buried in Kit Carson cemetery next to Ralph Meyers, a longtime friend, while Tony, who died early in 1963, lies in the little disheveled graveyard within the walls of the ruined pueblo church.

A book shop will have considerable contact with a local author of seven books, four of them concerned with the local scene. For years we saw Mabel often. When the shop first opened, her *Winter in Taos* was still available, and her final published work, *Taos and Its Artists*, was expected out soon. An autograph party for the latter was impossible, she said, for with unwanted trepidation for a woman of her temperament, she was firmly determined to be out of town when the book on her neighbors as artists would appear. But successive delays defeated her purpose; the book finally came out unannounced and found her in Taos.

Although she still would not agree to an autograph event, she was in every other respect over the years unfailingly cooperative and considerate. She volunteered to borrow from Victor Higgins, as a focal point for a shop window display, his large oil painting of a Pueblo woman, which had been reproduced on the jacket of *Taos and Its Artists;* and a telephone call when new shipments of her books arrived would bring her into the shop promptly to sign copies.

In addition she was that comparative rarity among writers, a buyer of other people's books. She bought them in quantity, read them with lightning speed, and turned them over to the community library of the Harwood Foundation. Later, as her health declined, she became the only Taos Book Shop customer to receive curb service, as she sat in her closely curtained car with Tony and the driver in front.

But in many things she could still be capricious and her span of interest was notably short. When we moved the book shop into Ralph Meyers's old trading post, which Mabel had known well, she was fascinated by the activity and the new plans. She resolved to take over a small unused apartment opening onto the back patio for the sale of some of her furniture, which she would not need in the new house she had built in order to escape winter heating problems in the big house nearby.

Since it was February and little but the actual necessities of life was sold in Taos in winter, we urged her to wait until summer. But she opened the shop with an attendant in charge, and when no customers appeared, impatiently closed it again before the winter was over. Such qualities could give one pause. Although she once suggested that Genevieve and I should rent one of the small, attractive adobe houses she had built at a short distance from her own, we declined after hearing a well-authenticated rumor that she had peremptorily ordered the last tenant out, practically over-night, because of an opinion he had expressed on some ordinary and quite uncontroversial matter.

She operated always on her own terms. We were sometimes invited to her home, but she might, with true arrogance, decline an invitation to ours on one occasion, yet arrive on another when she had not been invited.

"I heard you were having a party," she once explained, "so I thought I'd come."

Her final illness covered a period of several years, during which she became more and more incapacitated. I suppose one of her last appear-ances at an affair of any size was made at our house in Talpa, when we had invited a fair number of old Taos hands to hear Gustave Baumann, Santa Fe artist, reminisce about a horse-and-buggy trip he had made some time in the twenties from Taos to Abiquiu with the Luhans and Mary Austin.

When we telephoned Mabel, she promptly disclaimed any knowledge of having made such a trip, and was, of course, vague as to whether she could come. But she was intrigued. In the ensuing days she telephoned several times to make sure of the date and hour, and on the afternoon in question appeared with Tony a half-hour early. Though she made no com-ment, she listened to the reminiscences with obvious relish.

Baumann had been a house guest of the Luhans, he said, with the Lawrences and Mary Austin. Mabel, finding herself one morning at cross purposes with Lawrence and Frieda, had abruptly decided to walk out on the situation and go to Abiquiu, inviting her other guests to go along.

Abiquiu is sixty miles from Taos; in those prepavement days, the trip with horses was a matter of several days; but though the route was com-pletely devoid of public accommodations for meals or lodging, the four set out with full faith in their ability to live off the land. This plan they success-fully carried out by a cunning strategy which involved stopping at houses along the way to buy the fine old Rio Grande blankets for which the area is noted, and timing their stops to coincide with mealtimes or the approach of nightfall, when the kindly hospitality of the small Spanish ranchers would naturally serve to provide them with food and shelter. The sole disadvan-tage, Baumann recalled, was a deplorably frequent appearance of mutton stew.

Though Mabel's friendships in Taos included such frontier stalwarts as Ralph Meyers and that colorful old gambler and stage driver, John Dunn, they did not extend appreciably into the area of rank and file Taoseños, who accordingly knew considerable about her faults but little about her virtues.

Of her faults she wrote freely, of her jealousy, willfulness, promiscuity,

112

compulsion to meddle. Her reticence was somehow reserved for her virtues. And chief among these was a generosity, not only in community affairs, but also in money and personal concern for anyone in sickness or trouble.

Her gifts to Taos—a hospital with a large tract of land, a plaza bandstand, thousands of dollars in library books—these were known, though for the most part taken for granted, for this was a wealthy woman, who it was felt could well afford it. But few knew, and these never from her, of the help she had given to those in need, from whom she would never get, as she never wanted, a recompense.

But the scope of Taos's debt to Mabel Dodge Luhan is much greater than this. Her impact on its cultural life was tremendous and is still felt. Spud, in an article for a New York art magazine, has pointed out the major role she played in helping establish this village's international fame.

Although not a finished writer, a status to which she came closest in her quietly charming *Winter in Taos,* she was nevertheless highly articulate, in four of her books celebrating the beauty of the Taos landscape, the simplicity, warmth, and color of its life, the esoteric quality of its aura.

But she also employed for its interpretation a personal prestige which drew an amazing response. The extent of this talent was recalled again by Thornton Wilder, spending Christmas here in 1962. Relaxed and reminiscent at a small Christmas Eve supper and a "long Christmas dinner," he at one point described one of Mabel's New York gatherings.

She had begun a new series, at the first of which she had presented a psychiatrist and a physician as foils for each other. For the second, focal point was the controversial U.S. Indian commissioner, John Collier. Wilder himself was the third; he was to discuss one page of *Finnegans Wake.* The rooms were crowded with guests, when crashers began to appear—to appear in such numbers that men were stationed at the street door of the building to turn them away.[1]

It was on this talent that Mabel drew to call to Taos the creatively articulate in many fields, from John Marin to Robinson Jeffers. Although her already considerable ego was certainly served by this ability to surround herself at will by such notables, this was something more than mere lionizing. She was deliberately discriminating in bringing to Taos people whom Mary Austin would have included among those she described (in a different connection) as able to measure the exceptional quality of the privilege of having seen Taos, hopefully to respond with a noticeably richer content of themselves, and, to the extent of their involvement, to leave "repolarized in contact with this living tissue of our common past, this still kindling coal of the primitive hearth of society." [2]

Laura Gilpin

20.   *Young Taos Indian painter Joseph P. Romero and art instructor Constantine Aiello*

John Milton

21. *Church of Saint Francis of Assisi at Ranchos de Taos*

Laura Gilpin

22. *Dorothy Benrimo*

Laura Gilpin

23. *Mabel Dodge Luhan's old house*

Laura Gilpin

24. *Mabel Dodge Luhan*

Laura Gilpin

25. *Brett with two of her paintings of the Deer Dance*

26. *Frieda Lawrence, photograph collection of Louis F. Cottam*

Mildred T. Crews

27. *Brett's painting of Mabel, Frieda, and herself, with Lawrence in the background*

Laura Gilpin

28. *Looking westward from the Lawrence Ranch*

29. *The Lawrence chapel and Frieda's grave*

Mildred T. Crews

Mildred T. Crews

30. *Becky James*

Mildred T. Crews

31. Patrocinio Barela

32. *Gisella Loeffler*

John Stebbins

33. *Spud Johnson, photograph Milford Greer collection*

Laura Gilpin

34. Dennis Hopper

35. *doughBelly Price, photograph Charles B. Brooks collection*

Laura Gilpin

36. Frank Waters

37. *San Ysidro, collection Taylor Museum, Colorado Springs*

through with strong tones of mysticism, producing an interpretation devoid of distortion but set down on canvas with beauty and depth.

And as her insight grew, so also grew her competence as a painter. Two of her canvases now hang in major London galleries, a ceremonial at the Tate and her portrait of Lawrence at the National Portrait Gallery. Others have gone to major American art museums.

In middle age it was Brett who was lionized, as she still is, receiving a stream of important visitors, including seemingly every British celebrity who comes to the Southwest. Taos regards her with affectionate pride.

With the deaths of Frieda and Mabel, she alone remains of that amazing triumvirate.

"I'm a survivor," she chuckles. "That's what the newspapers call me."

But her present stature was not attained by default, by time's removal from the scene of her two famous contemporaries. She had attained it during their lifetimes. Obviously it came from creative strength and a massive Churchillian persistence.

So Brett emerged, and if there are scars, they seldom show, except in her writings. For strangely enough, her present lively and confident personality is not projected in her second volume of reminiscences, now under way, a section of which has been published in the *South Dakota Review*. Writing about those early times, she seems to revert to the old meekness and sense of rejection. But here in person, living her colorful life in Taos, only in occasional flashes does she reveal any bitter memory of what must have been devastating years.

One such occasion came in 1961 when CBS television came to Taos to make two films, one on the pueblo and the other on D. H. Lawrence.

The original plan having called for only the Indian project, John Ciardi with a technical crew arrived in Santa Fe to look around and decide on which of the Rio Grande pueblos to choose for the purpose. When they decided on Taos, Santa Feans pointed out the availability of Lawrence material here, which could be used for a second broadcast. They were also advised to get in touch with us for help in making contacts for the Lawrence feature. They telephoned to enlist Genevieve's aid, and shortly arrived at the shop.

Of the three Taoseñas who had been closest to Lawrence, Frieda had died, and Mabel was by this time seriously ill. We knew the success of the project depended upon whether Brett would consent to be interviewed. But she, though normally far from temperamental, had spent the day in Santa Fe and, arriving home late and tired, took a murky view of the whole proposal.

"What is there left to say about Lawrence?" she wanted to know. "Everything has been said. I know what they'll do. They'll just set me down in a big fancy chair and ask me a lot of silly questions. What good will that do?"

Ciardi had tried to secure Aldous Huxley to be interviewed with her, but had learned that he was in India. He had, however, lined up the well-known Lawrence specialist, Harry T. Moore. But even this announcement was no help with Brett.

"What does he know about Lawrence?" she snorted. "He wasn't even here."

The CBS men shrugged. If she wouldn't cooperate, it was regrettable. But they were here; they would go ahead and do what they could.

Their first problem was choosing a site for the shooting, so Genevieve took them to the "Tony House" in Mabel's compound, where Lawrence had first lived and worked, and then up to the ranch on Mount Lobo, where his later Taos writing had been done. In the shop we lent them Lawrence material, including a recording of Frieda's voice reading some of his poems, a section of which they taped for the broadcast.

Meanwhile pressure in Taos was mounting on Brett to go along with the project, and finally Jenny Vincent succeeded in wearing her down.

After the film was made at the ranch, Genevieve came home delighted with Brett's performance. Roundly photogenic at seventy-seven, she had responded with ease and with matter-of-fact verve.

Later that afternoon at Mary Goodwin's home with the television principals and a number of Taoseños, Brett received the plaudits of her fellow townsmen. She was obviously pleased with the outcome, impressed with Ciardi's handling of the interview, and at this point also delighted with Harry T. Moore.

"Brett," I told her, "everyone says you were magnificent."

Brett's face closed. Her eyes slitted, and she looked straight ahead.

"I should like," she said flatly, "to rub my father's nose in it."

Her rise to fame and a consequent improvement in her financial resources have made no change in her choice of wardrobe, though she has occasionally been known to substitute a skirt for the baggy old corduroy trousers. But Taos prefers her as she is, and finds strangely out of character even this minor concession to convention.

She has, though, in recent years become slightly clothes-conscious, remarking once or twice that at a recent party she had felt "a bit shabby among all those elegant women." For a trip to England a few years ago she assembled a creditable wardrobe. "I suppose they expected me to look like some kind of character," she said later. "Well, I didn't intend to." Upon her return she was still amused at an episode involving a hat she had chosen to wear for the glittering occasion when Queen Elizabeth II opened Parliament. Brett's sister-in-law, Lady Esher, had seen the hat the preceding day and had promptly disapproved. But Brett ignored the comment, wore the hat, and was entertained later to find that her sister-in-law had forgotten her first reaction, and now actually admired it.

It was during this visit that, back in Taos, the Stables gallery sold one of her Indian paintings for three thousand dollars and Leone Kahl, then Stables director, telephoned Brett at the family home in England.

"My, didn't my stock go up!" Brett reported.

Noticeably slowing down these days, she paints or writes little now in her disorganized studio on the mesa, but still receives a procession of notables and Lawrence devotees. Until recently she drove about town in an orange-colored camper of which she was extremely proud. Though with no slightest wish to use it for the itinerant outdoor life for which it was designed, she just liked to know that she could.

We are acutely aware of her less robust health at eighty-nine, for she has always seemed as permanent as Pueblo Peak. Yet unlike that other pinnacle on the Taos horizon, there is nothing brooding about Brett. Just seeing her has always given us a lift.

Frieda

Lawrence's great legacy to Taos, in Dorothy Benrimo's words, was the magnificent Frieda.

More than one biographer has noted about her in her later years something of the classic figure of the earth mother.

No one I know of has attempted to reconcile this with the fact that here was a woman who had abruptly left behind three small children to follow Lawrence. It would seem at first that one could resolve the paradox by going back to the archetypal situation of the mother-child relationships in the representations of primitive peoples. There is, for instance, Erich Neumann's reference to the Peruvian jar showing mother and child, "where the aspect of inhumanity almost outweighs that of magnificence" as the mother stares straight ahead, tremendous and unfeeling, "monumentally embodying nature's indifference toward the living things that depend on her."[3]

But the paradox in Frieda's life did not resolve so easily. She was obviously and painfully not unfeeling. If the role was classic, so, too, were the dimensions of her tragedy in the years when she mourned for her children and Lawrence suffered with her, even in the face of his mounting jealousy of her obsession.

A moving sequence in a British television portrait of Frieda is a description by her daughter, Barbara Barr, of one of the two occasions on which as children they saw their mother again. It is a picture of Frieda walking through the streets of Chiswick, not knowing which house they lived in, but finding it finally by recognizing the Nottingham curtains; of her creeping in at the back door and up the stairs to the nursery, there confronted by the furious grandmother and aunt. And so much had two years and that hostile household done to the children's memories that they, too, joined in and told her to go, "and she was pushed out of the house." [4]

Although years later she visited them in England, and Barbara and Monty, too, I think, came to Taos, the breach was never really healed until news reached them of her imminent death. Only then did they understand what emerged as "this stuffy thing that had condemned her . . . had made her lonely and defiant . . . had changed our childhood love to rancour." [5] But understanding came so late that it brought only grief for the wasted years.

Yet there was in Frieda's face when we knew her, in the last nine years of her life, nothing of bitterness, of suffering past or present, of defiance or resignation, of loneliness or the tempestuous love story she had lived with Lawrence. In her face there was none of this and all of it, for she seemed whole, with a wholeness bearing little resemblance to any of its parts.

She would have scoffed at any such solemn concept. And actually there was nothing solemn about her; there were other elements there, too —naturalness, and humor, and an aristocratic assurance combined with a peasant delight in people and things, especially little things in bright color, such as the gay little heart she once sewed over the hole in the yoke of a nightgown and the small primitive pictures she liked to paint.

Her short, plump figure was dressed in a peasant's full skirt and blouse, joined by a colored ribbon, with another tied in a bow in her white, bobbed hair. Memory is strong of the delighted smile on her broad face and her booming, gutteral German laugh.

"Ja! ja!" she would say, nodding her head vigorously.

In Taos she was generous and easy. In the homes of friends and at the parties she sometimes gave with Angie in the adobe house on the mesa, she usually just sat down somewhere and shortly would find herself chatting comfortably with a semicircle of people sitting on the floor. Genevieve has often noted her way of building someone's bit of small talk into something important and unobtrusively giving it back to him as his own.

One of these Taos affairs resulted in our most prolonged and intimate contact with Frieda. I had asked her about the condition of the mountain road, then unimproved, that led to the ranch where are the log cabin in which Lawrence did most of his work during that period, the larger house which she and Angie had later built, and the small chapel where Lawrence's ashes were placed.

"I don't know how the road is," Frieda said. "I haven't been up there this summer, and I must go soon. We will all go, you and Genevieve and I. We will spend the weekend. We will not let Angie go," she added. "It is not gay enough for him there, and besides, there is too much Lawrence."

We both felt we should not accept, since Frieda's health was not at its best, and when in a few days she followed up on the idea, we strongly demurred, agreeing to go finally only on the condition that we should bring all the food and do any work involved.

It was a sunny September weekend. Frieda seemed well and relaxed. There were long breakfasts in the kitchen of the big house, Frieda in robe and voluminous flannel nightgown, thinking back to other days and other people who had breakfasted in the big room.

"But I usually had to do most of the work," she said. "Not always, though. This is the only floor in the world to be scrubbed by both a Vanderbilt and a Guggenheim."

In the afternoons she slept in the big house, while we followed the wooded trail up the mountain, picked the apples on the old tree behind the house, and sometimes just sat looking out over the tremendous desert and mountain panorama spread out before us.

There were long evenings by the lighted fireplace, Frieda talking about her childhood in Germany in the home of her father, Baron von Richthofen, and of her life with Lawrence.

It was then that she expressed her dismay over the continuous flood of comment on him and his work, so many people painting so many Lawrences that her own image of him was sometimes threatened with fragmentation. Then, too, she spoke of his writings on sex, which had had to fight their way to publication, though they stood at the opposite pole from pornography.

He had written swiftly, making few corrections or interpolations. We remembered the beautiful little holograph manuscripts she had once shown us of the three versions of *Lady Chatterley's Lover*. At our request she and Angie had brought them out to our house one Sunday morning to show to Hans and Mimi de Schulthess, who had recently arrived in Taos and wished to meet Frieda in the hope of buying the manuscripts.

Here, written in Lawrence's small, neat hand, were the three little paper-bound volumes. Hans was more than ever eager to have them, but it was not until some time later that Frieda consented to let them go.

On the Sunday of our weekend at the ranch with her, we had by common consent decided to extend our stay through Monday, when Frieda told us that she had that morning bent the needle of the hypodermic which she used for a daily insulin shot.

"But I thought I would just skip a day," she said. "I will take a chance."

We had not known before of the diabetes and of course felt that the risk of skipping the insulin was too great and, furthermore, unnecessary. When Angie came up unexpectedly to join us for lunch, it was arranged that he should buy a new needle in Taos and that I should drive in the next morning to pick it up.

I returned from this errand to find that Frieda and Genevieve had spent the morning cleaning the log cabin, which had suffered from the litter of pack rats.

"Frieda knew that she would not be seeing the cabin again this fall," Genevieve told me later, "and that she would have to clean it all over again next summer. But it seemed to be something she had to do for Lawrence. Not that she spoke of it, but there was something in her manner. . . . She couldn't leave it like that. The cleaning seemed to be a sort of rite."

For though she was devoted to Angie, as he, though openly a playboy, was devoted to her, watching over her with considerate care, Lawrence was much in her mind.

As she became really wealthy from reprints of his books and from moving-picture rights, she remembered the scanty reward he had had from years of hard work and constant critical attack. The leanness of her own years with him largely forgotten, what remained now was almost a sense of guilt at profiting from what he had earned and never received.

Frieda did what she could. With Angie she built the chapel to his memory on the mountainside. The ranch she gave as a memorial to the University of New Mexico. And she published privately a new edition, a thousand copies, of one of his volumes of poems, *Pansies*.

This she asked us to distribute nationally from the book shop. We regretted the fact that the small green cloth volume had no jacket, so that its title, printed only on the spine, could not easily be seen, a factor which we knew would hamper its sale. But Frieda seemed almost completely uninterested in the sale of the book or recovery of the cost of publication. It seemed simply another memorial to Lawrence.

The focal point of the continuous Lawrence literary pilgrimage to Taos, she responded beyond her strength to the resulting demands in time

120

and effort and usually managed to circumvent Angie's constant efforts to protect her from even the youngest and rawest of Lawrence devotees and researchers.

There were few who knew her in Taos who did not really love her.

But Lawrence had said it best. "It ought to be lovely to be old," he had once written. "If people lived without accepting lies, they would ripen like apples."

So Frieda had ripened.

It was as simple—it was as complex—as that.

On her seventy-seventh birthday, August 11, 1956, she died here after a short illness.

On a late afternoon, rainy and smelling of the coming of fall, she was buried on the slope of Mount Lobo, in front of the chapel where Lawrence's ashes had been placed long ago. William Goyen, novelist and her friend, read the simple service—something he had written, something from Lawrence, and the 121st Psalm.

Below, the mountain sloped off to the tremendous wide mesa, with the western range beyond. As we turned to leave, the sun, obscured all day, shone briefly through the overcast and shed its familiar magenta glow over this vast and rugged landscape that Frieda had loved. It was at that moment that a hummingbird poised over her for one quick instant, then darted away.

One thought then of the final line of a prayer from the Navajo Night Chant: "In beauty it is finished."

Taos is old and wise and tough and resilient. Over more than four centuries it has felt wave after dynamic wave of influence and has absorbed them all into its always ongoing vitality. But there was a special vibrancy about that lengthy era over which these three women—Mable, Frieda, and Brett—jointly presided. Taos does not expect to see its particular like again.

15

Taos in D. H. Lawrence

It has been more than forty-five years since D. H. Lawrence last left Taos and with Frieda finally made his wandering way to Vence in southern France, where he died in 1930. He had been gone from this northern New Mexico mountain town for twenty-two years by the time I first saw Taos. But because of the book shop Genevieve and I are probably more aware of his continuing presence than are most other Taoseños except those few who, known to have been members of the Lawrence circle, attract the students, scholars, collectors, and simple enthusiasts drawn in steadily increasing numbers to the only American town where he lived, the village near which, on its mountain slope, sits the chapel which Frieda and Angie built in his memory and where his ashes are interred.

What identifies him so strongly with Taos? He lived here for a total of less than two years, and that in three periods, between 1922 and 1925. But here he wrote several of his major works. There are books written about his Taos phase—by Mabel, Frieda, Brett, Knud Merrild, Joseph Foster. There are lengthy references to it in the great bulk of Lawrenciana which has steadily over the years continued to pour from the presses. There are radio tapes and television films made here. There is the fact that Frieda and Mabel lived out the rest of their lives in Taos and that Brett is still here, as are several others who knew him. There is the small group of Taos writings by Lawrence himself: essays, poems, and a fragment of a play set in Mabel's kitchen. There is the recognizable use he made of Taos people as characters in novels and stories: Brett in *The Princess;* Mabel in *The Woman Who Rode Away;* Spud and Frieda in *The Plumed Serpent.* There is the fact that here, he said, he finally found something to believe in.

When all of this resulted in a 1970 commemorative observance here of the fortieth anniversary of his death, however, most of the Taoseños who had known him were less than enthusiastic. Lawrence would have hated it, they said. Brett felt that everything had been said about Lawrence and that everyone knew how great he was.

But did everyone know? I was remembering the time when the manager of La Doña Luz restaurant suddenly asked me, "What was so great about D. H. Lawrence?"

"You've got the chance of your life to find out," I said. "Harry T. Moore of Southern Illinois University comes here every day for lunch. He's one of the top Lawrence scholars."

I don't know whether he ever did get around to asking Moore, but I did.

"Tell him," he said, "to read *Sea and Sardinia.*"

Moore was spending that summer of 1967 here, revising his Lawrence biography, *The Intelligent Heart.* We saw him almost every day and since the conversation sometimes naturally turned to D.H.L., he once mentioned the date of his death.

"Then 1970 will be the fortieth anniversary," I said. "Maybe we should arrange some small commemorative observance here."

"Let's give it a little thought," he said.

As a result, I got in touch in Albuquerque with Dudley Wynn, the chairman of the General Honors Program at the University of New Mexico, to see whether that institution would be interested in taking an active part in such an affair.

"I should tell you, though," I said to him, "that Spud on second thought doesn't think much of the idea."

"Why not?"

"He thinks it sounds rather cheap."

He grinned. "You know," he said, "I saw quite a bit of Spud years ago when we were both connected with the *New Mexico Quarterly* down here and I don't think he ever really liked Lawrence."

I had wondered about that, too. For while Spud had been a member of the inner Lawrence circle here, had spent several months with him in Mexico together with Frieda, Brett, and Witter Bynner, and had typed some of his manuscripts, he was always reluctant to say much about him.

I remember asking him once about the fact that he had been the prototype for one of the characters in *The Plumed Serpent.*

"Yes," he said, "I was Villiers. I didn't come off very well, either. Villiers was a sort of callow youth. But I never took it personally. I felt he was just using me as a point of departure, as novelists usually do."

I wonder now, thinking it over, whether Spud ever really liked Frieda either. For once when I had told him of her comment that though she had known him and loved him for thirty years, she had never known whether he even liked her, he had just gone rather poker-faced and hadn't said anything. This being characteristic, I didn't think much about it. But there was another time I'd wondered about. I had learned, from the posthumous publication of her second volume of reminiscences and correspondence, of her affair (during Lawrence's lifetime) with Middleton Murry.

"How do you account for that?" I asked Spud.

"I suppose," he said flatly, "she was just a promiscuous woman."

But these two incidents might have meant nothing, Spud being Spud. Certainly the two had always seemed on the best of terms, and the first time Genevieve and I had spent more than a few minutes with Frieda was on a Sunday picnic on the grass before the big house on the ranch, with Spud and John Goldmark. That day we pried open a window and put Spud through to bring out some of the few remaining copies of her first book, *Not I, But the Wind.*

But whatever the survivors of the Lawrence circle thought of the advisability of a commemorative event, the university immediately warmed to the idea; so, too, did the New Mexico Arts Commission and the National Endowment for the Humanities. All three, with a handful of Taos people, financed the D. H. Lawrence Festival here in October of 1970. The event brought scholars from England, Scotland, Holland, France, and around the United States, attracting four hundred people from sixteen states and ten foreign countries.

The picture of Lawrence that finally emerged from the conference was that of a giant literary figure, with one of the most concerned and inquiring minds of modern times. And the conference was marked by an immense knowledge and expertise shown by many of the participants. But it was also a free-wheeling affair, and you could hear as many varied opinions of Lawrence at the ranch as you can in Taos—a range from Joe Foster's estimate of him as the man of the century to that of somebody else who calls him "that terrible man" who wrote sexy novels and threw dishes at Frieda.

"What about that last bit?" I once asked Spud.

"Oh, yes, it sometimes happened," he said. "Of course it was embarrassing for the rest of us there and we all felt sorry for Frieda."

But though Lawrence had (as Dorothy Parker wrote of Thomas Carlyle) "combined the lit'r'y life/With throwing teacups at his wife," [1] Frieda had not, like Jane Carlyle, further irritated her husband by meekly dodging; she had been quite up to fielding the crockery and throwing it back.

There was time for a lot to be said at the ranch in twenty-seven hours of discussion spread over four days. How great was he? Do his ideas mean

124

much today? What kind of person was he—kind, generous, magnanimous through an affinity with nature, quarrelsome, undependable, a firm and loyal friend? Had he ruined two or three women's lives by first seeming to offer and then withdrawing his affections? Was he impotent during his last years, perhaps because of the tuberculosis that caused his death? Was he a latent homosexual?

"You mean was he a fag?" Robert Bly, young American poet, inquired loudly.

"What do you mean—fag?" somebody asked.

"I mean was he a fag, a homosexual?"

And Bly stood up to demand: "And what if he was? He was interested in love among men, in its universal sense."

No conclusion was reached on this point (nor on any other in this kaleidoscopic affair) but a roomful of people burst out laughing when a member of the British contingent stood up to say stiffly, "For your information, Mr. Bly, in England a fag is a cigarette."

I am sure that never again will anyone be able to assemble in one spot so many people who have actually known Lawrence as were here during those five fall days. For they were his contemporaries and he would have been eighty-six years old.

Except for Jenny Vincent and panelist Joe Foster, the Taos contingent of D.H.L.'s friends remained discreetly absent from the affair, though Brett came in to tell me: "I don't want you to think I'm just being difficult. I'm just too old and too deaf."

They appeared at the ranch only in a BBC television film, "D. H. Lawrence in Taos," made here in 1968. Here were Bill and Rachel Hawk, Louie Cottam, Spud, Frank Waters, Tinka Fechin, Joe Foster—with Brett, looming larger than life in frequent closeups, zestfully vivisecting Mabel and Frieda and strewing the pieces around the Taos landscape.

How great was Lawrence and what was he trying to say? Answers came from London and Nottingham, Amsterdam, Edinburgh and Nice, and around the United States.

"He was probably the greatest English literary figure of the century."

"I've read very little by or about him and have been spectacularly bored by that."

"He was inferior to Katherine Mansfield."

"Mansfield's was a minor talent. Lawrence was one of the greats."

"He was the man of the century."

"What he said fifty years ago he is still saying. For he was concerned with the problems of a materialistic society and certainly they are far from solved."

An unmistakable excitement was sparked by this concentration on Lawrence—readings from his work, literary and graphic Lawrenciana, radio and television interviews with those who had known him, and this lively exchange of ideas based on his body of thought. And I suppose you can explain it in terms of an answer a student got to her question as to why James Branch Cabell, who once seemed to loom large in American letters, has long since receded into obscurity, while Lawrence after forty years remains a world figure.

Harry Moore answered it: "The difference was the flame. Lawrence had the flame."

Lawrence seems to have had very little effect on Taos. Awareness of his identification with this village comes less from living here than in waves from the outside world. Taos reacts to his work as it does to that of Joyce or Camus, in personal individual response to the achievement of any figure tall enough to command attention.

This was obviously the case with the Lawrence commercial films seen here in the recent past—*The Virgin and the Gypsy, Women in Love*, and *The Fox*. They were given no special fanfare and were greatly admired here by those responding to films of that caliber not because of the original authorship but simply because they are outstanding productions and had received high national critical acclaim.

You see Lawrence's name here only on a small sign on the highway a dozen or so miles north of Taos, which points to the ranch, and in connection with a group of nine of his paintings that are shown for a fee in a room off the lobby of a hotel on the plaza.

The house on the mesa here where Frieda and Angie lived for a number of years has changed hands several times since her death and has been greatly altered in appearance. Angie, finding Taos too lonely without Frieda, has long since returned to his native Italy. So the reminders are mostly at the ranch where, each year, a writer spends the summer on a Lawrence fellowship financed by a group sponsored by the University of New Mexico.

There was reason enough for Lawrence's lack of impact on Taos. He saw little of it as a village around a plaza.

During his brief initial stay in one of Mabel's houses on the edge of Taos, he found that her patronage had too many strings attached. They quarreled violently and he moved to the ranch, which Mabel had given to Frieda and for which she was more than repaid by the gift of the manuscript of *Sons and Lovers*. From then on, Lawrence had little connection with Taos, separated from it as he was by twenty miles of distance, at the end of a primitive road.

126

"We see little of Taos itself," he wrote. "There are some American artists, sort of colony; but not much in contact."

He spoke slightingly of the Taos painters of his time. "Taos was nice," he wrote in a letter to Jan Juta from the ranch, "but so much artistic small beer—paint purely in terms of dollars."

This was no real attempt on Lawrence's part at art criticism, according to Spud (speaking from personal contact) and Harry Moore (from research). Both say his comments came from the simple fact that he had a low opinion of painting as an art form, even after he took it up himself as a hobby.

His comparative isolation can be accounted for, too, by the amazing amount of work he accomplished during those less than two years at the ranch. Here he wrote, completed, or revised *The Kangaroo, St. Mawr, Birds, Beasts, and Flowers, The Woman Who Rode Away, The Princess, Mornings in Mexico, David, The Plumed Serpent*, and a number of lesser works.

And as he remained aloof from the Taos Anglos, he seemed to be little aware of the Spanish people. Only one of them appears in his writings, a character in *The Princess*, who, though given a sympathetic treatment, is cast as the villain.

Nor did he react to the individual Taos Indian. "He saw him only as a figure against the land," Scott Momaday has noted. It was "the old dark religion" of the Pueblo Indians to which he reacted, along with the sun and the land.

And the landscape he found extraordinarily beautiful. In an essay published in *Survey Graphic* he wrote:

> For a greatness of beauty I have never experienced anything like New Mexico. All those mornings when I went with a hoe to the Cañon, at the ranch, and stood in the fierce, proud silence of the Rockies, on their foothills, to look far over the desert to the blue mountains, blue as chalcedony, with the sagebrush desert sweeping grey-blue in between . . . the vast amphitheatre of lofty, indomitable desert, sweeping round to the ponderous Sangre de Cristo mountains on the east, and coming flush at the pine-dotted foothills of the Rockies! What splendour!

He had felt New Mexico's vitalizing influence when he had first stepped off the train at Lamy:

> . . . the moment I saw the brilliant, proud morning shine high up over the deserts of Santa Fe, something stood still in my

soul, and I started to attend. There was a certain magnificence in the high-up day, a certain eagle-like royalty, so different from the equally pure, equally pristine and lovely morning of Australia, which is so soft, so utterly pure in its softness, and betrayed by green parrot flying. But in the lovely morning of Australia one went into a dream. In the magnificent fierce morning of New Mexico one sprang awake, a new part of the soul woke up suddenly, and the old world gave way to a new.[2]

So while he made almost no impact on Taos, its effect on him was tremendous. It gave him, he said, his greatest experience from the outside world. "It certainly changed me forever."

Here, he said, he finally found a valid religion, in the "old human race-experience" of the Taos Indian. And as the monasteries of Europe had kept the spark of civilization alive while wolves were howling in the streets of Rome, he predicted that the cosmic religion of the pueblos, though temporarily beaten down by a materialistic age, would see a resurgence and "the genuine America, the America of New Mexico," would resume its course.[3]

He conceded that he could not identify himself with this primitive consciousness (no white man could, he believed), yet he felt close to penetrating its meaning. The Indian's one positive commandment was "Thou shalt acknowledge the wonder."

He elaborated with an interpretation of the San Gerónimo Day ritual races at Taos Pueblo, when the young men, painted with white clay stuck with bits of eagle down, run in relays down the track. He saw the race as run "in an effort to gather into their souls more and more of the creative fire, the creative energy that shall carry their tribe through the coming year . . . in the unending race of humanity along the track of trackless creation."

Though he had been happier here, Frieda said, than in any other place, an urge to wander prodded at his heels and he moved on.

16

Figures in a Mountain Landscape

I have missed seeing Kit Carson and Padre Martínez by a hundred or so years, but I can bear that cheerfully when I remember that if I'd been here then, I'd have missed, not only Brett and Frieda and Mabel, but Becky James and doughBelly Price, and Pat Barela and Spud and Gisella and Miss Lizzie Anderson and all those other authentic originals that have distinguished the Taos scene over the past two or three decades.

A few of them are still here, but their numbers are dwindling. And you can't replace people like that. As the man said, you can't get the material.

Becky James

For years, until she was beset by a chronic and terminal illness, Rebecca Salsbury James cut a swashbuckling figure on the plaza, her classic profile and white pageboy surmounted by a wide-brimmed black western hat, her cowboy jeans and shirt seen under a flowing black cape.

Becky linked two Taos worlds, that of the artist and that of the roistering frontier, from which this village has happily still not entirely emerged. An introverted extrovert, she was uncomfortably caught between two urges, instinctively reaching out to the world only to find her sensitive artist's skin flinch from the contact.

She was born in London, daughter of Nate Salsbury, who financed Buffalo Bill and managed his shows. Once married to the noted photographer Paul Strand, she came here from New York with Georgia O'Keeffe, who painted briefly in Taos at Mabel Luhan's invitation. O'Keeffe soon returned to the East and finally located in Abiquiu on the west side of the Rio Grande. But Becky later settled down here, and was married for many years to Bill James, Denver banker and gentleman cattle rancher.

As an artist she won national honors in two mediums, with brush and with needle. Her luminous paintings on glass are formally elegant florals and stark representations of Penitente crosses. And here, from Jesusita Perrault, she learned the famous *colcha* stitch, one of the most notable of New Mexican Spanish-Colonial folk arts. Her embroidered miniatures were sought and exhibited by museums here and throughout the country.

But it was clear that the people who most attracted her interest were frontier types who had nothing to do with writing or painting, and it was so much the better if their flamboyant careers had involved them with gambling, cattle wrangling, and the manufacture and sale of that potent Taos drink known as Taos Lightning. This interest finally resulted in a book, characteristically entitled *Allow Me To Present 18 Ladies and Gentlemen.*

Most of the survivors in the group came to an autographing party at the book shop, an affair which, sparked by a whiskey punch that Becky concocted, kept three hundred people happily involved until close to midnight.

doughBelly came because, he said, Becky had threatened to cut his throat if he didn't. Curley Murray, who had spent most of his life as a professional gambler, had intended to go down to the racetrack at Ruidoso that night but at the last minute remembered the autograph affair at the book shop and thought he'd look in for twenty minutes or so. At 11:30 he was still there, exchanging signatures with the rest of the characters in the book. Curley had arrived in Taos in 1929 after he had spent the summer hiding out in the mountains near Mora from Texas Rangers, who were looking for him on a trumped-up murder charge. By that time, though, they had given up and his long years of residence in Taos were untroubled by the law.

Pat Barela

Taos characters are in the nature of things cut to no single pattern and differ from each other as much as they differ from the run-of-the-mine rest of us. And so there was Patrocinio Barela, Spanish New Mexican woodcarver, son of a "wild weed doctor," whose vital sculptures had worked their way up after the middle thirties from the status of doorstops to prominence in galleries and museums, including the New York Museum of Modern Art.

Genevieve and I ran into Pat early, for we lived next door to him in Cañon during our first winter here. His son Robert, then about twelve, would usually be waiting to visit with us when we came home from the shop at night, and sometimes would come running in breathlessly on Saturday nights to ask us to call the sheriff to rescue the family from the effects of his father's bottle of cheap wine.

Pat, in spite of a smiling and roguish air, was a troubled man. A simple Spanish-American villager, he was a displaced man in his family, his town, and a world in which a man is expected to get along.

"I lead a heavy life," he told his biographers, Judson Crews, Wendell Anderson, and Kit Egri, who published a book about him built around a group of memorable camera studies by Mildred Crews.

From the resinous woods of the Taos mountain slopes he whittled his statement of the classic problems: sin and pain, loneliness and death, love and faith. As an artist he spoke in the tone of the Penitent Brother, usually in terms as austere, as grotesque and terrible as the problems themselves.

He spoke with compassion. It was a compassion he was not, in this life, able to evoke for himself.

He inherited from his national origin a preoccupation with death. And death came to him in his adobe studio one October day in a holocaust fed by the pine and cedar shavings fallen from the resinous figures through which he had spoken.

Gisella

If these Taos characters are a disparate and colorful lot, among them it is Gisella Loeffler who literally personifies color.

Color is her life. She wears it, peasantlike—raw yellows and purples, reds, high blues, shocking pinks and greens, all thrown together in full woolen skirts, gaily embroidered blouses, and Latin-American shawls and rebosos.

With them go the heavy exotic silver necklaces, bracelets, and long squash blossom earrings made by the Navajo.

All this, with her cap of brown hair and raven black eyes, adds up to a figure that might, when you see her in Taos, be one of those robust children she paints in a medley of roses and birds and flowers for schools, children's hospitals, toy rooms, and books.

Perhaps because they are sober-faced, she surrounds her painted children with reassurance, with madonnas and guardian angels, flowers and friendly animals, rocking horses and clowns. They appear in batik and embroidered wall hangings, in easel paintings, in felt and balsa wood Christmas tree ornaments, on Christmas cards, and in books, of which she has written two and illustrated four.

Color runs uninhibited in her house-studio, which might be mistaken for the Black Forest cottage of Hansel and Gretel.

Gisella's immersion in folk arts goes back to her childhood in the Austrian Alps. In a small mountain village she lived with her parents in her grandfather's inn.

It was a world of color, of flowers and gypsies and fairs and markets, of gaily garbed peasants. It was all, she felt, she could ever want. She would have liked, actually, to be a gypsy and used sometimes to stain her skin with walnut juice in true Maggie Tulliver fashion.

She was happy to stay behind with her grandfather when her parents decided to come to the United States to see the World's Fair in St. Louis, but desolate when word came that they had decided to stay in America, that she was to travel with friends to join them.

To Gisella at five the small brick house in mid–St. Louis was a bitter disappointment. Where were the great decorated beds, the wine cellar, the gypsies and fairs and flowers? The small area in front of the house was paved with bricks.

Rallying, her parents took her to playgrounds and amusement parks with merry-go-rounds; her father dug out the bricks of the courtyard, and soon she was swinging in a little hammock, again in a world of flowers.

Gradually her spirits rose, but she had not forgotten, and when as still a child she began to paint, her pictures showed gaily dressed children suffused in Austrian folklore.

Her first marriage unhappy, she came to Taos in the middle thirties with two small daughters, Aithra and Undine. And here she was happy again, among the folk arts of Indian Latin America. Her painted children began to look, as they do now, like roundheaded Navajo or Pueblo children, surrounded by European folklore.

Her daughters off and away with husbands and children of their own, she has followed her interests to Mexico and South America. Warm and receptive, she comes into the shop to sign her books with bright colored crayons and sometimes to add a bird or an animal for a special child.

Finding her gregariousness a problem to her working schedule, in summer she often retires to the flat roof of her adobe house to paint.

In her world of folklore her hold on reality is nevertheless firm, anchored by a kind of ingenuous wisdom. Troubled often by the ordinary details of everyday living, she has surrounded herself, as she has her painted children, with color and symbols of innocence and gaiety, and in Taos has chosen a solemn New England husband, Frank Chase.

Spud

If Spud (Walter Willard) Johnson had not come to Taos, I suppose we should have had to think him up. For Spud was the aesthetic and intellectual conscience of Taos. He warned when meretricious elements crept in with change; he was the watchdog of intellectual integrity and the voice of reason raised against ideological extremes.

As a newspaper columnist he served as the gentle crusader, the mildly buzzing, persistent gadfly. It was a role in which he moved about instinctively, advancing into each new sensitive area of controversy as if completely unaware of its potential threat to his peace and comfort, appearing among his friends after each backlash with the mildly surprised and faintly aggrieved air of one who has been unaccountably attacked while only going peaceably about his business.

For the peaceful tone of his comments did not impede his progress from one kettle of hot water to another, nor did it on one occasion (after a piece deploring the spreading infection of neon signs) protect the windshield of his car from a fusillade of shots.

His fragile frame he topped from time to time with a variety of headgear ranging from deerstalker caps to his last device, a wig. This topper he wore only intermittently, a practice which once brought him a letter (unquestioningly placed in his post-office box) addressed to "The Man Who Scalps Himself, Taos, New Mexico."

A professional bachelor, he was the only gregarious hermit I ever knew, and the only man who, in a roomful of people, could sit silently in a corner all evening, smoking his Sherlock Holmes pipe, and still often manage to give the impression of having taken a pleasant and active part in the proceedings.

A member of the D. H. Lawrence circle and every other Taos circle of cultural importance since the early twenties, he flitted through a couple of dozen books by major literary figures and was on first-name terms with an array of celebrities ranging from Georgia O'Keeffe to Emily Hahn.

Some of these associations stemmed from a short stint as a staffman on *The New Yorker;* some from his longtime editorship of a "little" magazine, *The Laughing Horse;* some from several periods as bookseller in Santa Fe and Taos; and many simply from spending most of his adult life in these two New Mexico towns.

Fruit of these years were fifteen issues of *The Laughing Horse*, irregularly published over thirty years; a small volume of polished and somehow haunting poems, *Horizontal Yellow;* publication for a number of years on his own press in Taos of a miniature handset newspaper, *The Horsefly;* articles for regional literary magazines; and, later, feature columns in Taos and Santa Fe newspapers and part-time stints as a cataloger of out-of-print books for the Taos Book Shop. His bundle of work, along with association papers and correspondence with the great and near-great, went ultimately to the Yale and University of Texas libraries.

The Laughing Horse was originated at the University of California by Spud and two fellow students as a horselaugh on what they considered the dull and conventional campus publications and, it developed, on the whole intellectual climate of the Berkeley scene.

The ruckus they raised there, with the aid of the more adventurous of the student writers and such famed early contributors as Lawrence and Upton Sinclair (the latter supplying a diatribe on the university's academic mores) quickly embroiled them with the authorities. It also embroiled them with the California courts on a charge against the editor (not Spud at that time) of publishing obscene literature. But a quick victory there (the case was dismissed in a matter of minutes) brought *The Horse* overnight national fame.

Later, as Spud took over the magazine and brought it to New Mexico, his stable of writers came to include such notables as Carl Sandburg, Lincoln Steffens, Sherwood Anderson, John Dewey, Miguel Covarrubias, and many others.

Although *The Laughing Horse* ceased publication years ago, Spud's youthful ardor only leveled off into a way of life as columnist, literary critic, poet, and casual philosopher.

An informal scholar whose books sat among jars of food on his kitchen shelves, he was the enemy of only ugliness, in thing or concept. Clothed in a modest air of mild benignity, punctuated occasionally by brief spells of seemingly unprovoked waspishness, he went his Taos way, one ear cocked for the half-truth and the false note, eyes quick to catch the bright flash of the piñon jay.

He was happy his last afternoon, riding with three friends through the rich fall color of the Rio Grande canyon. But happiness had not been his life condition.

This morning I took his book of poems down from the shelf and read again:

Autobiography
One of my dreams is very old
And never has been or will be told:

And three of them have long been sold
And ten have caught their death of cold. . . .

Miss Lizzie

That morning, when Miss Lizzie crossed the road to see Mr. Pitcher, he had a big new gadget hanging down from the ceiling in front of his living-room window. It seemed to be made of thin rods of different lengths, some wire, and a number of crystal balls.

"What is it?" she asked.

"Why, it's a mobile, Lizzie," Otto said.

"What does it do?"

"It doesn't do anything," he told her. "It just hangs there."

"Oh," she said.

The next time Miss Lizzie came, she surveyed the mobile again with a thoughtful eye.

"When do you light it up?" she asked.

Mr. Pitcher shook his head. "It doesn't light up. It doesn't do anything. It's an ornament."

On her third try a few days later Miss Lizzie took still a different tack.

"I expect it makes music," she said craftily.

"No," said Otto, "it doesn't make music; it doesn't light up. It doesn't do anything. It just hangs there."

Not long afterward, on the street in Taos, Otto ran into Mrs. John Dunn.

"I understand from Lizzie Anderson," she said slyly, "that you've got the only indoor lightning rod in Taos."

Otto was devoted to Miss Lizzie. Her sister Miss Jennie was another matter. But he saw quite a lot of both of them during those several years when he served as neighbor, chauffeur, adviser, and general troubleshooter for the Anderson Girls on their farm across the road from his house.

His volunteer unpaid services were often called upon at extremely short notice. For if the Andersons took no thought for the morrow, it was because the morrow seemed too far away. When they needed feed for their 120 chickens, they needed it *now*. When Miss Lizzie summoned Mr. Pitcher to drive her to town for chicken feed, he knew the hens were facing an immediate famine and that he must hastily drop any of his own concerns and do something about it.

In willingly spending so much time with Miss Lizzie, Otto was admittedly motivated by more than his affection for her and a humanitarian concern for the state of affairs in the henhouse. As an old pro actor, he was enormously diverted by his role of straight man in the deadpan, inadvertently comic routines Miss Lizzie continually provided.

Though Miss Jennie was in her eighties and her sister coming along only five years behind, they carried their water, winter and summer, from a spring three or four hundred feet from their dilapidated Victorian frame house. But when he was not at home, they would accept his neighborly offer to get it from Otto's house instead. After the first of these periods, Miss Lizzie approached him in a state of bright-eyed wonderment.

"Do you know, Mr. Pitcher," she asked, "that if you turn on that *other* tap, *hot* water comes out?"

Uncle Alex Anderson, when he had died forty years ago, had left the girls a hundred acres including some of the best land in Taos County, plus a few more acres and a small mine in Arroyo Seco, not far away. But Uncle had told them never to sell any of it. And he had known all about such matters.

Uncle had been a businessman and a man of property. He had owned the gristmill, with its sluice and waterwheel and its grain storage building, an establishment part of which has now become Otto's house. Besides this and the mine, with its showing of copper and a few other ores, he had had thirty beehives and sold the honey. He had raised prize dahlias and marketed them wholesale.

Furthermore, Uncle was much more than a memory. They were still grateful to him and loved him. They had first lived at Embudo, twenty-five miles south of Taos, where their father had worked in a little mine and had to be away from home a lot of the time. And when their mother had had a mental break and had to be taken away, Uncle had brought the two little girls home with him to Taos and given them solicitous care. So when he told them never to sell the land, they knew he was right. No matter how scarce cash got over the years, they hung on grimly.

For years they prepared dinners in the old house in Los Cordovas, three or four miles from Taos, for the town's elite. There would be chicken, potatoes cooked in two to seven ways at the same meal, three kinds of salad or slaw, two or three kinds of pie, and cake with ice cream.

Of course, no matter what time the guests arrived, dinner was never ready, for there were still the dishes to do from previous meals, and one of the gentlemen had to be detailed to turn the ice cream freezer. Nor could you, in contemporary Taos fashion, fill in the wait with a sociable highball. The girls didn't hold with any such sinfulness, which had to be carried on, if at all, surreptitiously among the lilacs at the side of the house. So strongly did they feel on this subject that in later years, when Miss Lizzie saw a bottle of rum with which Otto was mellowing a Christmas cake, she sadly reported to Elsie Weimer, "Mr. Pitcher has taken to drink."

As age began to catch up with the Anderson Girls and more and fancier restaurants opened in Taos, they gave up serving the dinners and settled for selling eggs, the cream from their four cows, and the angelfood cakes which they still liked to bake. Miss Lizzie brought these to town on weekly trips.

I don't think I ever laid eyes on Miss Jennie. She couldn't, she felt, leave the property unprotected. This was the reason why, after the road commission had ripped out Uncle's old wooden bridge, replaced it with a culvert, and piled the old timbers up at the side of the road, Miss Jennie broke out her shotgun and sat by the pile through all of one chilly autumn night. If she hadn't, you never could tell who would have stolen her timbers.

But while Miss Jennie seldom left the old homestead, I saw Miss Lizzie about every week, though, since we bought only eggs, we never saw her during those periods when the hens were moulting. It was, it appeared, impossible for them to lay when they were moulting or else to moult when they were laying. Whichever it was, these physiological phenomena never occurred simultaneously, the fact interrupting Miss Lizzie's visits to us.

Her spare New Englandish figure was garbed in winter in a long dogskin coat; in spring and fall in a long fitted black one of cloth. In summer she came in her countrywoman's dress of cotton. Her wide-brimmed hats, felt in winter and black straw in summer, were anchored in place with a scarf that tied under her chin and produced a sunbonnet effect.

Her speech, coming out in a high, thin voice, was brisk and chipper. But it was hard for me to keep my mind on what she was saying because of the interruptions that happened once or twice in each sentence when her upper dentures began to slip from their proper place. When this happened, she was, of course, forced to arrest their fall by a brisk upward movement of her lower jaw, and so had her choice of muttering through clenched teeth or waiting until things had settled down and she could reopen her mouth to finish her sentence. This had to be accomplished with all possible speed before the same thing began to happen again.

The procedure, fascinating to see, caused Miss Lizzie no concern or embarrassment. And if, after she had brought out the eggs from one of the two pasteboard cartons she carried by their rope fastenings, her visits were always short, it was only because she had to hurry to the Safeway to meet Mr. Pitcher and get a ride home.

At the Safeway she would buy an Eskimo Pie, an addiction she had learned to finance by raising the price of eggs to a few cents above the figure she would report to Miss Jennie. Then on the way home, Mr. Pitcher would have to stop the car under a friendly shade tree, while she ate the delicacy with leisurely relish.

When Miss Jennie finally slipped on an icy spot and died as an indirect result of a broken hip, everyone worried about Miss Lizzie. What would she do now, all by herself in that old rattletrap of a house? Miss Jennie had always taken the lead; what would Miss Lizzie do without her?

But Otto was not apprehensive. He knew Miss Lizzie had only been scared to death of her sister.

He was out of town when Miss Jennie died, and got home a few days after the funeral. When Miss Lizzie asked him to drive her over to the cemetery, he complied with more than his usual alacrity. There was something he was curious about.

He knew there was room for five graves in the Anderson family plot. Father and Mother and Uncle Alex had long been there, side by side in a neat row. There was one more prized spot, right next to Uncle. But the fifth Anderson would have to settle for a crosswise place at the foot of the row.

As he and Miss Lizzie reached the plot and stood looking down, she nudged Otto's elbow and a slow grin spread over her face.

"See where Jennie is," she said. "Across the feet."

Now after more than eighty years, Miss Lizzie discovered freedom. For one thing, she sold some land. Though this radical move was rather forced upon her by the staggering size of the bills attending Miss Jennie's passing, she decided to use what money was left over to pay back the loans that had been made to them over the years by some of their longtime friends. She was touched when most of them refused the payments; they'd written those loans off years ago. Miss Lizzie was pleased, too, with the new checkbook she took around to use in paying the debts.

It was during this period that somebody paid her a check that bounced.

"Well, Mr. Pitcher," she said, "I see the bank's run out of money."

"Oh, I don't think so," Otto replied. "How do you know?"

"Well," said Miss Lizzie, "I took in this check and they didn't give me the money. They said they didn't have any more."

Soon she made another bold move—she went up in the attic. Miss Jennie had never allowed her to go up there; she might fall down the stairs and break a hip. But now in the attic she came upon Uncle's old wind-up phonograph with horn and a bunch of cylinder records. There was one, though, that she didn't find that she wanted to hear again. She was especially fond of "Birmingham Jail." Mr. Pitcher, when she asked him about it,

138

didn't have this record, either, but he did have a tape recording. Miss Lizzie watched his contraption with interest.

"That's the funniest phonograph I ever saw," she declared. "It eats up the record as it goes along."

Now she decided to fix up an old radio that Mabel Luhan had once given them for Christmas. You could run it with batteries or you could plug it into the wall. Miss Lizzie tried to find batteries, but the model was obsolete, so she had the kitchen wired for electricity and put in just one outlet where she could plug in the radio. Otto discovered her there one evening, blissfully listening in a dim room still lighted by an old kerosene lamp.

"What, no electric light?" he inquired.

"Oh, that's too expensive," Miss Lizzie said. Unless it cost too much, nobody who had electricity in his house would eat his dinner by candle-light, as she had often seen Mr. Pitcher doing. But after he had explained that he just thought it was nicer to have candles at dinner, she agreed to having an electric light, so Otto went to a rummage sale, found an old lamp, and hitched it up with a double plug to the radio outlet.

Thus reassured on the question of expense, she soon afterward bought an electric refrigerator. And the first thing she got to go into it was a hundred Eskimo Pies.

But her pleasure in what you could do by plugging things into the wall was dashed one day when she overloaded the line and blew out a fuse. Again she repaired to Otto's house, this time at seven o'clock in the morning.

"Mr. Pitcher," she asked, "have you used up all of *your* electricity yet?"

"I don't think so," he said, flipping a switch.

"Well, I guess I've used all of mine," she said. "The radio hasn't said a word since six o'clock."

Now she settled down to enjoy life. She sold some more land and drilled a well. In fact, life was improving so much that she didn't accept when her cousin in California wrote and asked her to come and live with him and his wife. He'd visited her once and he liked her. He worried about her there all alone in the winters in that old, cold house with its wood-burning stoves. But she was not yet ready to go.

Nor did she get ready until finally it happened—Miss Lizzie fell and struck her head against the cast-iron oven door of the kitchen stove. The door broke, and while her own injuries were, comparatively speaking, less serious, the neighbors took her off to the hospital, where she stayed for three weeks.

When the time came to go home, she found she couldn't face that cold house. In the hospital the heat sort of came out of the walls; hot water came out of the other tap there, too; and somebody cooked your meals and brought them right to you.

She went home only long enough to sell her house and the rest of her land. They brought enough money to live on the rest of her life. When her cousin came to take her to California, she walked out of the house with only two suitcases and scarcely a backward glance. Miss Lizzie knew she had had it.

And California was wonderful. Her cousins lived in Concord, just outside San Francisco. Their house was warm and pretty, and they were pleasantly attentive. Not too attentive, either. She could come and go as she liked. And Miss Lizzie, who had been known to get lost in Taos, found she could get around out there with no trouble at all. The thing was, there were so many more policemen.

She did slide into things gradually. At first she just went to the supermarket, which was only a block or two away. Then she saw she could range farther afield on the bus that stopped right in front of the supermarket and stopped there again on its way back. And if you got off downtown and didn't know how to get home again, you could just ask one of those nice policemen. He wouldn't just tell you how to get home; he'd *take* you there in his car.

Things got more and more interesting. If you wanted to, you could just stay on the bus and ride for two hours for twenty-five cents, up through Lafayette and Walnut Grove and back again, and get off at the supermarket. Her cousins got so they didn't even worry about her much. There seemed to be lots of policemen.

Emboldened by these successes, she remembered some other cousins in Glendale and went off to visit them, an all-day trip on the train. There were some relatives in Vancouver, too, and Miss Lizzie even went up there, two or three times, to help them pick strawberries.

These trips she made by herself, though of course when she took in the World's Fair in New York, she went with her cousins.

A while ago she jetted in from San Francisco to Albuquerque to visit an old friend, and came up to Taos for a day. Otto said he missed seeing her, but Pat McCarthy saw her.

"Just as full of juice as ever," was the way Pat put it.

And, of course, why not? She was only eighty-seven.

Here in Taos she is still the subject of amused and affectionate remembrance. At least, every time a few people gather at Otto's, somebody is sure to ask, "Now just what was it Miss Lizzie said about the mobile?"

And I will say, Otto always tells it the same way.

Dennis Hopper

There's more than a generation gap between Miss Lizzie and Dennis Hopper. There's about every other kind of gap one can think up. But the contrast only serves to point up the variety of characters Taos has attracted over the years.

The village is full of new people these days—the new left, the fairly far right, and everything in between; the new poor and the comfortably affluent. Everybody notices that if you go to a public event here now, you don't know a fourth of the people you see. And a lot of the newcomers are very attractive. But with the exception of Dennis Hopper, they don't seem to qualify with the colorful figures Taos has been used to seeing around the plaza.

Hopper came here from Los Angeles in 1967 looking for a location for filming *Easy Rider,* in which he starred and which he wrote and directed. The filming took seven weeks, two of them in Taos.

He's been here a lot of the time since, having bought Mabel Luhan's beautiful old house, which he's left in its original state except for hanging the walls with modern paintings (which would have delighted Mabel) along with some of his own "photographic constructions," which he made in the fifties and early sixties. He lives, though, in the "Tony house," a small one nearby, while the big house has stood empty much of the time.

Hopper arrived in Taos at about the time that *Life* magazine published an unfavorable cover story about him in which it accused him of using hard drugs.

"But I went on the Dick Cavett show," he says, "and said I considered it highly irresponsible of the magazine to put me on the cover and report from secondhand sources that I used heroin and other narcotics. I've never used hard drugs. I've smoked marijuana, though, for twenty years."

Does he still smoke it?

"Once in a while," he said, "but mostly I drink, like everybody else in Taos."

Hopper's careless style of dressing, old blue jeans and shirt, long, black straggly hair surmounted by a wide black hat, got him into trouble in his early days here, which coincided with the first invasion of the hippies, who were at the time extremely unpopular with a group of young Spanish-American boys.

"Six of them jumped us [him and his brother David] one night, and I held them off with a gun until the police came. They charged us with assault with a deadly weapon, but they let us out on eight thousand dollars' bail.

141

"So we went around and saw the boys' families and told them that if they pressed charges against us, we'd have to press charges against the boys, too. So they dropped the whole thing.

"That was during that period when there was all that violence here, but it's died down now and we have very good relations with people."

Hopper says he's settled down here. He has opened an art gallery, showing modern art and photographs.

"I love Taos; it's marvelous. I'm going to stay here. This is my home."

After *Easy Rider* he shot a film, *The Last Movie*, in Peru, then came back here to edit it. Writing and editing keep him busy. Twentieth-Century Fox released his film *Kid Blue* in mid-1973.

He is thirty-seven years old. Of his three marriages, the first lasted eight years, the second eight days. On May 14, 1971, he married Daria Halprin of San Francisco, daughter of Lawrence Halprin, city planner, and Anna Halprin, who directs a modern dance workshop in that West Coast city. Daria is a screen actress who starred in Michelangelo Antonioni's film *Zabriski Point*.

Dennis has two daughters, a baby named Ruth and an eleven-year-old, Marin.

His big black hat is his identification badge. He seldom seems to take it off, even at private parties.

17

Taos Observed

Taos knows very little about Mr. Burns's fathers, but in any case he has now been gathered to them. His unkempt, bearded figure no longer enchants newly arrived visitors to the plaza here with the belief that at last they are looking upon a Real Live Old Prospector of the Real Old West.

We always called him Mr. Burns, and we miss him. Local legend hinted that he had been a Harvard man and a classical scholar, who still indulged his tastes for such rich fare as black caviar through the intermittent courtesy of certain faroff affluent relatives. Actually he had followed the prosaic profession of surveyor, but somehow he managed to cast the aura of a broken old prospector. All day, every day, he shuffled about the plaza or huddled precariously against the ledge of a store window. As he sat there, his head drooping forward as if he were looking down his ragged beard to his tattered shoes, he seemed indeed lost in a hopeless and formless regret over something sought for in the mountains and never found.

An old Taos hand tells a fine story about Mr. Burns. It seems the late Miriam Golden, a well-known Taos figure of two decades ago, had agreed to give a public reading of *The Trojan Women*, for which a charge was to be made. Someone, bethinking himself of the old man's reputed interest in the classics and also of the unrelieved dreariness of his days, thought it would be a courtesy to provide him with a complimentary ticket for the event.

Approaching him on the plaza, he made his offer.

Mr. Burns passed a grimy hand across his rheumy eyes.

"I presume," he inquired, "it will be read in the original Greek?"

"Well, no," he was told, "it will be read in translation."

"In that case," said Mr. Burns, "I don't believe I'd be interested."

It is one of the paradoxes of our remote New Mexico village, seven thousand feet up in the Sangre de Cristo Mountains, that while most of its residents lead serious and logical lives and Taos artists may look, and frequently do, like highly successful businessmen or hard-bitten old ranchers, one secret of comfortable life here is a capacity for absorbing the unexpected.

It is this quality which one summer provided us with a popcorn man who used to sit all day in his stand on the plaza, lightening the intervals between customers by reading Thoreau.

This quality in the Taos milieu has resulted in such happenings as one that took place some years ago, when the late Maggie Gusdorf, prominent citizen and daughter of a noted army officer, single-handedly stood off with a shotgun the resident priest at the famous and beautiful church of Saint Francis of Assisi in Ranchos de Taos. The padre had assembled a crew of workmen for the purpose of changing the church's authentic old flat roof for a new pitched one of tin.

This Taos "difference" is seen in such matters as the appearance in *El Crepusculo* of a classified ad bearing the caption, "For Sale—Stolen Wood." An extra *l* appeared in the word "stolen," but it turned out to mean just what we'd thought it meant. One of our citizens had stolen some wood, for which offense he had been apprehended and lodged for some days in the village jail. After his release, still unaccountably in possession of the wood and having, he reasoned, already paid for his peccadillo under highly uncomfortable circumstances, he simply recouped his losses by offering it for sale.

The thought of buying wood of any kind in Taos is a matter of rueful amusement for me, in view of the time I bought some aspen for a *sombra* to shade our back patio from the intense New Mexico sun.

I got in touch with an Indian from the pueblo who said he could supply the small poles.

Aspen poles would be best, I thought.

"Oh, no," he objected. "Aspen no good—aspen get all black and slicky."

"Well, what should I use?" I asked him.

"Fruze, that be the best," he said. "But fruze, that cost more. Fruze harder to get. That cost maybe six dollars more for a load."

I had no idea what fruze might be, and his explanation was vague. But the deal was made. However, unwary in these earlier days of Taos life, I made no point of being at home when the poles arrived. That night, when I saw them, they certainly appeared to be aspen.

"Look," I said the next day when he came for his money, "these look like aspen."

"Aspen, sure," he replied. "They aspen, all right."

"But you said I had to have fruze."

My friend looked blank.

"Fruze?" he said. "Oh, fruze no good. Fruze get all black and slicky."

While Santa Fe refers to its degree of uniqueness by calling itself "the City Different," Taos just trudges along, occasionally startled but usually enjoying, sometimes enduring, and always expecting the unexpected.

Even some major events in community life are infected with this oblique quality—for example, the two bank robbery attempts made here within the recent past.

One of them ended in tragedy for a twenty-two-year-old boy, who made the attempt carrying in his pocket a suicide note to his father. But before its grim denouement was known, it produced a series of comic incidents. For instance, a Taos funeral director bustled into the bank in the midst of the drama, noticed something unusual about the customers frozen in their tracks, and, in his first uninformed moment, inquired loudly, "What's the matter with you people? You look funny."

The other robbery attempt was pure comic opera. For us it was preceded by the arrival at the book shop of two puzzled strangers.

"Perhaps you can tell us," they began. "We've just seen two people on the street wearing funny costumes. Would you have any idea—"

We thought of some of the Taos painters—for instance of Brett, whose fame as a distinguished interpreter of Indian ceremonials and membership in the British nobility do not deter her from wearing a heterogeneous assembly of garments including a Russian-style fur hat bearing something resembling Her Majesty's coat of arms; a long, fur-lined coat to which over the years she has applied leather patches of various shades; a pair of ancient corduroy breeches; and high shoes of brindle cowhide.

"Maybe it was one of the artists . . ." we suggested cautiously.

"Well, no," one of our customers said. "This is different. They seemed to be men wearing women's clothes."

We shook our heads and gave up until, a half-hour later, news drifted up from the plaza of the most bizarre robbery attempt in the history of banking.

A Santa Fe editorial writer described it in the next afternoon's edition of the daily *New Mexican*.

Taos, that most remarkable of towns, has done it again. Somehow our lively neighbor to the north has managed to have a bank robbery attempt with all the hilarity of a Gilbert and Sullivan opera.

Apparently the would-be badmen weren't both residents of the community, which makes the incident all the more remarkable.

It seems just entering the light-hearted town—even with ill intentions—can have infectious results.

Where else, we wonder, would a bank robber don high heels, a fur stole, and Hollywood-style makeup to pull off a deed of derring-do? And where else would bandits become so embarrassed by the attention of curious natives that they would self-consciously throw up their hands and flee from an unaware and unrobbed bank?

And then to put a final slapstick touch to the whole affair, our badmen found themselves being chased wildly down the streets by a minister armed only by righteous indignation.

They finally fired off their pistols at the clergyman, probably in a desperate attempt to get someone at long last to take them seriously.

We contend that had the same set of bungling badmen tried the same deed anywhere else, it wouldn't have been funny. Somebody likely would have been shot.

But at Taos, where Taoseños don't take mundane affairs such as bank robberies very seriously, it was bound to be ridiculous.

Long live Taos and may she never grow old and stodgy.[1]

I am reminded of a passage in Mary McCarthy's discerning and beautiful book, *Venice Observed:* "Everything that happens in Venice has this inherent improbability," she wrote. "It is another world, people say. . . . And it is another world, a palpable fiction, in which the unexpected occurs with regularity; that is why it hovers on the brink of humor." [2]

It interests me to note that unexpectedness in Taos is largely fortuitous. I make an exception, of course, in the case of our female impersonator bank robbers, whose choice of technique was certainly premeditated—advised, if ill-advised. One cannot guess how the two could have been unaware of the ludicrous aspect of their project, unless, as is theorized, they were temporarily disoriented by the influence of Taos Lightning.

I make a different kind of exception in the case of Taos's well-known late doughBelly Price. This ex-cowpuncher, gambler, rodeo hand, and autobiographer, dubbed by *Life* magazine as "low pressure real estate dealer," purposely exploited the interest in incongruity he knew can be found in the general public.[3]

146

"dough," as everyone called him here, was as insistent as e. e. cummings on an unorthodox use of lowercase and uppercase letters in spelling his name—a nickname he found much better suited to his business than the Christian name of Carrell with which his parents had launched him. His office was officially listed as "doughBelly's Clip Joint" and his advertising offered to clip you more thoroughly than could be accomplished by any other dealer you might come across. This technique naturally served to imbue the veriest newcomer with a vast confidence in his reliability in a deal, a naive trust which on the whole seemed at least partly justified. As Richard G. Hubler put it in an introduction to Price's book, *Short Stirrups,* "doughBelly is honest, but not to the point of desperation."

Despite such instances as the two cited above, and whatever has been happening in Venice over the long haul, here in Taos unexpectedness usually sneaks up on us, no matter how well we learn to expect it. But whether or not humorous, whether or not deliberate, it is an undeniable part of life in Taos, where the burglary suspect unhurriedly lets himself out of the county jail on the jailer's night off.

And when Taos is funny, Taos is the first to know it. Caught in a new incongruity, it roars with appreciative laughter. And it is eminently tolerant of the follies of others, having, in Dylan Thomas's words, so many, ripe and piping, of its own.

18

Taosiana

In May one can drive over to Los Cordovas, five miles west, to see the processional honoring San Ysidro, patron of the fields. Out from the church they will carry the carved wooden figure of the saint, with his plough and oxen and the angel behind him. They will hold him up to bless all the lands of the valley, the north, the south, the east and west. Behind him the men will stand and the women, brooding over the fields in a prayerful fertility rite.

You can read about him and the people of Los Cordovas in Joseph Krumgold's magnificent book, *And Now Miguel,* and see him in Krumgold's documentary film by the same name. Both are based on the life here of the Blas Chávez family of sheep ranchers, and chiefly on their boy, Miguel, who was twelve when the book and film were done and wanting to grow up and go with the men to take the sheep to the high meadows of the nearby Picuris range. The film is distributed by New York's Museum of Modern Art, and Lawrence Clark Powell has called it almost unbearably beautiful.

Later Hollywood made a longer film of the same thing, but in this we were all disappointed. They could at least have learned how to pronounce the name Chávez, with the accent on its first syllable, and we resent still more their substitution of the Grand Teton Mountains for our own beautiful Sangre de Cristos, which Miguel could see from his father's ranch.

When the book came out, illustrated by Jean Charlot, it won the Newbery Medal as the year's most distinguished contribution to children's literature. Actually, as is often the case with the best books for children, it appeals to adults even more.

Miguel is grown now, but he doesn't herd sheep, after all. Until recently we saw him whenever we went to the supermarket, where he checked out our groceries.

I wonder sometimes where all the Taos books come from. We are always having to tell people that few writers are working here at any one time. Yet over the past century and a third an amazing bulk of Taosiana has accumulated, if one includes only the literature for which this village is the setting or main theme or is of major import in its action. The town emerges in the forefront of a massive literature on the Southwest and West —on prehistoric times, the waves of Spanish and American conquest, the frontier exploration and trade, the mountain men, the padres.

Of the books that are definitely Taos, four stand at the top as finest and most popular. They are *And Now Miguel*, Frank Waters's *The Man Who Killed the Deer*, Mabel Dodge Luhan's *Winter in Taos*, and Dorothy Benrimo's *Camposantos*. Another of comparable stature but done in such a small edition that it has never seen general circulation is *Taos Pueblo*, whose text was written by Mary Austin to accompany a sheaf of extraordinary photographs by Ansel Adams.

Krumgold came here from the East to do *Miguel* as a documentary film for the State Department to beam at sheep-raising countries such as Iraq. He reworked it into an equally successful book and then turned his attention to other themes.

Waters, on the other hand, has been in and out of Taos for more than thirty-five years and has lived here for long stretches. He has so absorbed the Taos life and scene that he seems, in his two books on the area, to write from inside the people. His first book after he came here, *People of the Valley*, did for the Spanish villages, in terms of Mora, fifty miles away, what he later did for the Taos Indians in *The Man Who Killed the Deer*, dramatizing the motivating forces of their lives as if he had always been a part of them, and describing with understanding and compassion the painful wrench of changing times and thought.

As the northernmost and most isolated of the pueblos, Taos has always been the most resistant to inquiry into its way of life. Elsie Clews Parsons's anthropological study, *Taos Pueblo*, done in the thirties, its publisher once wrote us, so offended the Indians here that its distribution west of the Mississippi River was prohibited. (A new edition has been published by an Eastern reprint house and one wonders what will happen to that.) But Waters's book, *The Man Who Killed the Deer*, has been freely sold and read in Taos, with only minor repercussions.

The Deer is a wonderfully perceptive novel, set in the twenties, in which his protagonist, a young Taos Indian returning from an "away school," works his uncertain way through the problem propounded by the conflict between the old ceremonial ways of his fathers and the new ways of the outside world.

Of Waters's dozen or so books, *The Deer* and *The People* are the finest. Later he wrote a Colorado trilogy, which he has recently condensed into one lengthy novel, *Pike's Peak.* He has also written *The Book of the Hopi; Pumpkin Seed Point,* an account of his life among the Hopi while he was writing about them; and *Masked Gods,* a study of Pueblo and Navajo ceremonialism. He is still here and working busily.

I sometimes find myself thinking of Mabel Luhan as an idle woman. But nobody is idle who has written eleven books (seven of them published), handled an immense volume of correspondence, and entertained in her home any number of notable figures.

Of her four-volume autobiography, *Intimate Memories,* the fourth, *Edge of the Taos Desert,* recorded her arrival and early days here. Later she went on to write *Lorenzo in Taos* (the Lawrence years), *Winter in Taos,* and *Taos and Its Artists.* Except for *Winter* and the art book, which is largely encyclopedic, her books were full of sound and confusion, as most of her life had been. But *Winter in Taos* is a true Taos book, serene and bucolic, telling in simple terms of her life at home with her Indian husband, Tony, of the round of the seasons, the quiet in which she had time and mood to hear the water running in the ditches, the Penitente pito, the doves in their cotes outside her door; time to smell the wild plum blossoms.

The book has long been out of print. But books like *Winter in Taos* are needed; they should, as May Sarton said of Peggy Pond Church's biography of Edith Warner, be sold in drugstores because of their healing quality.

There is a comparable feeling in Dorothy Benrimo's *Camposantos,* a collection of magnificent photographs, taken over thirty years, of old crosses of wood, stone, and metal in the little Spanish cemeteries of northern New Mexico. Their endless variety and consummate grace, their high stature as an art form, are shown for the first time in Dorthy's camera study, supplemented by two explanatory and historical essays by Taos's late Rebecca Salsbury James and E. Boyd, curator of Spanish-Colonial affairs at the Museum of New Mexico.

A whole group of Taos books have circled about D. H. Lawrence, English novelist, essayist, poet, and playwright who lived here for three brief periods in the twenties. There are Brett's two volumes of memoirs, one published years ago, the other still being written. There are Frieda Lawrence's two books of memoirs and correspondence. There is Knud Merrild's account of a winter spent as neighbor to the Lawrences at their ranch near Taos; first published as *A Poet and Two Painters,* it is now in print retitled *With D. H. Lawrence in New Mexico.* There is Lawrence's own small sheaf of Taos writings, essays and poems, most of them collected now in a recently published reprint of his *Phoenix*, with the second volume in print for the first time. A new Lawrence book, a biographical memoir, has been written by Joseph Foster.

But there is no lofty literary theme in a group of Taos books about the always fascinating Manby murder case. Or was it a murder case? And if it was, did somebody kill Manby or did he kill somebody else and leave his victim there in his place (for the body seemed not definitely identifiable)? If you wish to spend an entire Taos evening on one topic of conversation, you need only mention the Manby case. But it is wise to delay the whole matter until after dinner; there is no more unpalatable murder case in the world than this one.

I should be glad to give you at least the bare facts if I or anyone else knew what they were. But any statement I might be so rash as to make would be loudly contradicted by every Taoseño who happened to see it. Perhaps a few things will be firmly established by Frank Waters's book, *To Possess the Land*, due out in the fall of 1973. He has been probing diligently into such records as are available, though some of them seem to have been spirited away.

His will be the first nonfiction account of the lurid affair except for Chapter 7 in Erna Fergusson's book, *Murder and Mystery in New Mexico*, which came out in 1948 to an accompaniment of loud dissent on her theories. But two novels have been based on the case, Frank O'Rourke's *A Texan Came Riding* and another one, *The Man Who Lost His Head*.

It was an apt title, for Manby had literally lost his. Some people say it was found on the mantel, others that it was in the next room. All are agreed that it was not where it should have been—on his neck. The big question, though, was whether it had been neatly snicked off or gnawed off by one of his big police dogs, which was found locked up in the house with the body.

Arthur Manby was an English remittance man: a chap whose family was happy to keep him supplied with an income, so long as he never went home. Manby lived here for thirty years and was an old man when his body was discovered that hot July 3, 1929, by a deputy U.S. marshal who had come to collect from him on a $14,000 breach-of-promise suit he had lost. In Taos he had been hated and both feared and afraid; he had kept his doors and windows locked and bolted, owned five fierce police dogs, and carried a revolver, even in the house.

The Manby story is studded with wild improbabilities: an $827 million trust fund; a bag of diamonds said to have been found under his mattress; membership in a secret society, "The United States Civil and Secret Service, Self-Supporting Branch"; Mexican revolutions controlled from Taos;

crooked mining ventures and mysterious deaths, one of them another de-capitation; Manby's mistress, known to him as "Princess Teresita" (who ap-pears here also in the chapter on witchcraft); sinister signals from airplanes flying over.

Did it all add up to nothing in the end? Did Manby die really of pa-resis, with which he was believed to have been afflicted, and were the wild yarns the result of its accompanying delusions? At least he had made some of them sound plausible enough to extract for his schemes the savings of a number of ostensibly sensible Taos citizens. Did his estate turn out, as was rumored, to consist of a two-dollar bill and a buffalo nickel?

Maybe Waters can establish the facts. But whatever he finds out, he'll have to listen to a lot of arguments for the rest of his life.

As for the coroner's jury, hastily assembled (for five hot days had passed since Manby's death), its finding reduced things to simplicity: death was due to natural causes. And everyone had to admit that it was indeed natural for a man to die if his head had been removed, by whatever means.

Frank Waters wrote another book that turned out to be controversial, as I'm sure he knew it would be, and for quite a different reason. It would be hard to imagine two more completely different books written about the same person than Peggy Pond Church's biography, *The House at Otowi Bridge*, and Frank's novel, *The Woman at Otowi Crossing*. Both centered on Edith Warner, a shy little Pennsylvania schoolteacher who for twenty years lived near the pueblo of San Ildefonso and the atomic city of Los Ala-mos.

Peggy is a native Taoseña now living in Santa Fe. Her father years ago had established at Los Alamos a notable school for boys, for which her hus-band, Fermor S. Church, had long served as headmaster. But with the on-slaught of World War II the government preempted this remote and peaceful spot on its high mesa as a perfect place where in essential secrecy it could develop the atomic bomb.

Miss Warner had come out on vacation and remained to settle natu-rally into the New Mexican scene. To earn her living she had first taken a job as freight agent for the little narrow-gauge railroad (since dismantled). Later she set up a tearoom where Los Alamos scientists, restricted by secu-rity measures to their small area, found they could congregate without fear of making indiscreet disclosures. Edith Warner became their friend and comforting presence, as she had already become for the San Ildefonso Indi-ans.

The Church family had by this time returned to Taos, but not before Peggy had learned to know and to love Miss Warner. And later in writing about this exceptional woman, she was able to sketch in her warm wisdom,

152

her identification with nature, and her amazing two-way communication with the new thing that science was saying and the old thing she felt in her Indian neighbors.

How close Peggy came to a true picture of Edith Warner seems clear to me from her book as seen in conjunction with even one short paragraph from Miss Warner's personal journal:

> On gray days like this I often think of the wild geese flying south. I heard their honking one October day and went out into the gently falling rain to see the swaying black line of them against the gray sky. Soon they entered the canyon and I watched them closely, following against the dark mesa the darker line. Now above, now below the broken mesa rim they flew with never a moment of hesitation, with always the memory of warm, plentiful feeding grounds, and an old trail leading to them. Where the river turns again, they rose above the mesa, and my last glimpse of them was that swaying line against the lighter clouds, winging southward. Death could be like that.

I wonder if she had a prescience of her death as Waters says she had about the bomb. For before we had come to know Peggy well enough even to think of a possible meeting with her friend, Miss Warner was deep in a terminal illness with cancer.

One cannot criticize the Waters novel for the fact that its woman protagonist, though based on Edith Warner, emerged as quite a different figure, for that as a novelist he had intended. But by both his choice of locale and specific circumstance he had identified Miss Warner with his central figure, and it is also true that she did not come through with the same stature. This was a matter of great distress to Edith's friends and resulted in a sharp division of adherence to one book or the other. But I feel myself that as literature, Peggy's *House at Otowi Bridge* does tower over the novel. Frank's reputation as a writer is assured by his other writings, Peggy's by this one book and her poetry, which as yet has had only regional publication. She is working now on a biography of Mary Austin.

The list of books centered on Taos itself goes on and on. Of the Spanish-American people there are several good novels: Robert Bright's *Life and Death of Little Jo;* Joseph Foster's *In the Night Did I Sing; Dayspring,* by Harry Sylvester. Harvey Fergusson's *Grant of Kingdom,* set in the frontier period, told of the marriage of a Taos mountain man to the daughter of a don, a part of whose dowry was the fabulous Maxwell Land Grant, known in the book as the Ballard Grant. Miss Grant's novel, *Doña Lona,* took as its central figure a Taos girl, Doña Tules, who in territorial times hitchhiked to Santa Fe and became a notorious gambling hall proprietress and political figure. Doña Tules also became the protagonist of Ruth Laughlin's novel, *The Wind Leaves No Shadow*.

Lorraine Carr's *Mother of the Smiths* (said to have been a candidate for the Pulitzer Prize) recorded the struggles of an Anglo mother to bring up a brood of children in the harsh Taos economic climate. Frank O'Rourke's *The Man Who Found His Way* followed the fortunes of a conscience-stricken bank robber, whose life was complicated by a Questa witch and decomplicated through the efforts of a Taos witch doctor. O'Rourke also wrote a very popular historical novel, *The Far Mountains*, whose main characters lived through the New Mexico economic, social, and political changes of the first half of the nineteenth century, which brought them to Taos and took them through the Taos Rebellion of 1847. Background for Irwin Blacker's novel, *Taos*, is the 1680 revolt of the Pueblo Indians, fomented here. These are two fine historical novels. But even more distinguished is Elliott Arnold's *The Time of the Gringo*, which, like O'Rourke's book, covers the last thirty years of the area under Mexican rule, ending with the beginning of the American occupation. In both of these books we meet Taos's famous controversial priest, Padre Antonio José Martínez, who figures so prominently in Willa Cather's *Death Comes for the Archbishop*. Padre Martínez is an important character in Arnold's novel, and if one is looking for a balanced portrait of the notorious priest, one comes much closer to it here than in Miss Cather's book.

According to her own memo, she based her novel on the situation as presented in the Reverend W. J. Howlett's *Life of the Right Reverend Joseph P. Machebeuf, D.D.*, which gives the church's view of the rebellious Taos priest against whom it had felt forced to invoke the dread sanction of excommunication. The key to the Cather picture of Padre Martínez is contained in the final sentence of her description: "His mouth was the very assertion of violent, uncurbed passions and tyrannical self-will; the full lips thrust out and taut, like the flesh of animals distended by fear or desire."

This was the man, she said, who held the Santa Fe clergy under his thumb through fear of his power; who lived in a wallow of squalor and immorality, shamelessly admitting to having a common-law wife and five children; who had fomented the bloody rebellions of 1837 and 1847; who had bilked the Taos Indians out of a large tract of land; who openly admitted having broken his vows, defied the order to cease any churchly functions, set up a schismatic church of his own in Taos, and died unrepentant.

This was Padre Martínez as his superiors saw him; but the picture painted by many laymen, Catholic or not, of his time or this, is a different thing. Typical is an unsigned article appearing in 1949 in the Taos weekly

154

newspaper, then called *El Crepusculo*. Here he emerges as "the most out-standing man of his time, a simple boy of Taos, a devout student entering Holy Orders, a parish priest serving his community for over forty-two years, a great educator, a famous politician. . . ."

Yes, the account concedes, he was a controversial rebel and "we may believe what we like about his extracurricular activities," but here he is ab-solved from complicity in the two rebellions and any charge of obtaining Indian land by trickery. What mattered most to laymen was their belief in his pastoral concern for his poor parishioners: his fight for their land rights, for the abolition of heavy fees for conducting marriage, burial, and baptis-mal services; for religious tolerance and the separation of church and state.

Arnold in his novel, *The Time of the Gringo*, recognizes what actually seems to me to have been the case—that the good-bad Taos padre was ex-actly that: that he broke his clerical vows; indulged himself beyond accept-able limits; but at the same time saw some of the evils of his time (igno-rance, superstition, injustice, poverty, political and diocesan indifference to individual need) and did his valiant best to correct them. Some of the other sins attributed to him must remain controversial.

With two exceptions, Miss Cather has used the actual names of historical figures in *Death Comes for the Archbishop*. So five Taos charac-ters can be found: Father Martínez; his associate in rebellion, Father Mari-ano de Jesús Lucero of Arroyo Hondo; Father Martínez's successor, Father Damaso Taladrid; and two Anglo laymen, Kit Carson and trader Ceran St. Vrain. The two high churchmen appear under different names, Archbishop John B. Lamy as Jean Marie Latour and Bishop Joseph P. Machebeuf as Jo-seph Vaillant. Much of the Cather novel was written in Taos.

Padre Martínez takes a prime role in any discussion of Taos writers and writing; it was he who began it all with a little orthography, written of course in Spanish, and printed in Santa Fe in 1834.

Douglas C. McMurtrie, one of the top historians on the subject of early American imprints, is one of the authorities establishing Martínez's authorship of the first book written in Taos. In 1929 McMurtrie published in Chicago 120 copies of *The First Printing in Taos*, a facsimile edition of the little orthography to which he appended a commentary. Here, however, he definitely demolished the often-heard claim that the padre turned out in 1834 the first imprint to appear west of the Mississippi. Martínez, he points out, would not have sent his little textbook manuscript to Santa Fe to be printed if he had had a press of his own in Taos. Actually, it appears from other sources, the honor for the first trans-Mississippi printing must go to two St. Louis imprints dated 1808.

Another claim in general circulation in New Mexico, that Padre Martínez turned out in either Santa Fe or Taos four issues of a weekly newspaper called *El Crepusculo de la Libertad,* may turn out to be a myth. The point is being investigated by Jack Rittenhouse of the University of New Mexico Press. No one, so far as is known, has ever set eyes on a copy of the newspaper.

It is known that in 1834 Ramón Abreu set up in Santa Fe the first press to operate in New Mexico, though no one seems to know where he obtained it. It is also known that "about 1837," Padre Martínez bought the press and brought it to Taos, where he began the printing of textbooks for his school for children and manuals for young men studying for the priesthood in his Taos seminary.

In 1968 one of these manuals printed here in 1839 was found in the Taos area and came into our possession. It was bound in rawhide and tied with thongs, and went to a delighted collector of Taosiana.

The writing activity that the Taos priest initiated has gone on in one form or another since his day, though a great deal of it is out of print and nearly forgotten. Such is the case, for instance, with Maxwell Anderson's dark drama, *Night Over Taos,* which once had a week's run in New York. It concerns the last twenty-four hours in which the Taos dons finally faced the grim truth that U.S. domination over New Mexico was inevitable.

The most prolific in writing Taos history was Blanche C. Grant. And whatever the other writers here at the time thought of her works, they came later to pick up considerable prestige as Southwestern Americana. She wrote the only full-scale history of the place, under the title *When Old Trails Were New,* along with three little paper-covered studies, which she published privately: *One Hundred Years Ago in Old Taos, Taos Today,* and *Taos Indians.* And she provided the first publication of *Kit Carson's Own Story of His Life.*

A considerable volume of writing has built up over the years around that doughty Taos Indian agent, scout, and army guide, beginning with Dewitt C. Peters's biography, *Kit Carson's Life and Adventures, from Facts Narrated by Himself,* and still continuing. Latest biographies are Marion Estergreen's *Kit Carson: A Portrait in Courage,* which came out a few years ago, and a new one by Harvey L. Carter called '*Dear Old Kit*': *The Historical Christopher Carson.* Marion's is a good sound job of writing and especially useful because of her patient hunting down of new documentary material. '*Dear Old Kit,*' however, purports to make important corrections in all previous Carson accounts.

Carson, who had dictated to Peters a short statement on his life, considered the resultant book rather "too prettied up." But he did nothing himself with the transcript of his statement. It remained in Peters's posses-

156

sion and later in that of the latter's son William, an impecunious poet who ultimately died in Paris. Found in his trunk, it was brought back to the United States by his brother Clinton, who had two typed copies made. The original manuscript went finally to the Newberry Library in Chicago, but Blanche Grant obtained one of the typed copies from Charles L. Camp of Berkeley, who had published some long excerpts in the *California Historical Society Quarterly*. Miss Grant published the complete work at Taos in 1926.

At the time of her death about two years after our arrival in Taos this item was believed to be out of print and scarce, and one copy, in a blue silk slipcase, was said to have sold in New York at $32.50. But after her death her sister found tucked away in her studio a hundred or so copies of each of her paper-bound items, which we sold to a Denver dealer. Now all are again out of print, except for the Carson work, which is available in two paper-bound editions and one cloth.

One maverick in the Carson literature is a book entitled *Thirty-one Years on the Plains and in the Mountains*, by William F. Drannan, an old western roustabout who claimed to have been adopted by Kit and taken about with him in his travels. The book has long since been heartily debunked by historians, a fact which seems to have no effect on its fans, most of them men who read it as boys, remember it with delight, and will pay any necessary price whenever we can turn up a copy.

Our first experience with this book came early in the life of the book shop, when a cowboy came in with his wife, spotted the title, and pounced on it eagerly.

"I'd come a thousand miles to get this book!" he exclaimed, hastily producing the seven dollars at which the copy was then selling. But his wife took one disgusted look and put up a vigorous protest. Seven whole dollars for that book! For any book, for that matter! After a feeble defense, the cowboy followed her out, empty-handed. But he slunk back in alone the next morning and bought the book.

Mrs. Estergreen, incidentally, has turned her attention now to another local frontier figure and is writing a biography of Lucien Maxwell, of Maxwell Land Grant fame.

Joseph Foster has been living and writing here for many years. Besides his work on Lawrence, previously mentioned, he has produced a book on Montezuma and four novels on the Southwest's Spanish Americans. One of these, *Street of the Barefoot Lovers*, has been sold to Hollywood. Joe recently worked closely with a television man whose film on Lawrence was done for the British Broadcasting Corporation.

Another movie based on a book by a Taos writer is Max Evans's *The*

Rounders, a film which drew considerable national attention as a superior comic western. Max, though still a young man, is an experienced ranch and rodeo hand and gambler. He is so much of an extrovert that nobody thought he could sit still long enough to write even one book. But he has sat long enough to write six and is still going strong. Early in his work he did a biography, *Long John Dunn of Taos,* of our late and locally famous gambler, stage driver, and admitted rascal, but his other work has dealt with cowboy themes in fiction.

The list of Taos books seems endless. Among books about the Indians is Elsie Clews Parsons's collection of folklore, *Taos Tales,* which supplemented her general book on the pueblo. And there is the whole bulk of work done by John Collier, Sr., ending with his autobiography, *From Every Zenith,* written here during the last years before his death at the age of eighty-four. Probably his greatest work is *Patterns and Ceremonials of the Indians of the Southwest,* reprinted under the title *On the Gleaming Way.*

Murder mysteries with Taos settings have been written by Frances Crane and Frederick Brown, both of whom worked here for several years. Eric Sloane's *Return to Taos* is an account of his revisit after thirty years' absence.

The art movement in Taos has accounted for several books: Mabel Luhan's *Taos and Its Artists;* Laura Bickerstaff's *Pioneer Artists of Taos;* Van Deren Coke's *Taos and Santa Fe; Patrocinio Barela: Taos Wood Carver,* by Mildred Crews, Wendell Anderson, and Judson Crews; Frank Waters's *Leon Gaspard;* Harold McCracken's *Nicolai Fechin;* Eric Gibberd's *The Paintings of Gibberd;* Jerry Baywaters's *Andrew Dasburg;* and Doel Reed's *Doel Reed Makes an Aquatint.* Bainbridge Bunting's *Taos Adobes* is an important architectural record of classic Taos houses, complete with text, photographs, and drawings.

Where does one stop in drawing together Taos books, after one has gone back to mention doughBelly's autobiography, *Short Stirrups,* Becky James's book on village characters, *Allow Me to Present 18 Ladies and Gentlemen,* and that famous classic of the mid-1800s, Garrard's *Wah-to-Yah and the Taos Trail?* And how does one keep track of the new books coming out, like *Hollering Sun* by Nancy and Myron Wood?

There are still the juveniles, some on Taos, by Barbara Latham, Gisella Loeffler, Ann Nolan Clark, Barbara Harmon, Ila McAfee, and Marcia Keegan.

There are highly specialized works, for instance, two studies of Taos economics: *Forgotten People* by George I. Sánchez and *It Happened in*

Taos by J. T. Reid. There are lengthy monographs on the geology of this immediate area and several on archaeological digs. Polly Schaafsma's *Rock Art in New Mexico* is a publication of the New Mexico State Planning Department.

And finally there are the people who have used this village as a fine place to hole up in and write on themes far afield.

Victor White over a period of ten years wrote a tetralogy around a character named Peter Domanig, whom he brought from Vienna to Santa Fe. The most successful of the series was subtitled *Morning in Vienna*, a distinguished novel in the great European tradition. Others who have written here for several years at a time are Myron Brinig, Walt Sheldon, Richard G. Hubler, and Robert Wilder, with Edward Abbey and William Goyen here for shorter periods.

Working here for long annual stretches is Helen Hoover, writing nature material. Her latest book is *The Years of the Forest*. Her husband, Adrian Hoover, furnishes illustrations.

Others are settling in to stay: Cecil Dawkins, author of the novel *The Live Goat;* John Nichols, known for *The Sterile Cuckoo;* and Dr. Paul B. Sears, professor emeritus of ecology at Yale University, who has written a number of books in that field, such as *Deserts on the March*. Writing in a different vein is Dr. Charlotte I. Lee of the Oral Interpretation Department of Northwestern University, author of several texts in her field for high schools and colleges.

You wouldn't think we need another Taos book. But if you notice, no one before has really tried to pull the whole scene together, to show the pattern of the mosaic in all its colors. If I have approached the matter with at least a minor degree of trepidation, it's because of an old saying: If you want to write about Taos, you should do it during your first two weeks here; after that you don't know enough about it.

19

Piñon Smoke

After a little spell of chill rain, touched up with a few growls of thunder and an hour or so of spitting hail, the finest kind of Indian summer came this year and lingered. One could imagine that the earth, as well pleased as we with the rich effect it had achieved, had decided to arrest its turning for a few weeks to allow full admiration of an incredible Taos compound: burnished sun, turquoise sky, heady air, mild wind, reddish gold cottonwoods, yellow aspen, the small furtive sounds of dry leaves skittering across the bare ground, and the first faint autumn whiff of piñon smoke. . . .

"No man," Kit Carson is supposed to have said, "who has seen the women, heard the bells, or smelled the piñon smoke of Taos will ever be able to leave."

Carson's wife, a native of Taos, would seem to have borne out his opinion of the women of this New Mexican village a century ago, for though in a lifetime as trapper and government scout, guide, and Indian agent, he apparently could spend little time with his señora in the adobe house which still stands across the street from our book shop, her beauty has been duly noted in the records of that day.

Certainly she made an immediate though involuntary conquest of seventeen-year-old Lewis H. Garrard, who came out of Missouri in the caravan of a Taos trader and arrived here in 1847 just in time to attend the trial and execution of the murderers of Governor Charles Bent. In *Wah-to-Yah and the Taos Trial* he describes Mrs. Carson, who as an eyewitness to the massacre had been called upon to testify at the trial.

"The wife of the renowned mountaineer Kit Carson was also in attendance," Garrard wrote. "Her style of beauty was of the haughty, heart-breaking kind—such as would lead a man, with a glance of her eye, to risk his life for one smile. I could not but desire her acquaintance." [1]

Garrard's desire was frustrated. He left soon after, with no further reference to the glamorous Taoseña.

The women of Taos today have not, so far as I know, been the subject of special comment. Nor are the bells now of particular moment, doubtless because there are fewer of them and because they are not, as tradition reports of the bells of the early missions, cast of an alloy containing silver and gold jewelry melted up in sacrifice by the church's devoted followers. But Taos fragrances have lost none of their haunting charm.

My earliest sharp memory of the book shop, after we had brought it from its first small spot on the plaza to this famous old adobe building, was of a wonderful odor which greeted us there on the first winter morning.

"Gray cedar," said Johnny Romero. And there on the top of the old "Warm Morning" coal stove were the ashes of the grayish green twig whose aroma lingered throughout the day. Even many Taoseños do not, until they come into the shop, seem to know the oriental fragrance of gray cedar, which Johnny picked for us on his walk in from the pueblo.

Nor do many know of the smell of the burning oshá root, which Mabel Luhan celebrates in *Winter in Taos*—a versatile New Mexican herb credited with being a cure for afflictions ranging from fevers to snakebites.

These odors, like many other Taos pleasures, are things one comes upon gradually. But others are offered to the newest arrival. There is the herbal smell of sagebrush under the wet snow or rain, or crushed in the hand, the memory of which can induce a deep nostalgia in the farthest wanderer who has ever known Taos. There is the spring gift of the wild plum blossom's pungent fragrance. This follows by a few weeks that memorable day when the pueblo's religious leader, the cacique, has noted that the sun has reached its appointed notch in the mountains, and the pregonero, the crier, has from the housetop announced that the day has come to open the ditches and let the cherished mountain water flow down through the fields.

But a special mark and blessing of Taos is the smell of piñon smoke, which in winter pervades the valley.

Its prevalence is due to the number of small Indian fireplaces with which Taos houses are so generously furnished. For continuous heating purposes, stoves burning oil or gas are used, with a few furnaces. Yet the primitive appeal of these hospitable corner adobe hearths and the strength of the warmth they give out are so happily a part of Taos life that still, as in the first old houses, you will find them in nearly every room.

And for this use, besides its celestial fragrance, piñon is a perfect fuel.

If dry, it will ignite when you hold a match to a resinous spot. Unlike cedar, which also grows here but is given to snapping and shooting out showers of sparks, piñon heartwood burns for a long time with intense and steady heat.

The piñon, dwarfed, long-needled evergreen denizen of the slopes and some of the mesas, is a doubly generous tree. For it bears the delectable piñon nut, which seems to appear in few other parts of the country.

Two years ago the piñon nuts, for which traditionally there is a crop only once in seven years, were to be found in abundance and the slopes of the foothills were alive with seekers for these succulent morsels.

Luckily the party of five which I joined one day in September included Corina Santistevan, who, as native to these parts, knew the proper technique. So we were not misled by recent state newspaper accounts of what the knowledgeable piñon nut hunter does, nor by the sight of people beating the branches with sticks to knock the nuts down onto blankets spread on the ground.

Equipped only with small baskets, we took to the slopes that build up to the Picuris range and crawled about under the low trees, retrieving the glossy, deep-brown nuts that had fallen in their own good time. It really meant picking them up one by one, and since they are tiny and lie among the fallen needles of other years, it was not a rapid process.

Long familiarity, we could see, would speed up the work and enable one to decide more quickly which was a good nut and which was a bad one, likely to hold only a worm or air and disappointment. It was a matter of depth and shade of color, and we learned from Corina to avoid the shell with a lackluster tone of light brown.

After two hours the rest of us had gathered less than a quart apiece and had acquired a high degree of respect for the suppliers of that elderly gentleman who in summer sits all day in his wheel chair on the plaza selling piñon nuts to passersby.

There is no more tasty nut in the world, but he who enjoys one has earned it. After he has brought it home from the hills, he has made only the merest start toward his ultimate goal. Next it must be roasted. And then it must be shelled.

There are only two ways of shelling a piñon nut. One is by a machine. So far as I know, there is only one in the area, invented and owned by an Albuquerque confectioner, who refuses to sell his shelled nuts, preferring to add their ineffable flavor to his candies. The other way is by an ingenious method of mastication. The nuts enter your mouth at one side and undergo a sort of cement-mixer technique, after which the soft shells, mysteriously separated from the meat in the process, are deftly ejected from the other side of the mouth, while the meat itself is swallowed.

Just as only a Cornishwoman can make a meat pasty, so only a native New Mexican (and that man in Albuquerque) can shell piñon nuts. The result is that after you have brought home a pailful, you are still in the position of a sailor adrift on a raft stocked to the edges with canned food, yet unfortunately lacking a can opener.

But though the generous piñon tree reserves its fruit for the initiated, the warmth and fragrance that its trunk and its branches can give are bestowed upon all in Taos.

In this high village all five senses are nourished with special foods. For the eye, the great skyline of the Sangre de Cristo Mountains or the design created by long, slanting shadows of vigas upon the outside wall. For the ear, the drums' throbbing, the chanting, the soft murmur of Spanish and Tiwa tongues mingling with harsh Anglo-Saxon under the portales around the plaza; perhaps occasionally still to be heard out on the mesa or in the foothills the weird strain of the Penitente pipe, the pito, during Holy Week; and the merry, sour tune of the mariachis' fiddles during summer fiesta. Let the fingers feel the rough perfection of the old Navajo blanket on the earth bench by the fireplace, and the earth paint, tierra bayeta, on the wall. As for the taste, if not the piñon nut or the seldom obtainable wonderful coarse Indian bread, then the *pozole, sopaipilla, chalupa.*

But of all these, only the skyline can haunt you as does the piñon smoke of Taos.

These last few days the earth, apparently satisfied with having staged the year's finest show, seems to have resumed its dutiful turning. From the deep, recessed windows of our old house we look out across the muted russet tones of the Talpa Valley to Picuris Mountain, where in summer the sheep and their herders go to the high meadows. But today, summer and autumn having lapsed into November, early snows dapple the mountain's scarred flanks; cold clouds hang low in the crevasses.

We are ready for winter. The piñon wood is piled high along the stone wall, and its smoke from the little fireplace beside me as I write drifts along the ridge and blends with that of a hundred other small fireplaces to sweeten the valley air. With slow and pleased acceptance, Taos drifts into winter.

163

Notes

Chapter 1

1. Mabel Dodge Luhan, "Holiday from Science?" *Southwest Review* 31, no. 3 (Summer 1946): 223.

Chapter 2

1. Specialists in Indian prehistory are understandably vague on this point. But John Collier, for one, places the migration "at a date so far back that the long extinct horse and camel, the giant beaver and giant bear, the four-horned antelope and the dire wolf and mammoth were their foes and their prey. . . . The time of their coming was within the Pleistocene or glacial epoch. Most archaeologists believe it was near the close of the last glacial period, somewhere between fifteen and twenty thousand years ago." John Collier, *The Indians of the Americas*, p. 30.
2. Mary Austin, *The Land of Journey's Ending.*
3. Mary Austin and Ansel Adams, *Taos Pueblo*, p. 2.
4. Mabel Dodge Luhan, *Taos and Its Artists*, p. 11.

Chapter 3

1. Mary Austin and Ansel Adams, *Taos Pueblo*, p. 4.

Chapter 4

1. Emily Dickinson, *The Poems of Emily Dickinson*, Martha Dickinson Bianchi and Alfred Leete Hampson, eds., p. 2.

Chapter 5

1. Louis H. Warner, "Wills and Hijuelas," *New Mexico Historical Review* 7 (January 1932): 75–89.

2. William A. Keleher, "Law of the New Mexico Land Grant," *New Mexico Historical Review* 4 (October 1929): 350–71.

3. In a September 1973 study, *Thomas Benton Catron and His Era*, Victor Westphall writes, "The Santa Fe Ring had no fixed membership or formal organization." It consisted of Republican leaders and Westphall believes application of the term "Ring" was politically motivated. The connotation of violence, deception, fraud, and other nefarious implications gave the land speculators associated with it in the popular mind a sinister reputation, which was in some cases far from deserved, Westphall believes (see pp. 98 and 99).

4. Victor Westphall, *The Public Domain in New Mexico 1854–1891*, p. 49.

5. See, however, note 7 in connection with the Tierra Amarilla grant.

6. Michael Jenkinson, *Tijerina: Land Grant Conflict in New Mexico*, p. 44.

7. Myra E. Jenkins to author. The attorney referred to was Thomas B. Catron of Santa Fe, said to have become the largest landholder in U.S. history. Westphall (p. 48 of *Thomas Benton Catron and His Era*) observes: "It has been popularly supposed that Catron virtually stole much of the land that he acquired in the form of land grants. This is not substantiated in the case of Tierra Amarilla. Land grants were sold for minimal amounts in the 1860s and the first few years of the 1870s, but prospective sellers seem to have realized the potential value of property by the middle 1870s. Persons initially satisfied with the price they received later thought they had been bilked when the economy of the territory became more affluent and the price of land increased."

8. Herbert O. Brayer, *William Blackmore: The Spanish-Mexican Land Grants of New Mexico and Colorado 1863–1878*, pp. 313, 313n33, 322, 330.

9. Keleher, "Law of the New Mexico Land Grant."

10. Myra E. Jenkins to author.

11. Margaret Meaders to author.

12. White, Koch, Kelly and McCarthy, Attorneys at Law, *Land Title Study*.

13. Myra E. Jenkins to author.

Chapter 6

1. Father Cuesta to author.

2. For information relating to the general background of Taos poverty problems, the author is indebted to Mary Alexander, County Director of the Social Service Agency, Public Welfare Department.

3. Edward Abbey, "Let Us Now Praise Mountain Lions," *Life* (March 13, 1970), pp. 52B ff.

4. Rudyard Kipling, "Namgay Doola," in *My Own People* (New York: United States Book Co., 1891).

Chapter 7

1. Mary Austin and Ansel Adams, *Taos Pueblo*, p. 2.

Chapter 8

1. L. Bradford Prince, *Historical Sketches of New Mexico, From the Earliest Records to the American Occupation* (New York: Leggat Brothers, 1883), p. 288.
2. For all official reports concerning this insurrection, see U.S., Congress, Senate, *Insurrection against the Military Government in New Mexico and California, 1847 and 1848*, Sen. Doc. No. 442, 56th Cong., 1st Sess.
3. Lewis H. Garrard, *Wah-to-Yah and the Taos Trail*.

Chapter 9

1. Elsie Clews Parsons, *Taos Pueblo*.
2. Parsons writes, "I have also to thank Dr. Aurelio M. Espinosa for a fragment of the Emergence myth which throws light on ritual and ceremonial organization" (*Taos Pueblo*, p. 6). This material, as paraphrased in English and told to Dr. Espinosa, is repeated by Parsons on p. 113 of *Taos Pueblo*.
3. John Collier, *On the Gleaming Way*.
4. Ibid.

Chapter 10

1. Weston La Barre notes, "In the early 1930s Parsons was dubious about any wider spread of peyotism at Taos, but it has since flourished, cult members increasing from about 130 in 1936 to approximately 300 in 1960, out of a total of some 900" (*The Peyote Cult*, p. 213). But I believe that a more accurate estimate (closer to 50 now) is given by a highly knowledgeable Taoseño who, because of close ties with the pueblo, will not consent to be identified with even so minor a piece of information.
2. Elsie Clews Parsons, *Taos Pueblo*.
3. G. MacGregor, aided by Oliver La Farge, "Peyote and the Native American Church of the United States," *Indian Affairs* 41A, Supplement (1961), newsletter of the American Indian Fund and the Association on American Indian Affairs.

Chapter 11

1. D. J. Flynn, "Holy Week with the Penitentes," *Harper's Weekly* (May 26, 1894): 489–90.
2. This evaluation of materials was made by Mills and Grove in a 1966 revision of their work, *Lucifer and the Crucifer: The Enigma of the Penitentes*, pp. 6 ff.

3. Lorayne Horka-Follick, *Los Hermanos Penitentes: A Vestige of Medievalism in Southwestern United States*, p. 203.

4. "Los Hermanos Penitentes," *El Palacio* 8, no. 1 (January 31, 1920): 5.

5. Santa Fe *New Mexican*, January 29, 1947.

6. "Los Hermanos Penitentes," pp. 6, 7.

7. First published in *La Hermandad* 1 (April 1899), Pueblo, Colorado. Republished by the Taylor Museum, Colorado Springs Fine Arts Center, in a brochure at the time of a summer-fall exhibition in 1955.

8. Alice Corbin Henderson, *Brothers of Light*, pp. 21–22, 35.

9. Charles F. Lummis, *Land of Poco Tiempo*, p. 92.

10. Harvey Fergusson, *Rio Grande*, pp. 121–22.

11. Clinton E. Brooks and Frank D. Reeve, eds., "James A. Bennett: A Dragoon in New Mexico 1850–1856," *New Mexico Historical Review* 22 (January 1947): 51–97.

12. Reverend J. M. Roberts, "Home Mission Letter to Children," *Rocky Mountain Presbyterian*, Denver, 7 (December 1878): 12.

13. Mills and Grove, *Lucifer and the Crucifer*, p. 116.

Chapter 12

1. The late Dr. R. D. Jameson of New Mexico Highlands University.

2. Meldrum K. Wylder, *Rio Grande Medicine Man*, p. 111.

3. Elsie Clews Parsons, *Taos Pueblo*, pp. 60–62.

4. Information on "the Frog Man of Mora" case came from Justice of the Peace Vincent Romero, who held the hearing, and his niece, Mrs. Adelina Rudolph, who also heard the testimony. Their account agreed essentially with details of news stories published December 30, 1939, in the Las Vegas (New Mexico) *Daily Optic* and the Santa Fe *New Mexican*.

5. "Witchcraft in New Mexico," *Journal of American Folk-Lore* 1, no. 2 (July–September 1888): 167–68.

6. Adolph F. Bandelier, *Final Report of Investigations among the Indians of the Southwestern United States*, p. 35.

7. Watson Smith and John M. Roberts, *Zuni Law: A Field of Values*, p. 49.

8. Frank Hamilton Cushing, *My Adventures in Zuni*.

9. Smith and Roberts, *Zuni Law*, pp. 41–42.

10. T. F. Ealy in *Annual Report of the Commissioner of Indian Affairs to the Secretary of the Interior for the Year 1880*, p. 135.

11. Irving Telling, "New Mexican Frontiers: A Social History of the Gallup Area 1881–1901" (Ph.D. diss., Harvard University, 1952), pp. 131–34.

12. Elsie Clews Parsons, "Witchcraft among the Pueblos: Indian or Spanish?" *Man* 27 (1927): 108–9.

13. Ruth L. Bunzel, *Introduction to Zuni Ceremonialism*, p. 479.

14. L.S.M. Curtin, *Healing Herbs of the Upper Rio Grande*, pp. 64–65.

15. Blanche Grant, *When Old Trails Were New*, p. 273.

Chapter 14

1. Thornton Wilder to author.
2. Mary Austin, *Taos Pueblo*, pp. 5–6.
3. Erich Neumann, *The Great Mother*, p. 129.
4. A. Alvarez, "A Portrait of Frieda," radio script for the BBC, 1961.
5. Ibid.

Chapter 15

1. Dorothy Parker, "A Pig's-Eye View of Literature," in *Sunset Gun*, p. 31.
2. D. H. Lawrence, "New Mexico," *Survey Graphic* (May 1931), reprinted in *Phoenix: The Posthumous Papers of D. H. Lawrence*, vol. 1, pp. 141–47.
3. D. H. Lawrence, "Taos," *Dial* (March 1923), reprinted in *Phoenix: The Posthumous Papers of D. H. Lawrence*, vol. 1, pp. 100–103.

Chapter 17

1. Santa Fe *New Mexican*, November 13, 1957.
2. Mary McCarthy, *Venice Observed*, p. 25.
3. "Low-Pressure Salesman," *Life* 27 (October 3, 1949): 85–86.

Chapter 19

1. Lewis H. Garrard, *Wah-to-Yah and the Taos Trail*, p. 208.

Bibliography

Abbey, Edward. *Desert Solitaire: A Season in the Wilderness*. New York: McGraw-Hill Book Company, 1968.

Amsden, Charles Avery. *Prehistoric Southwesterners from Basketmaker to Pueblo*. Los Angeles: Southwest Museum, 1949.

Anderson, Maxwell. *Night Over Taos*. New York: Samuel French, Inc., 1932.

Arnold, Elliott. *The Time of the Gringo*. New York: Alfred A. Knopf, Inc., 1953.

Austin, Mary. *The Land of Journey's Ending*. London: George Allen and Unwin, 1924.

—— and Ansel Adams. *Toas Pueblo*. San Francisco: Grabhorn Press, 1930.

Ayer, Mrs. Edward E., trans. *The Memorial of Fray Alonso de Benavides*. Chicago: privately printed, 1916.

Baldwin, Brewster and Frank E. Kottlowski. *Santa Fe, New Mexico*. Scenic Trips to Geologic Past no. 1. 2d ed. Socorro, N.M.: New Mexico Bureau of Mines and Mineral Resources, 1968.

Bancroft, Hubert H. *History of Arizona and New Mexico*. San Francisco: The History Co., 1889.

Bandelier, Adolph F. *Final Report of Investigations among the Indians of the Southwestern United States, Carried on Mainly in the Years from 1880 to 1885*. Papers of the Archaeological Institute of America, vol. 3–4, 1890.

—— and Edgar L. Hewett. *Indians of the Rio Grande Valley*. Albuquerque: University of New Mexico Press, 1937.

Benedict, Ruth. *Zuni Mythology*. 2 vols. New York: Columbia University Press, 1935.

Benrimo, Dorothy. *Camposantos*. Photographic essay with commentary by Rebecca Salsbury James and historical notes by E. Boyd. Fort Worth, Tex.: Amon Carter Museum of Western Art, 1966.

Bickerstaff, Laura. *Pioneer Artists of Tcos*. Denver: Sage Books, 1955.

Blacker, Irwin R. *Taos*. Cleveland: The World Publishing Company, 1959.

Boyd, E. "The New Mexico Santero." *El Palacio* 76 (1969): 1–24.

——. *Saints and Saint Makers of New Mexico*. Sante Fe: Laboratory of Anthropology, 1946.

Brayer, Herbert O. *William Blackmore: The Spanish-Mexican Land Grants of New Mexico and Colorado 1863–1878*. Denver: Bradford-Robinson, 1949.

Brett, Dorothy. "Autobiography: My Long and Beautiful Journey." *South Dakota Review* 5, no. 2 (Summer 1967): 11–71.

————. *Lawrence and Brett, A Friendship*. Philadelphia: J. B. Lippincott Co., 1933.

Bright, Robert. *The Life and Death of Little Jo*. Garden City, N.Y.: Doubleday, Doran & Co., Inc., 1944.

Bunting, Bainbridge. *Taos Adobes: Spanish Colonial and Territorial Architecture of the Taos Valley*. Fort Burgwin Research Center Publication no. 2. Santa Fe: Museum of New Mexico Press, 1964.

Bunzel, Ruth L. *Introduction to Zuni Ceremonialism. Forty-Seventh Annual Report to the Bureau of American Ethnology*, pp. 467–544. Washington, D.C.: U.S. Government Printing Office, 1932.

Bywaters, Jerry. *Andrew Dasburg*. New York: American Federation of Arts, 1959.

Carr, Lorraine. *Mother of the Smiths*. New York: The Macmillan Company, 1940.

Carter, Harvey L. *'Dear Old Kit': The Historical Christopher Carson*. Norman: University of Oklahoma Press, 1968.

Cather, Willa. *Death Comes for the Archbishop*. New York: Alfred A. Knopf, Inc., 1927.

Christiansen, Paige W. and Frank E. Kottlowski. *Mosaic of New Mexico's Scenery, Rocks and History*. Pamphlet no. 8. Socorro, N.M.: New Mexico State Bureau of Mines and Mineral Resources, 1967.

Church, Peggy Pond. *The House at Otowi Bridge*. Albuquerque: University of New Mexico Press, 1960.

Coke, Van Deren. *Taos and Santa Fe: The Artist's Environment 1882–1942*. Albuquerque: University of New Mexico Press, 1963.

Collier, John. *The Indians of the Americas*. New York: W. W. Norton & Company, Inc., 1947.

————. *On the Gleaming Way*. The Swallow Press, Inc., 1949.

Condit, Lester D., ed. *Check List of New Mexico Imprints and Publications 1784–1876*. Historical Records Survey, American Imprints Inventory. New York: Kraus Reprint Corp., 1964.

Corke, Helen. *D. H. Lawrence: The Croydon Years*. Austin: University of Texas Press, 1965.

Cowan, James C., ed. *D. H. Lawrence's American Journey*. Cleveland: The Press of Case Western Reserve University, 1970.

Crews, Mildred, Wendell Anderson, and Judson Crews. *Patrocinio Barela: Taos Wood Carver*. Taos, N.M.: Taos Recordings and Publications, 1962.

Curtin, L.S.M. *Healing Herbs of the Upper Rio Grande*. Reprint. Los Angeles: Southwest Museum, 1965.

Cushing, Frank Hamilton. *My Adventures in Zuni*. Santa Fe: Rydal Press, 1941.

————. *Outlines of Zuni Creation Myths. Thirteenth Annual Report of the Bureau of American Ethnology*, pp. 321–447. Washington, D.C.: U.S. Government Printing Office, 1896.

————. *Zuni Breadstuff*. Indian Notes and Monographs, vol. 8. New York: Museum of the American Indian, Heye Foundation, 1920.

————. *Zuni Folk Tales*. Reprint. New York: Alfred A. Knopf, Inc.., 1931.

Díaz, Albert James. *A Guide to the Microfilm of Papers Relating to New Mexico Land Grants*. Albuquerque: University of New Mexico Press, 1960.

Díaz-Plaja, Fernando. *The Spaniard and the Seven Deadly Sins*. New York: Charles Scribner's Sons, 1967.

Drannan, William F. *Thirty-one Years on the Plains and in the Mountains; Or the Last Voice from the Plains*. Chicago: Rhodes and McClure Publishing Co., 1900.

Dustin, C. Burton. *Peyotism and New Mexico*. Farmington, N.M.: privately printed, 1960.

Dutton, Bertha P. *Sun Father's Way*. Albuquerque: University of New Mexico Press, 1963.

Ealy, T. F. Untitled letter. In *Annual Report of the Commissioner of Indian Affairs to the Secretary of the Interior for the Year 1880*, pp. 134–35. Washington, D.C.: U.S. Government Printing Office, 1880.

Estergreen, M. Morgan. *Kit Carson: A Portrait in Courage*. Norman: University of Oklahoma Press, 1962.

Evans, Max. *Long John Dunn of Taos*. Los Angeles: Westernlore Press, 1959.

——. *The Rounders*. New York: The Macmillan Company, 1960.

Fechin, Alexandra. *March of the Past*. Santa Fe: Rydal Press, 1937.

Fergusson, Erna. *Murder and Mystery in New Mexico*. Albuquerque: Merle Armitage, 1948.

Fergusson, Harvey. *Grant of Kingdom*. New York: William Morrow & Co., Inc., 1950.

——. *Rio Grande*. New York: William Morrow & Co., Inc., 1931.

Fewkes, J. Walter. *Tusayan Katcinas. Fifteenth Annual Report of the Bureau of American Ethnology*, pp. 245–313. Washington, D.C.: U.S. Government Printing Office, 1897.

——. *Two Summers' Work in Pueblo Ruins. Twenty-Second Annual Report of the Bureau of American Ethnology*, part 1, pp. 3–195. Washington, D.C.: U.S. Government Printing Office, 1904.

Flynn, D. J. "Holy Week with the Penitentes." *Harper's Weekly: A Journal of Civilization* (May 26, 1894): 489–90.

Foster, Joseph. *D. H. Lawrence in Taos*. Albuquerque: University of New Mexico Press, 1972.

——. *The Great Montezuma*. Ranchos de Taos, N.M.: Ranchos Press, 1945.

——. *In the Night Did I Sing*. New York: Charles Scribner's Sons, 1942.

——. *Street of the Barefoot Lovers*. London: Alvin Redman Limited, 1954.

Garrard, Lewis H. *Wah-to-Yah and the Taos Trail*. Cincinnati: H. W. Derby & Co., 1850.

Gibberd, Eric. *The Paintings of Gibberd*. Denver: The A. B. Hirschfeld Press, Inc., 1969.

Gladwin, Harold Sterling. *A History of the Ancient Southwest*. Portland: Bond Wheelwright Co., 1957.

González, Nancie L. *The Spanish-Americans of New Mexico: A Heritage of Pride*. Albuquerque: University of New Mexico Press, 1969.

Grant, Blanche C. *Doña Lona: A Story of Old Taos and Santa Fe*. New York: Wilfred Funk, Inc., 1941.

——. *One Hundred Years Ago in Old Taos*. Taos, N.M.: privately printed, 1925.

——. *Taos Indians*. Taos, N.M.: privately printed, 1925.

——. *Taos Today*. Taos, N.M.: privately printed, 1925.

——. *When Old Trails Were New*. New York: The Press of the Pioneers, Inc., 1934.

——, ed. *Kit Carson's Own Story of His Life*. Santa Fe: Santa Fe New Mexican Publishing Corp., 1926.

Hackett, Charles Wilson. *Revolt of the Pueblo Indians of New Mexico and Otermin's Attempted Reconquest, 1680–1682*. Introduction and annotations by Charles Wilson Hackett, translations of original documents by Charmion Clair Shelby. Coronado Cuarto Centennial Publications, 1540–1940, edited by George P. Hammond. Vols. 8 and 9. Albuquerque: University of New Mexico Press, 1942.

Harrington, John P. *An Introductory Paper on the Tiwa Language, Dialect of Taos, New Mexico.* Papers of the School of American Archaeology, no. 14, Archaeological Institute of America, 1910.

Henderson, Alice Corbin. *Brothers of Light: The Penitentes of the Southwest.* New York: Harcourt, Brace & Co., 1937.

"Los Hermanos Penitentes." *El Palacio* 8, no. 1 (January 31, 1920): 3–20.

Hewitt, Edgar L. *Ancient Life in the American Southwest: With an Introduction on the General History of the American Race.* Indianapolis: The Bobbs-Merrill Co., Inc., 1930.

——. *The Chaco Canyon and Its Monuments.* Albuquerque: University of New Mexico Press, 1936.

——. *Pajarito Plateau and Its Ancient People.* Albuquerque: University of New Mexico Press, 1938.

—— and Adolph F. Bandelier. *Indians of the Rio Grande Valley.* Albuquerque: University of New Mexico Press, 1937.

—— and Bertha P. Dutton. *The Pueblo Indian World.* Albuquerque: University of New Mexico Press, 1945.

—— et al. *The Physiography of the Rio Grande Valley, New Mexico.* Bureau of American Ethnology Bulletin 54. Washington, D.C.: U.S. Government Printing Office, 1913.

Horgan, Paul. *Great River: The Rio Grande in North American History.* New York: Rinehart & Company, 1954.

——. *The Saintmaker's Christmas Eve.* New York: Farrar, Straus and Cudahy, 1955.

Horka-Follick, Lorayne Ann. *Los Hermanos Penitentes: A Vestige of Medievalism in Southwestern United States.* Los Angeles: Westernlore Press, 1969.

Howlett, Rev. W. J. *Life of the Right Reverend Joseph P. Machebeuf, D.D.* Pueblo, Colo.: The Franklin Press Co., 1908.

James, Rebecca Salsbury. *Allow Me to Present 18 Ladies and Gentlemen and Taos, N.M., 1885–1939.* Taos, N.M.: El Crepusculo, 1953.

Jaramillo, Cleofas M. *Shadows of the Past (Sombras del Pasado).* Santa Fe: Ancient City Press, 1972.

Jeançon, J. A. *Archeological Investigations in the Taos Valley, New Mexico, during 1920.* Smithsonian Miscellaneous Collections, vol. 81, no. 12. Washington, D.C.: Smithsonian Institution, 1929.

Jenkinson, Michael. *Tijerina: Land Grant Conflict in New Mexico.* Albuquerque: Paisano Press, 1968.

Johnson, Spud. *Horizontal Yellow.* Santa Fe: Rydal Press, 1935.

Keegan, Marcia. *The Taos Indians and Their Sacred Blue Lake.* New York: Julian Messner, 1972.

Keleher, William A. "Law of the New Mexico Land Grant." *New Mexico Historical Review* 4, no. 4 (1929): 350–71.

——. *Maxwell Land Grant, A New Mexico Item.* Santa Fe: Rydal Press, 1942.

Kidder, Alfred Vincent. *An Introduction to the Study of Southwestern Archaeology: With a Preliminary Account of the Excavations at Pecos.* New Haven, Conn.: Yale University Press, 1924.

Krumgold, Joseph. *And Now Miguel.* New York: Thomas Y. Crowell Company, 1953.

La Barre, Weston. *The Peyote Cult.* 1938. Enlarged edition. New York: Schocken Books, Inc., 1969.

Latham, Barbara, illustrator, and Lily Duplaix. *Pedro, Nina and Perrito.* New York: Harper and Brothers, 1939.

Laughlin, Ruth. *Caballeros.* Caldwell, Idaho: The Caxton Printers, Ltd., 1945.

——. *The Wind Leaves No Shadow.* Caldwell, Idaho: The Caxton Printers, Ltd., 1956.

Lawrence, D. H. *Apocalypse.* Florence: G. Orioli, 1931.

——. *Mornings in Mexico.* New York: Alfred A. Knopf, Inc., 1927.

——. *Phoenix: The Posthumous Papers of D. H. Lawrence, 1936.* Edited and with an introduction by Edward D. McDonald. New York: The Viking Press, Inc., 1968.

——. *Phoenix II: Uncollected, Unpublished, and Other Prose Works by D. H. Lawrence.* Collected and edited with an introduction and notes by Warren Roberts and Harry T. Moore. New York: The Viking Press, Inc., 1968.

Lawrence, Frieda. *Frieda Lawrence: The Memoirs and Correspondence.* Edited by E. W. Tedlock. London: Heinemann, 1961.

——. *Not I, But the Wind.* Santa Fe: Rydal Press, 1934.

Lee, W. T. *Building of the Southern Rocky Mountains.* Geological Society of America Bulletin 34, 1923, pp. 285–300.

Loeffler, Gisella, illustrator, and Elizabeth Willis De Huff. *Little-Boy-Dance.* Chicago: Wilcox and Follett, Inc., 1946.

Luhan, Mabel Dodge. *Edge of the Taos Desert.* New York: Harcourt, Brace and Company, 1937.

——. *Lorenzo in Taos.* New York: Alfred A. Knopf, Inc., 1932.

——. *Taos and Its Artists.* New York: Duell, Sloan & Pearce, 1947.

——. *Winter in Taos.* New York: Harcourt, Brace and Company, 1935.

Lummis, Charles F. *The Land of Poco Tiempo.* New York: Charles Scribner's Sons, 1893.

McCarthy, Mary. *Venice Observed.* New York: Reynal and Hitchcock, Inc., 1956.

McCracken, Harold. *Nicolai Fechin.* New York: The Hammer Galleries, Inc., 1961.

McMurtrie, Douglas C. *The First Printing in New Mexico.* Chicago: John Calhoun Club, 1929.

Martínez, Padre Antonio José. *Cuaderno de Ortografía.* Santa Fe: Imprenta de Ramón Abreu, 1834.

Martínez, Rowena. *Land Grants in Taos Valley.* Taos, N.M.: Taos County Historical Society, Publication no. 2, 1968.

Matthews, Washington. *The Night Chant, a Navaho Ceremony.* New York: Memoirs of the American Museum of Natural History, vol. 6, 1902.

Melton, F. A. "Ancestral Rocky Mountains of Colorado and New Mexico." *Journal of Geology* 33 (1925): 84–89.

Merrild, Knud. *A Poet and Two Painters: A Memoir of D. H. Lawrence.* 1938. Reprint. *With D. H. Lawrence in New Mexico.* New York: Barnes & Noble, Inc., 1965.

Miller, Merton Leland. *A Preliminary Study of the Pueblo of Taos, New Mexico.* Chicago: University of Chicago Press, 1898.

Mills, George and Richard Grove. *Lucifer and the Crucifer: The Enigma of the Penitentes.* Reprinted from *The 1955 Brand Book of the Denver Westerners.* 2d ed. Colorado Springs, Colo.: The Taylor Museum of the Colorado Springs Fine Arts Center, 1965.

Moore, Harry T. *The Intelligent Heart: The Story of D. H. Lawrence.* New York: Farrar, Straus and Young, 1955.

Nabokov, Peter. *Tijerina and the Courthouse Raid.* Albuquerque: University of New Mexico Press, 1969.

Nehls, Edward. *D. H. Lawrence, A Composite Biography.* 3 vols. Madison: University of Wisconsin Press, 1957, 1958, 1959.

Neumann, Erich. *The Great Mother, An Analysis of the Archetype.* Bollingen Series 47. 2d ed. New York: Pantheon Books, Inc., 1963.

"Note on the Extinct Glaciers of Arizona and New Mexico." Abstract. *Scientific American* Supplement, vol. 52 (1901); *Science* (new series) 14 (1901).

O'Rourke, Frank. *The Far Mountains.* New York: William Morrow & Co., Inc., 1959.

——. *The Man Who Found His Way.* New York: William Morrow & Co., Inc., 1957.

——. *A Texan Came Riding.* New York: The New American Library, Inc.

Ortiz, Alfonso. *New Perspectives on the Pueblos.* School of American Research Advanced Seminar Series. Albuquerque: University of New Mexico Press, 1972.

Parsons, Elsie Clews. *Pueblo Indian Religion.* 2 vols. Chicago: University of Chicago Press, 1939.

——. *Taos Pueblo.* General Series in Anthropology, no. 2. Menasha, Wis.: George Banta Publishing Co., 1936.

——. *Taos Tales.* The American Folk-Lore Society. New York: J. J. Augustin, Inc.—Publisher, 1940.

——. "Witchcraft among the Pueblos: Indian or Spanish?" *Man* 27 (1927): vol. 6, no. 70, pp. 106–12; no. 80, pp. 125–28.

Peters, Dewitt C. *Kit Carson's Life and Adventures, from Facts Narrated by Himself.* Hartford, Conn.: Dustin, Gilman and Company, 1875.

Price, doughBelly. *Short Stirrups: The Saga of doughBelly Price.* Los Angeles: Westernlore Press, 1960.

Rael, Juan B. *The New Mexican Alabado.* Transcription of music by Eleanor Hague. Stanford, Calif.: Stanford University Press, 1951.

Reed, Doel. *Doel Reed Makes an Aquatint.* Santa Fe: Museum of New Mexico Press, 1965.

Reid, J. T. *It Happened in Taos.* Albuquerque: University of New Mexico Press, 1946.

Salpointe, Most Rev. John Baptist. *Soldiers of the Cross.* Reprint. Albuquerque: Calvin Horn, Publisher, Inc., 1967.

Sánchez, George L. *Forgotten People: A Study of New Mexicans.* Albuquerque: University of New Mexico Press, 1940.

Schilling, John H. *Taos–Red River–Eagle Nest, New Mexico Circle Drive.* Pamphlet no. 2. Socorro, N.M.: New Mexico State Bureau of Mines and Mineral Resources, 1956.

Scholes, France V. "The First Decade of the Inquisition in New Mexico." *New Mexico Historical Review* 10, no. 3 (July 1935): 195–241.

Sloane, Eric. *Return to Taos: A Sketchbook of Roadside Americana.* New York: Wilfred Funk, Inc., 1960.

Smith, Watson and John M. Roberts. *Zuni Law: A Field of Values.* Papers of the Peabody Museum of American Archaeology and Ethnology, Harvard University, vol. 43, no. 1, Reports of the Rimrock Project Values Series no. 4, Cambridge, 1954.

Steiner, Paul and Meredith Maran. *Chamisa Road: Doing the Dog in Taos.* New York: Random House, Inc., 1971.

Steiner, Stan. *The New Indians.* New York: Harper & Row, Publishers, 1968.

———. *La Raza: The Mexican-Americans.* New York: Harper & Row, Publishers, 1970.

Stevenson, Matilda Coxe. *The Zuni Indians: Their Mythology, Esoteric Fraternities, and Ceremonies. Twenty-third Annual Report of the Bureau of American Ethnology,* pp. 3–608. Washington, D.C.: U.S. Government Printing Office, 1904.

Sylvester, Harry. *Dayspring.* New York: D. Appleton-Century Co., 1945.

Tate, Bill. "The Penitentes of the Sangre de Cristos." *The Rio Grande Sun,* Española, N.M., 1966.

Telling, Irving. "New Mexican Frontiers: A Social History of the Gallup Area 1881–1901." Ph.D. dissertation, Harvard University, 1952.

Tiverton, Father William. *D. H. Lawrence and Human Existence.* New York: Philosophical Library, Inc., 1951.

Twitchell, Ralph Emerson. *The Leading Facts of New Mexico History.* 2 vols. Cedar Rapids, Iowa: The Torch Press, 1911.

———. *The Spanish Archives of New Mexico.* 2 vols. Cedar Rapids, Iowa: The Torch Press, 1914.

University of New Mexico, Institute for Social Research and Development, Bureau of Business Research. *New Mexico Statistical Abstract.* 1972 ed. Albuquerque: University of New Mexico, 1973.

Vestal, Stanley. *Kit Carson: The Happy Warrior of the Old West.* Boston: Houghton Mifflin Company, 1928.

Villagra, Gaspar Pérez de. *History of New Mexico.* Los Angeles: Quivira Society, 1933.

Wagner, Henry R. *The Spanish Southwest 1542–1794.* 2 vols. New York: Arno Press, Incorporated, 1967.

Warner, Louis H. "Conveyance of Property, the Spanish and Mexican Way." *New Mexico Historical Review* 6, no. 4 (October 1931): 334–59.

———. "Wills and Hijuelas." *New Mexico Historical Review* 7, no. 1 (January 1932): 75–89.

Waters, Frank. *The Book of the Hopi.* New York: The Viking Press, Inc., 1963.

———. *Leon Gaspard.* Flagstaff, Ariz.: Northland Press, 1964.

———. *The Man Who Killed the Deer.* New York: Farrar and Rinehart, 1942.

———. *Masked Gods: Navaho and Pueblo Ceremonials.* Albuquerque: University of New Mexico Press, 1950.

———. *People of the Valley.* New York: Farrar and Rinehart, 1941.

———. *Pumpkin Seed Point.* Chicago: The Swallow Press, Inc., 1969.

———. *The Woman at Otowi Crossing.* Chicago: The Swallow Press, Inc., 1966.

Weigle, Marta. *The Penitentes of the Southwest.* Santa Fe: Ancient City Press, 1970.

Westphall, Victor. *The Public Domain in New Mexico 1854–1891.* Albuquerque: University of New Mexico Press, 1965.

———. *Thomas Benton Catron and His Era.* Tucson: University of Arizona Press, 1973.

White, Koch, Kelly and McCarthy, Attorneys at Law. *Land Title Study.* Santa Fe: New Mexico State Planning Office, 1971.

"Witchcraft in New Mexico." *The Journal of American Folk-Lore* 1, no. 2 (July–September 1888): 167–68.

Wood, Nancy and Myron Wood. *Hollering Sun.* New York: Simon & Schuster, Inc., 1972.

Wylder, Meldrum K., M.D. *Rio Grande Medicine Man.* Santa Fe: Rydal Press, 1958.

Zytaruk, George J. *The Quest for Rananim.* Montreal: McGill University Press, 1970.